RIGHTS TO CULTURE

Heritage, Language, and Community in Thailand

T0369720

Edited by

Coeli Barry

Silkworm Books

Funding for this project was provided by the Culture and Rights in Thailand
Project of the Princess Maha Chakri Sirindhorn Anthropology Centre.

ISBN: 978-616-215-062-3

Published in 2013 by
Silkworm Books
6 Sukkasem Road, T. Suthep
Chiang Mai 50200 Thailand
info@silkwormbooks.com
http://www.silkwormbooks.com

Cover photo courtesy of Majid Bagheri

Typeset in Minion Pro 10 pt. by Silk Type

Printed and bound in China

5 4 3 2 1

Contents

Illustrations

Foreword

This publication on cultural rights matters in Thailand is both a timely and welcome contribution to the discussions on cultural rights, which have remained a relatively underdeveloped area of human rights despite numerous references in international instruments and the practice of human rights. The complex issues of culture and human rights have started to be debated in many venues in the international arena: within the United Nations, in national and transnational, mainstream and alternative media outlets, and across civil society groups and academia. Yet, the right to culture and cultural rights continue to evoke heated debate and controversies. Partly, this is due to an insufficient understanding of the nature of these rights.

As I elaborate in my reports to the United Nations, cultural rights are pivotal to the recognition and respect of human dignity: they protect the rights of each person – individually, in community with others, and as groups – to develop and express their humanity, world visions, meanings assigned to life and understanding of development. Core aspects relate to the right of everyone to access, participate in and contribute to cultural life in all its diversity. Cultural rights encompass important freedoms connected to collective identity and the pursuit of specific ways of life, but equally to individual identity and self-expression; they are inextricably linked to a host of other rights such as: freedom of expression and belief, information and communication, language, and education.

In promoting the cultural rights of all without discrimination and on a basis of equality, it is vital to understand that culture itself is ever-evolving and that all collective identities entail contestations over meanings and definitions; processes that are inevitably linked to the underlying structures and dynamics of power related to accessing and exercising control over economic, political and cultural resources. Hence, the right to access and contribute to cultural life necessitates access to tangible and intangible cultural heritage and well as contemporary cultural expressions of one's own community *and* that of others. Cultural rights thus include the right, without fear of punitive actions, not to participate in particular cultural activities; to challenge existing precepts and norms; to leave and rejoin communities; to critique, reject and innovate; to hold multiple identities simultaneously. All individuals must be recognized as active and legitimate producers of culture(s).

Grounded in existing norms and principles of international human rights law, cultural rights enrich our understanding of the principle of universality of human rights. Taking into consideration cultural diversity, they can serve as essential tools for building social cohesion, mutual respect and understanding between individuals and groups. Cultural diversity must never be equated with cultural relativism, however, and no one may invoke cultural diversity to infringe upon human rights guaranteed by international law, nor to limit their scope. Not all cultural practices accord with international human rights law and, notwithstanding the challenge of identifying exactly which cultural practices may be contrary to human rights, the endeavor always must be to modify and/or discard all practices pursued in the name of culture that impede the enjoyment of human rights by any individual. The diversity of opinion within communities is as important as the diversity across communities.

Some cultural practices may be particularly detrimental to the rights of women and girls. All harmful practices, regardless of provenance and justification must be eliminated. All States, regardless of their political, economic and cultural systems, have an obligation to uphold the principle of non-discrimination and to respect, protect and fulfill the cultural rights of all persons. There is a need to work simultaneously at the level of both society and state; legal measures by themselves are rarely, if ever, sufficient. Within every tradition and structural limitation, people have a certain relative power to act differently, including by drawing upon different aspects of the same cultural traditions. Upholding the cultural rights of all without discrimination will encourage the promotion of universal human rights in all communities of shared cultural values by encouraging the development of new thinking, cultural practices and context-specific vocabulary, which uphold the universality, indivisibility, interdependence and inter-relatedness of human rights. In this it is important to stress that States must exercise due diligence to address rights violations by non-state actors, including those undertaken in the name of culture and religion.

Concepts of human rights, including cultural rights, are constantly evolving on the basis of new studies and thinking. Hence this book investigating issues related to cultural rights in Thailand and critically interrogating existing concepts will undoubtedly make an important contribution towards the promotion of a better understanding and recognition of cultural rights in all their facets.

Farida Shaheed
United Nations Special Rapporteur
in the field of cultural rights
April 2013

Preface

In 2010 the Princess Maha Chakri Sirindhorn Anthropology Centre launched the Culture and Rights in Thailand (CRT) project, the findings of which serve as the core of this book. The CRT took its place alongside international academic, activist, and policy debates around cultural diversity, cultural heritage management, and the sustainability of cultural practices. Academics, activists, and leaders from affected groups recognize that more effective means to protect diversity or encourage better management of change around it are needed in the face of forces like globalization, tourism, migration, and economic development. Some argue rights-based approaches may be a viable option.

In *Rights to Culture*, we map the landscape of rights and culture in Thailand, deepening and broadening the avenues through which these complex issues can be addressed. We reveal multiple meanings of the right to culture and cultural rights through original, ethnographic research. Marginalization and discrimination as well as modes of belonging experienced by ethnic and religious minorities in Thailand are explored and explicated through the prism of rights.

The right to culture and the concept of cultural rights are controversial for scholars and activists alike. For some human rights activists, as well as for feminist critics of human rights, the assertion of a right to culture opens the door to the weakening of core human rights in general and the human rights of women in particular. In the name of "culture" and "tradition", governments and social leaders can resist the full application of rights for women. From other vantage points, critics of cultural rights maintain that inasmuch as cultural rights are special entitlements to certain groups, these entitlements can become a kind of incentive for group members to maintain fixed boundaries of collective identity, and to impose the maintenance of a fixed set of cultural practices by all the members, ignoring power differentials and inequities within groups.

To investigate rights is not to endorse the idea of rights in an uncritical way: rights constitute only one set of norms, albeit powerful ones in transnational discourse at present. *Rights to Culture* positions itself as a critical engagement with rights, and the authors are aware that where hegemonic discourses are present, unequal power relations can readily be re-inscribed even if the normative claims are emancipatory. In this volume, we heed the call of socio-legal scholars and anthropologists for nuance and humility in writing about rights, especially in non-Western countries, and the authors have been open to the vernacular conceptions of justice and existing social and political hierarchies through which rights may (or may not) be adopted.

Acknowledgments

This book would never have been possible without the help of many people who contributed at different stages. For their work conceptualizing this project, special thanks go to Helaine Silverman, Chewasit Boonyakiet and Alexandra Denes. In her capacity as director of the Culture and Rights in Thailand project, Alexandra's commitment to research in the service of scholarship and public debate inspired members of the project and steered the research findings towards publication. Support for the Culture and Rights in Thailand project and for the production of this book came from the Princess Maha Chakri Sirindhorn Anthropology Centre. We would like to acknowledge this support. We wish to thank Paritta Chalermpow Koanantakool, the director of the center during the first two years of the project, and Suvanna Kriengkraipetch, who served as director during the final year as the manuscript was being prepared. Niti Pawakapan offered valuable feedback at different stages of the research process.

The resource people who guided this Culture and Rights project and mentored researchers were exceptional as scholars and intellectual colleagues. They include Kimberly Christen, William Logan, Frank Munger, Yukti Mukdawijitra, Thanapol Limapichart, in addition to Helaine Silverman. As this volume encompasses such a range of theoretical and disciplinary issues, we relied heavily on their expertise. We are fortunate that they were so generous with their time and their knowledge.

Two workshops were convened to develop the research papers that became the chapters of this book. We would like to thank the presenters of the 2010 workshop including Anan Ganjanapan, Rustom Bharucha, and Varaporn Chamsanit, as well as members of the project who contributed in workshops and meetings. They include Worapong Charoenwong, Isara Choosri, Rungroj

Chorbwan, Sittisak Rungcharoensuksri, Thanwadee Sookprasert, Sumittra Surartdecham, and Surachai Vaivanjit.

Our thanks as well to those who contributed to the preparation of this book in different stages: Thanet Aphornsuvan, Chris Baker, Alexandra Dalferro, Alexa Johns, Mary Beth Mills, Judy Pine, and Anusorn Unno. This manuscript could not have been completed without the expert editing of Alan Feinstein, whose patience and exacting standards improved this volume immeasurably.

1

Rights to Culture: An Introduction

Coeli Barry

The right to culture is among the most challenging of concepts to have emerged from the rights "revolution" that took place in the wake of the Cold War. Although culture as a right was inscribed in core human rights declarations, the idea that an individual or a group's culture could be claimed or defended by invoking rights is one that has only recently begun to take form in rights discourse revealed through activism, scholarship, or policy. Cultural rights remained an underdeveloped concept within core international human rights instruments written from the 1940s through the 1980s. But with the rise of indigenous rights movements and the growth of ethno-nationalism in the 1990s, cultural rights assumed greater significance on the global stage. In response to these changes, the United Nations and regional rights organizations drafted a number of international cultural rights instruments. Currently, many rights scholars and advocates argue that cultural rights should not be regarded as a subsidiary category of human rights; rather, cultural rights ought to be considered as inextricably bound to human rights. As Bryan Turner (2006, 45) notes, "In an increasingly hybrid and multicultural global context, cultural identities are politically contested—and hence securing cultural rights is an important precondition for the enjoyment of other human rights."

Rights to Culture investigates the interplay between transnational discourses of rights and their appropriation in Thailand across a range of topics including heritage, identity, language, and livelihood issues. The ethnographic, historically grounded research that connects the chapters of this book investigates the ways that rights and culture intersect in Thailand at present and how the politics of culture at present is informed by nation-building ideologies and development practices from the past half-century or more. In *Rights to Culture* we reveal how community and state actors manage cultural heritage and the resources needed to ensure more equitable belonging in Thai society.

Rights to Culture maps the terrain in which a "human right to culture," cultural rights, and the culture of rights in Thailand can be explicated. This deliberately wide swath allows us to bring together topics that might not otherwise be considered side by side. In investigating cultural rights, then, we open the conceptual and empirical inquiry to culture *and* rights. Across the chapters in this book we speak to crosscutting issues that together reveal the conditions that encourage or discourage individuals and communities from adopting discourses advocating for, or claiming, rights.

Rights to Culture intervenes in debates on culture and rights—and on how cultural rights relate to human rights—by focusing on a geographical region where these issues remain under-explored. In Southeast Asia in general and in Thailand in particular, the politics of identity and contestations over heritage are shaped by state interactions between minorities, migrants, and communities who have been on the periphery for much of the country's period of "modernization." The possibilities for claiming rights to culture in Thailand were often constrained by a combination of factors, including decades of militarized or authoritarian rule and a developmental state that laid claim to natural resources as well as cultural patrimony, invoking its role as guardian over the nation. State authority, however, is not monolithic, and anthropologists of ethnicity and the politics of development remind us of the spaces that are open to negotiation and assertions of agency by groups and communities when dealing with the state (Walker 2009; Pinkaew 2003).

The authors in *Rights to Culture* refer to the working definitions of cultural rights that circulate in global discourse. These rights, although inherent in core human rights documents, have a character of their own inasmuch as they are collective or group rights. If political and civil rights reside in the individual, cultural rights are group rights, and it is this quality that sometimes raises concern.

As Kymlicka and many others have pointed out, there are some conditions of life—the right to speak a language, for example—that cannot be protected by individual rights alone. . . . At the same time, however, all collective rights provisions have to be balanced with individual rights guarantees, so that individuals do not end up being denied substantive freedoms for the sake of the group. (Ignatieff 2001, 75–76)

Cultural rights can encompass an exceptionally wide range of issues including arts and creative expression, the maintenance and assertion of identity, and access to the resources that are crucial to a group's sustainability. In *Rights to Culture* we build on Cowan's formulation (2006) of the conjunctions between rights and culture: for example, when rights are treated as antithetical to a particular aspect of culture; when a legal claim is made to protect the right to culture; or when rights are approached as constituting a "culture" in and of themselves. This collection forges a theoretically informed approach to the study of cultural rights and culture and rights. We come to these different conjunctions fully attuned to substantial critiques of rights discourse and of the ways it gets mobilized in particular social and political contexts.

Critics of cultural rights point to the dangers and attendant risks inherent in invoking group identity in order to claim rights (Wilson 2003; Cowan 2001). As Gledhill writes,

We still need to ask how basing claims to recognition on identity can avoid re-subjugating actors historically subjugated through identity; what kinds of politicization, in what kinds of political context, could sustain subversion of the power structures producing such subjugation? (1997, 105, citing Brown 1995, 53)

Will Kymlicka, a leading political theorist of multiculturalism, is an advocate of cultural rights but acknowledges that

the tendency to equate culture with tradition (and hence to interpret a "right to culture" as a right to cultural preservation) raises several potential dangers: it may inhibit constructive relations between cultures (by privileging cultural purity over cultural hybridity); it may erode the freedom of individuals within groups (by privileging authoritarian or

conservative elites over internal reformers); it can be invoked to deny the
existence of universal human rights; and it may threaten the space for civil
debate and democratic negotiation over cultural conflicts. Given these
dangers, some critics have dismissed the whole idea of "cultural rights" (and
associated ideas of "multiculturalism," "identity politics," or "the politics
of recognition") as sociologically naive, historically inaccurate, illiberal,
and undemocratic. (Kymlicka 2004, 8)

This "strategic essentializing"—in which one or another aspect of a group's
culture is emphasized and legitimized—has been challenged by theorists of
identity, by anthropologists, and particularly by feminists who oppose the
reification of "culture" as defined often by male leadership within communities.
In the studies brought together in *Rights to Culture* we assess the terms by
which strategic essentializing takes place. For example, the chapters by Sirijit
and Bencharat (chapters 7 and 4, respectively) illustrate how minorities and
communities fighting for state support and official recognition of their status
can legitimize claims to land, citizenship, or development aid by deploying
the very same "essentialist" categories the state has adopted. The decision to
adapt such strategies seems best understood as part of the ongoing process
of negotiation between communities and the state for recognition that allows
the former to claim a right to state resources. In *Rights to Culture* we bring an
awareness of the uses of "culture" in state-community relations and of the
concern that asserting cultural rights could also lead to what the philosopher
Kwame Appiah (2004) terms the "tyranny of [group] identity".

Culture, Identity, and National Development

For much of the twentieth century, diversity in Thailand was yoked to national
integration and development projects in ways that limited the space for
minority groups to express differences that could not be subsumed within
the nation-state-building goals. State-driven concepts of culture, national
identity, and national development have largely essentialized Thailand's
cultures and seen the country's diversity as a security threat, a topic that
has been well covered in the historiography of Thailand (Reynolds 1993).
Hayami observes that

[Thailand's] homogeneity has been incessantly stressed in official and other discourse while repressing differences in the process of nation-building throughout the twentieth century. Those who do not fit into the narrowly defined "Thai-ness" have therefore been deemed "others" and outsiders, threats to the unity of the homogeneously conceived nation. . . . With the end the of the Cold War . . . "Thainess" became open to contestation, and the various waves of recognizing Thainess in varied locations and stress on local cultures began. Culture seems to have been handed to the people and their localities. . . . (2006, 283, 285)

Hayami goes on to say that, "In place of the overall [lack of] interest in the cultures of the others, and the eagerness to assimilate and incorporate them into the national development effort," state support for tourism development as well as official promotion of diversity have resulted in what she calls a "benign recognition of difference" (285).

The process of nation-building in Thailand was one of defining Thainess versus Otherness both within and across its boundaries. "Others" here might include not only the more obvious national and ethnic Others, but also those whose various loci of identity (religious, sexual, occupational, etc.) are marginalized in the normative social order. This normative social order does not remain static, nor is it free from contradictory dimensions. For example, attitudes in Thailand towards sexual minorities are considered rather open, though this statement cannot capture the varieties of experiences of different sexual minorities across space and time (Sinnott 2011).

The preeminent historian of Thailand's cultural politics, Craig Reynolds, captured a defining dynamic between Thailand's drive to secure the supremacy of the Thai-speaking majority over diverse ethnic and religious groups and to legitimize the use of the military in governing the country for much of the twentieth century: namely, that Thai identity was under threat and needed to be defended (Reynolds 1993; see also Connors 2005).

The centralized education system was a crucial vehicle for instilling in children the necessary behavior and values about "being Thai" (Vail 2006). Learning central Thai and learning via central Thai were essential to the nationalizing project, and those minorities who did not master central Thai were regarded as un-Thai. The Malay-speaking Muslim Thais are a striking example of this. At present the Muslim minorities in southern Thailand continue to live with the consequences of being marked as different because of language and "culture." Violence and arbitrary detention continue to worsen in the Muslim-dominated southern provinces, and the security-minded outlook that has informed central Thai government policies for decades is in evidence. As Mark Tamthai and Somkiat Boonchoo note in their study on national security policies in the southern border provinces over a thirty-year period, "Because of their deep-seated fear of communism, the authorities' way of thinking proved difficult to change" (Tamthai and Somkiat 2009, 39). Though Thailand participates actively in the international rights regime and has a rich discursive and political history of contesting civil and political rights, thinking through, let alone enacting, cultural rights is a political and epistemic challenge owing in part to the fact that official cultural policy and national identity were inextricably bound to the notions of loyalty and national security.

In the case of the Khmer speakers of Thailand's northeastern, or Isan, region, Vail and Panuwat note in chapter 6 in this volume that state discourse on monolingualism helped naturalize the idea that to speak Khmer was to mark oneself as a "second-class citizen." Hence, Khmer identity politics focused on language and heritage appear low-key, especially when viewed in contrast with the many ways Khmer-Thais take part in highly politicized, even radicalized, politics on other fronts:

> Observers of northeastern Thailand may find it curious that Northern Khmer speakers are so passive about linguistic rights and apathetic about their ethnic identity and heritage, given how highly politicized, and even radicalized, southern Isan has so often proved to be in other respects. Indeed, Isan is typically at the forefront of rights-claiming behavior when it comes to political enfranchisement, resource management, and even the validation of "local wisdom." (Vail and Panuwat, chap. 6)

But when it comes to identity politics, Khmer-Thais face a tension between being proud of their ethnic Khmer heritage, on the one hand, and being "loyal" Thai citizens, on the other.

Through the prism of rights, the ideologies and practices around "Thai-ness" can be seen as legitimizing some forms of exclusion and establishing the terms by which claims to rights get voiced as claims for recognition to those with greater status or authority. The studies in this volume draw attention to the ways in which claims-making in Thailand can be a matter of a group's petitioning the center for recognition rather than confronting it outright.

From the country's beginnings as a constitutional monarchy (the 1932 coup marks the end of absolute monarchy in Thailand), there have been two distinct streams of thought about the best way for the country to modernize politically. One group advocated liberal constitutionalism and the other a paternalistic approach. As Pasuk and Baker in their *History of Thailand* (2009, 197) note,

> By the late 1940s, the aspirations for the nation-state held by the old aristocrats, officials, generals, and new businessmen in Thailand's narrow political elite were divided in two broad camps. One side upheld the ideal of a diverse, liberal, egalitarianism achieved by the rule of law, a constitutional framework and democratic representation. The other upheld the ideal of a strong paternal state with the duty to protect, discipline, and educate its citizens within a hierarchic social order.

The struggle between these competing visions of Thailand's democracy continues into the present, but for much of the country's history the paternalistic vision was more influential—especially from the 1940s through the 1980s, when nationalist, military-led regimes ruled. In a deeply hierarchical society like Thailand, claims are often framed as petitions—not demands—for patronage and expressed in idioms of gratitude for recognition by those more powerful. State-driven concepts of culture, national identity, and national development were given life in policies that essentialized Thailand's cultures and rendered the country's diversity as either a security threat (during the Cold War especially) or a depoliticized lifestyle and tourism embellishment. The Thai state's capacity to appropriate ideas about development, culture, and identity reflects the importance it puts on the notion of "stewardship" over the citizenry, and past experience suggests that ideas of rights can be just as readily appropriated as other ideas were in the past.

The Culture of Rights, and the Meanings of
Culture and Rights in Thailand

The word for culture in Thai, *watthanatham,* was coined in 1934. As Thanapol notes in his study of this neologism (2001), *watthanatham* contained contradictions from the start. Culture represented simultaneously the embodiment of tradition, as well as modernity and progress. By the 1940s, the "Culture Master Plan" used the word *watthanatham* to indicate and promote social prosperity, orderliness, national unity and development, and morality of the people (Connors 2005). This extensive and overburdened definition of culture has never been entirely shed, even as the official renderings of the word have been adapted over time.

The word *culture* as used in this book allows for fluidity and contestation. We take our cue from the words of the eminent anthropologist of Thailand, Shigeharu Tanabe: "Culture is acquired, accumulated, and modified by an individual through the learning process from his or her experiences. It is not a reified product such as 'Thai culture' or 'community culture,' which has been constructed as a discourse . . ." (2008, 2). The power of the "reified product" called Thai culture, nonetheless, must be not be minimized, because, as research findings here suggest, it can be asserted in many situations, particularly when rights are being contested.

For example, in the heat of current debate about the possibility of reforming the Thai monarchy (and draconian laws about defamation of the crown), an opponent of this initiative railed against it on the grounds that Thailand's democracy, history, and culture constituted one—and only one—chapter in a long history. The author juxtaposed the 1932 coup, which introduced democracy in Thailand, against the "unique and ages-old identity" Thais enjoyed well before that:

> At the end of the day, we may need to separate the issues, amending Section 112 [the article in the Thai constitution on lese majesty], and the reformation of the monarchy especially for those people [who favor reform] whose perspectives keep them naively limited to Thai history and norms only from 1932 to the present. The Thai people must learn to preserve their unique and ages-old identity. "Internationalizing" things wrongly will only end up enslaving us to outlandish perceptions.

Should our present actions end up causing future generations of Thais an immense and irreparable loss, it will only show what sad fools we have been. (Donavanik 2012)

There are inevitably formidable challenges in finding apt ways to render English-language legal and political theory terminology into Thai, an issue that historians, sociologists, and anthropologists, as well as activists, confront in scholarship in general and in writing about rights and justice in particular (Engel 2000; Harrison 2010). A leading anthropologist of rights among Thailand's forest-dwelling communities and an active participant in the community forestry movement, Anan Ganjanapan, reflects that

In advocacy or negotiations with the government, local people do not only talk about customary rights, but they also generate other kinds of rights in order to set up institutional arrangements. They emphasize participatory rights, because the community is not necessarily monolithic in its opinions about the management of community forestry. People's opinions are sometimes different from or in conflict with each other. . . . Their discussion is not confined to the false dichotomy of participatory versus exclusive rights. Rather they talk about the multiplicity of rights, namely management rights, monitoring rights, and of course, usufruct rights which can coexist in the same forest. (2008, 9)

An anthropology of rights in Thailand is still in the making. Some anthropological studies on rights engage recent English-language socio-legal theory, particularly the theory of vernacularization elucidated by Sally Engle Merry (Merry 2006; Levitt and Merry 2009), which examines the dynamics by which the global rights lexicon is diffused and localized alongside preexisting idioms of justice (Munger 2006/7; Suchat 2009). A community rights movement in Thailand that took shape in the 1990s embodied the complex aspects of vernacularizing rights. The community rights movement had as one of its goals the preservation of the "traditional rural community"—though, in the view of many critics, this community was already a somewhat mythic entity by the 1990s.

The community rights movement drew on both Buddhist and Marxist-influenced ideas in a way that distinguishes Thailand's discourse around rights (in the post-Cold War era) from the so-called Asian Values debates. Thai intellectuals and activists distanced themselves from the patriarchal practices and capitalist development policies endorsed by the more vocal proponents of Asian Values. Acknowledging that the Western-derived concept of rights might not fit with "the Asian context," Thai intellectuals nonetheless believed community rights could serve as a new paradigm of thought to "save local and traditional communities" from development incursions coming from the national center and from globalization (Choltira 2000). Saneh Chamarik, Thailand's first National Human Rights Commission chairman and director of the country's most extensive research project on community rights in the 1990s, emphasized the need for cultural pluralism, local wisdom, and community learning, much of which drew upon Buddhist ideas as he interpreted them (Saneh 1993).

In northern Thailand during the 1990s as well, a community forestry movement and its supporters in academe insisted on the inseparability of cultural practices and beliefs and land use (Anan 2000). The interrelatedness of natural resource management and the perception of non-dominant groups is concisely stated by Andrew Walker (2001, 155): "The defining features of ethnic identity deserve ongoing discussion and debate precisely because these features not only generate the cultural content of identity, but lay down frameworks of inclusion and exclusion that shape access to the rights and resources being sought."

Civil society leaders from academe and nongovernmental organizations (NGOs), including those active in the community rights and community forestry movements, were influential in the writing of the 1997 Constitution, especially in the effort to promote community-based approaches to development and natural resource management (Walker 2009).

Being able to establish that a community existed long enough to be considered traditional is one important component, but the culture a community is entitled to conserve must be "good culture." These ideas were enshrined in the 1997 Constitution and then resurfaced in the 2007 Constitution (emphasis added):

> Persons so assembling as to be a local traditional community shall have the right to conserve or restore their customs, local knowledge, arts or *good culture* of their community and of the nation and participate in the

management, maintenance, preservation and exploitation of natural resources and the environment in a balanced fashion and sustainably as provided by law.

Bencharat Chua's study (chapter 4) on the contemporary community forestry movement scrutinizes the uses of "culture" as a strategic framing device by those whose livelihoods depend on recognition by the state in bargaining for some space to continue harvesting the forest.

The legal arena, embedded as it is in social life, often operates removed from or in uneasy coexistence with everyday life. The divide between these realms can be especially marked in developing countries outside the West, such as Thailand, because foreign legal concepts were imposed on existing systems of power and justice that did not necessarily correspond to ideas from Europe. The concept of rights is one site where the disparities reveal themselves.

The modernization of Siamese law was a crucial component to the effort of the ruling elites to maintain the country's status as (quasi) independent.[1] But the transculturation of Western legal concepts into the Thai language, and the mixing of traditional Thai ideas about justice with Western legal principles, resulted in a curious and very particular entity called Thai law. Whereas the concept of personhood enshrined in the liberal legal framework assumed autonomous individuals, free and equal in the eyes of the law (an ideal frequently honored in the breach in the courts of these same liberal regimes), Siamese law as practiced in the early decades of the twentieth century carried with it relational, contingent ideas of individuals' worth as based on their status. As Loos' research into court cases from the end of the nineteenth and early twentieth centuries evidences, subjects who came before the law were in no way assumed to be equal if their status outside the court indicated otherwise. While democratic development in Thailand over the last nearly eighty years (and particularly over the last twenty to thirty years) has witnessed a strengthening of the ideal of equality before the law, the practice of law and the legal consciousness expressed by many in Thailand throughout this same period also suggest a great deal of circumspection about the possibilities of realizing that ideal.

The idea of rights circulating in Thailand in the late nineteenth and early twentieth centuries contained meanings that would never be echoed in the founding documents of the United Nations and that continue to inform the framing and practice of rights at present. Alexandra Denes has written (2010b) about the Museum of the Living, where corpses from HIV/AIDS sufferers who were cared for at a temple in Lopburi province (central Thailand) are on display so that visitors can meditate on the dead—a traditional Buddhist practice. Although permission to use the corpses this way was granted by all of the people while they were alive, their families and HIV/AIDS activists have challenged the temple's right to continue this practice on the grounds that the display of the corpses violates the rights of the deceased and their families. This is a rather gruesome, but pointed, reminder that "universal human rights principles centered on the individual (in this case, rights of the dead) can come into conflict with historically embedded, cultural constructions of selfhood (in this case, Buddhist constructions of selfhood) which challenge the primacy of individualism and the 'self'" (ibid).

Justice, law, and rights in Thailand at present also contain within them the vestiges of a transculturation process whereby Thai law was modernized beginning in the late nineteenth century along the lines of Western law (Loos 2006), and the limits of positive law continue to be felt in Thailand. The country's leading social critic and historian, Nidhi Eoseewong, argues (2003) that Thailand has a "cultural constitution" that enshrines the practices and beliefs by which ordinary people resolve disputes and agree to some manner of social order that is far more enduring and relevant than any of the kingdom's many written constitutions. Appeals to state law and or the intercession of its guardians are often avoided by common people for fear of exposing themselves to the costly and protracted procedures that the pursuit of formal legal justice entails (Engel and Jaruwan 2010; Suchat 2009). Alongside formal law, then, more informal mechanisms for pursuing justice flourish, sometimes relying on recourse to spirits and supernatural assistance. Identifying and explicating the sources of gaps in understandings about rights and culture, the meanings embedded within them, and the normative, institutional, and discursive practices that perpetuate or challenge them are tasks taken up by different contributors to this volume.

Chapter Summaries

The book is organized in two parts. In the first half, chapters by Denes and Tiamsoon (2), Ho and Pornpan (3), and Bencharat (4) explore questions of "rights to culture" concerning contested claims between local communities and national heritage authorities. Haberkorn's chapter (5), also in the first half, investigates the tensions between state representations of Thai national identity and international standards of human rights norms. In the second half, the chapters by Vail and Panuwat (6), Sirijit (7), Hayes and Mullen (8), and Mukdawan (9) look at questions of "rights to culture" as they relate to the presence of distinctive "ethnic" identities and migrants within the Thai nation.

Alexandra Denes and Tiamsoon Sirisrisak's study (chapter 2, "A Rights-Based Approach to Cultural Heritage Management at the Phanom Rung Historical Park in Northeast Thailand") highlights the tensions between local communities and heritage authorities over the management of religious sites in Thailand's northeastern province of Buriram. These Angkor-era, Khmer sites have been incorporated into the Phanom Rung Historical Park. The authors argue that, although local meanings of the sanctuaries were eclipsed after the sites became listed as a historical park, living memory of rituals that tied community members to the temples attest to how important it was for people to honor the guardian spirits of these places. Denes and Tiamsoon see the revival of these rituals as a cultural rights claim against the rationalizing discourse of heritage officials. They acknowledge that, in contrast to conventional understandings of rights-claims, this type of claim can be seen as reinforcing social hierarchy and displacing agency onto the spirit realm. Their analysis challenges scholars of cultural rights in Thailand and more widely to see cultural rights-claiming as likely enmeshed in local beliefs and as emerging from existing hierarchical social relations to challenge newer, more alienating hierarchies.

In chapter 3, "Conserving Bangkok's Premier Heritage District: Ambitious Plans and Ambiguous Rights," K. C. Ho and Pornpan Chinnapong focus on Krung Rattanakosin, Bangkok's premier heritage district. The authors assess the heritage claims of two communities living there, at Tha Tien and Fort Mahakan. Interviews with stakeholders from the communities, with government officials, and with mediating groups such as NGOs and academics, reveal differing visions for the district and raise questions about whose heritage is being privileged. These questions in turn lead the authors to reflect on the salience of cultural rights in urban neighborhoods more generally. They maintain that in cities cultural rights claims are complicated by many factors, notably cultural practices and locality. Ho and Pornpan argue that heritage claims based on practices tied to place, but that are not necessarily tied to the groups who originated those practices, and community rights claims are not necessarily linked to cultural rights.

Chapter 4, "Rights Claims and the Strategic Use of Culture to Protect Human Rights: The Community Forest Movement in Thailand," by Bencharat Sae Chua, compares two communities in northeastern Thailand and their different experiences in mobilizing cultural arguments for resource and livelihood claims via the community forestry movement. Bencharat asks how "culture" is used, constructed, and performed by members of the community forest movement as they claim the right to the forests. She argues that an environmentalist frame forces the community forestry movement to limit itself to the official definition of permitted forest use. These communities attempt to challenge the Thai state's claim to control the forests but the burden is on these same communities to demonstrate that they possess "traditional knowledge" on how to live in harmony with their forest environment. Her study raises important questions about how or whether claims using local cultural rights to natural resources (with the community members in the role of "traditional protectors of the forest") can be formally recognized in policy and legal frameworks. While the communities need access to forestland for commercial agriculture, they must strategically frame their case in terms the Thai state, as well as the environmental movement, have set for them.

Beginning in 1946, Thailand began filing yearly reports with the United Nations with information on progress towards the protection of human rights within the country. Haberkorn's study in chapter 5, "An Uneasy Engagement: Political Crisis and Human Rights Culture in Thailand, 1958 to 1988," examines these annual reports along with preparatory documents drafted at the Office of the Juridical Council. Her critique of the Thai state's engagement with international human rights norms over a thirty-year period, in which Thailand "moved through a series of governments that were dictatorial, democratic, and variations in-between," draws attention to shifts in Thai understanding of human rights compliance and asks what the reporting reveals about how rights norms have changed both domestically and internationally. From the perspective of Haberkorn's study, a rights-based culture of transparency and accountability in Thailand appears elusive at best.

The second half of this volume begins with Peter Vail and Panuwat Pantakod's chapter "The Politics of Scripts: Language Rights, Heritage, and the Choice of Orthography for Khmer Vernaculars in Thailand," a study that examines the ways in which distinctive "ethnic" and migrant groups navigate belonging within the Thai nation. Vail and Panuwat's study maps the politics of choosing a script to teach Northern Khmer and links this issue with the cultural revitalization of the Khmer-speaking minority. The authors argue that the choice of script has implications for claims to Northern Khmer heritage and identity. Advocates of Khmer scripts maintain that using Thai script reinforces the notion that there is only one way to be a minority in the Thai polity: namely, to keep the group within the confines of nationally prescribed majority-minority relations. But the different script styles—*mul* or *crieng*—also evoke different understandings of heritage: where *mul* script evokes local religious traditions, *crieng* script is associated with Cambodian modernization. The authors raise questions about how heritage and language rights can be pursued, questions that imply divergent understandings of what "culture" means to different members of a group. Access to Thai-language education is crucial to social mobility for this and other minority groups. Vail and Panuwat's study demonstrates the complexities of pursuing language rights in the face of long-term effects of assimilation policies that have had very mixed effects on Northern Khmer-speakers and their descendants.

In chapter 7, "Negotiating with the Center: Diversity and Local Cultures in Thailand," Sirijit Sunanta offers a very different analysis of another minority in northeastern Thailand. She scrutinizes the ways that concepts of ethnic and cultural diversity as well as "localism" challenge or reify center-periphery relations in Thailand and asks how the enactment of these concepts implicates the articulation of rights. Phu Tai villagers in a village in northeast Thailand present themselves as good rural Thai citizens who have attained high levels of economic development, are loyal to the monarchy, and have thus earned their village an official designation as a "Cultural Village." Sirijit contends that, while Ban Phu villagers assert their rights to relative economic autonomy, they do not demand cultural autonomy or challenge the pre-modern cultural hierarchy in which Bangkok is the center of civilization and symbolic power. Thus, claims that might be seen as claims to cultural rights are defined by, and oriented towards, compliance with state authority and the dominant values of Thai-ness. Minority ethnicity is mobilized (and manipulated) as a resource to attract state attention and resources.

Mike Hayes and Matthew Mullen in the chapter entitled "Culture and Rights for Urban Minorities in Bangkok" (chapter 8) focus on immigrant urban groups in Bangkok and investigate how their legal standing and socioeconomic status shape the access they have to state protection and rights. The groups include long-standing Thai residents who have full citizenship, undocumented migrants, and those who come expecting to stay long enough to engage in some enterprise in Bangkok. The authors ask, what sort of "rights to the city" do these members of culturally distinctive communities enjoy? And under what conditions are they able (or inclined) to be visible in all aspects of their lives as a minority in Bangkok? Their study invites further investigation into the ways that minorities—both new and old— negotiate rights to culture in complex urban environments.

In the closing chapter of the volume, chapter 9, "Controlling Bad Drugs, Creating Good Citizens: Citizenship and Social Immobility for Thailand's Highland Ethnic Minorities," Mukdawan Sakboon examines citizenship and education programs for ethnic minorities in northern Thailand arguing that, although purportedly aimed at integrating these groups into the Thai nation, the pursuit of each can in fact make these minorities feel more conscious of how differently they are positioned within the national polity. The dominant ethnic Thai majority is portrayed as the norm, but this norm also depends upon the construction and reconstitution of non-Tai people (such as the hill tribe minorities) as dangerously different. Her study demonstrates how the path to citizenship can be made even more arduous for marginalized minorities whose "culture" is denigrated by the same state officials on whom they must rely as they seek to participate in more meaningful ways in Thai society.

Diversity and Rights: Some Concluding Thoughts

This volume's empirically grounded, historically informed approach to culture and rights elucidates the theoretical, conceptual, and normative challenges that scholars, activists, and policymakers alike must face when thinking through cultural rights and encourages critical reflection on how cultural rights can contribute to genuine diversity in Thailand. By looking at a range of settings in which cultural rights research and policy programs may take root, *Rights to Culture* invites audiences from other countries to appreciate the complexities involved in the choice of whether or how to adopt a rights-informed approach to "culture" in its multiple manifestations.

Bill Logan notes in a seminal article, "Opening Pandora's Box" (2007), that cultural rights as a concept does not yet have a single overarching meaning. Because scholars and practitioners use the term cultural rights in at least two different ways, their approach to diversity also diverges. While some understand cultural rights as a subset of human rights, (that is, a set of norms already laid out in core international human rights instruments), others invoke cultural rights in the defense of cultural diversity. These divergent interpretations can lead quickly to the problem of cultural relativism and point towards rather profound differences in the ways human rights agendas are pursued: if human rights are to be universal and derive their force from being applicable in *any* setting where a human right may be violated, how much room for cultural diversity can be permitted if the cultural diversity being invoked sanctions practices that contravene international human rights norms?

Logan observes that the tension between these two uses of cultural rights is either downplayed or left to the sidelines. Yes, we want diversity, Logan maintains, but what *kind* of diversity and who will decide? As Bryan Turner notes,

> If human beings are to have the capacity to articulate their needs and interests, then cultural rights to language, religion, and identity are fundamental to the generic right to enjoy rights. Yet securing universal cultural rights is deeply problematic; it is difficult to justify them without confronting the problem of cultural relativism, and it is also difficult to know how these rights could be enforced. (2006, 45)

Scholarship and policy discussions about cultural rights and human rights continue to return to this question: is it possible to have genuine diversity *and* defend a single, internationally recognized standard of human rights if you find instances where cultural practices contravene human rights? Proponents of cultural rights maintain that the conflict between culture and rights would be diminished if rights conventions were formulated with due attention to cultural difference and if cultural practices that directly violated individuals' human rights were prohibited. "International norms prohibit the exercise of cultural practices that contravene internationally proclaimed human rights" (Stamatopolou 2004). This is a point that the United Nations Special Rapporteur on Culture, Farida Shaheed, has advocated very publicly, as well.

> The principle of universality of human rights, one of the core principles of international human rights law, on the one hand, and cultural rights and cultural diversity on the other, are sometimes considered as opposed. This view stems partly from a misplaced tendency to equate cultural diversity with cultural relativism, which has the effect of raising fears and misunderstandings regarding the recognition and implementation of cultural rights. (2010, 12)

As noted in the first part of this introduction, anthropologists of rights in particular remain skeptical, but advocates of cultural rights maintain that more specificity about cultural rights is needed for this problem to be more systematically addressed.

Rights to Culture responds to the call for specificity about cultural rights in part by opening a space for these ideas to be examined in the context of Thai history and politics. Attention to cultural rights began as social and socio-legal movements on the part of indigenous peoples in the United States, Canada, and Australia (Brown 2003), and cultural rights conventions were subsequently drafted and given force in response to the rise of ethno-nationalism in Europe in the 1990s (Stamatopolou 2004). But Thailand's cultural politics have been forged in very different conditions. Thailand was never fully colonized or "settled" by Europeans (hence there were no indigenous peoples), and the Thai state's authoritarian, or at least heavily militarized, governments over the past eighty years promoted and defended a royal-nationalist development agenda that preempted ethno-regional autonomy politics.

As the studies in this book illustrate, changes over the past fifteen years or so have made cultural rights more salient in Thailand. Some of Thailand's upland minorities, for example, have recently begun to apply to themselves the term "indigenous" (Prasit et al. 2008) in order to extend the range of resources they might draw upon in their decades-old struggle for citizenship and to earn a more just recognition from the Thai government and from the lowland populations who continue to regard them with such suspicion or apathy. The recent declaration of special cultural zones for a few minority communities (in the north and for the Andaman Sea peoples) also suggests that some measure of "positive discrimination" on behalf of these disadvantaged groups will be instituted to facilitate the preservation of cultural heritage practices. In other spheres as well, the Thai government's concern for protecting national heritage in both its tangible and intangible forms is an inducement to take cultural rights conventions seriously.

Rights to Culture evaluates the expanding domain of heritage politics and critically assesses how "culture" and "heritage" come to be strategically invoked by communities and activists as they attempt to secure rights to land, language, housing, and citizenship. Discourse and practices relating to heritage increasingly include claims by groups attempting to legitimize their demands for access to resources and for participation in decisions on how they can continue to practice their cultural traditions. As Denes observed about the rise of heritage in Asia as a site of discourse and practice,

> The widespread concern for heritage preservation in the region is directly linked to the rapid pace of socio-economic change and the perceived "losses" of cultural diversity and traditional lifeways to the seemingly relentless juggernaut of globalization. One significant outcome of this increasing attention to heritage has been the revival and celebration of the cultures of historically marginalized, indigenous and minority ethnic groups. (Denes 2011, 168)

Rights to culture may not merit the same attention that other human rights do. Helaine Silverman's recent writings on human rights and heritage address this problem as well, calling for ongoing research and discussion.

> Human rights [are rights] such as: life itself without fear of intimidation or physical abuse by the state or its agents; adequate food and health care; freedom of religious practice (or not to practice religion); group expression of cultural traditions (and the right to leave that tradition); political expression; unfettered mobility; gender equality. Not all cultural

rights rise to the level of these human rights. Indeed, some cultural rights as locally practiced might be argued to abrogate human rights. The challenge is to defend those cultural rights that are human rights—but who decides? and how?—without provoking disastrous resistance by oppositional forces. (Silverman n.d.)

Taking up Silverman's call for pushing forward with research on the relationship between heritage and rights, *Rights to Culture* also brings us face to face with the complex interrelationship between social justice and culture and requires that we acknowledge how problematic the question "who decides?" can be when a country is as politically divided as Thailand has been for much of the past decade. The so-called "color politics" that has held Thailand in its grip since the 2006 military coup has had a deleterious effect on civil society and social movements, whose growth seemed so promising in the 1990s. Freedom of expression became politicized, with an alarming rise in the number of charges being filed against people accused of insulting the monarchy.

Over this same period, in Thailand's predominantly Muslim southernmost provinces violence between state security forces and militants from within the ethnically Malay Thai-Muslim population increased, resulting in the imposition of martial law in the south since 2004, and the declaration of an Emergency Decree since July 2005. This divisive climate has proved inhospitable for the protection of rights. If the culture of rights needs strengthening in Thailand, *Rights to Culture* also invites readers to think about the possibilities for and constraints to adopting rights idioms when negotiating with the state for access to resources or for rights to participate in managing heritage located within communities.

Modern Thai history offers ample evidence that those deemed disloyal or "dangerously different" because of political views or because they belong to one among the many groups who make up what the Thai historian and social critic Thongchai Winichakul has termed "the Others within" (2000) are judged harshly. While, for much of the past decade or more, Thai state policies encouraged tourism and local development and promoted pride in diversity of cultural identities, these policies relied (and continue to rely) on nationalist and developmentalist frameworks that allow limited room for rights consciousness to develop. Some of the cases highlighted in this book illustrate the willingness on the part of some of these historically marginalized groups to assert claims to their cultural heritage and their identity, suggesting that rights-informed approaches to cultural diversity and the management of cultural heritage may become more widely embraced in Thailand. As the global rights regime continues to exercise hegemony in international relations, in transnational activism, and in local battles for more equitable access to political security and cultural recognition, the Thai state and minority groups are also being drawn into debates over rights to culture.

Notes

1. Throughout the book, we use Siam to refer to Thailand in the period before 1939, when the country's name was officially changed.

References

Anan Ganjanapan. 2000. *Local Control of Land and Forest: Cultural Dimensions of Resource Management in Northern Thailand*. Chiang Mai: Regional Center for Social Science and Sustainable Development, Faculty of Social Sciences, Chiang Mai University.

————. 2008. *Multiplicity of Community Forestry as Knowledge Space in the Northern Thai Highlands*. Working Paper Series 35. Kyoto: Afrasian Center for Peace and Development Studies, Ryukoku University.

Anderson, Benedict. 2003. "Nationalism and Cultural Survival in Our Time: A Sketch." In *At the Risk of Being Heard: Identity, Indigenous Rights and Postcolonial States*, edited by Dean Bartholemew and Jerome M. Levi, 165–90. Ann Arbor: University of Michigan Press.

Appiah, Kwame A. 2004. *The Ethics of Identity*. Princeton, NJ: Princeton University Press.

Baker, Chris, and Pasuk Phongpaichit. 2005. *A History of Thailand*. Cambridge: Cambridge University Press.

Brown, Michael. 2003. *Who Owns Native Culture?* Cambridge, MA: Harvard University Press.

Castellino, Joshua, and Elvira Dominguez Redondo. 2006. *Minority Rights in Asia: A Comparative Legal Analysis*. Oxford: Oxford University Press.

Cholthira Satyawadhna. 2000. "Community Rights in Thailand and Southeast Asia." *Tai Culture: International Review on Tai Cultural Studies* 5 (2): 8–14.

Connors, Michael K. 2005. "Ministering Culture: Hegemony and the Politics of Culture and Identity in Thailand." *Critical Asian Studies* 37 (4): 523–51.

Cowan, Jane K. 2001. "Ambiguities of an Emancipatory Discourse: The Making of a Macedonian Minority in Greece." In *Culture and Rights: Anthropological Perspectives*, edited by Jane Cowan et al., 152–76. Cambridge: Cambridge University Press.

———. 2003. "The Uncertain Political Limits of Cultural Claims: Minority Rights Politics in South-east Europe." In *Human Rights in Global Perspective: Anthropological Studies of Rights, Claims and Entitlements*, edited by Richard A. Wilson and Jon P. Mitchell, 140–62. New York: Routledge.

———. 2006. "Culture and Rights after *Culture and Rights*." *American Anthropologist* 108, (1): 9–24.

Cowan, Jane, Marie-Benedicte Dembour, and Richard Wilson, eds. 2001. *Culture and Rights: Anthropological Perspectives*. Cambridge: Cambridge University Press.

Denes, Alexandra. 2010. "Lopburi's 'Life Museum' and the Rights of the Dead: Reflections from a Thai Human Rights Commission Forum." Culture and Rights in Thailand blog posting, 16 July 2010. Accessed at http://cultureandrights.wordpress.com/2010/07/16/lopburis-life-museum-and-the-rights-of-the-dead-reflections-from-a-thai-human-rights-commission-forum/.

———. 2011. "The Revitalization of Khmer Ethnic Identity in Thailand: Empowerment or Confinement?" In *Handbook of Heritage in Asia*, edited by Patrick Daly and Tim Winters. New York: Routledge.

Donavanik, Jade. 2012. "Talking Publicly about Thai Monarchy." *Bangkok Post*, 15 February. Accessed at http://www.bangkokpost.com/opinion/opinion/279862/talking-publicly-about-thai-monarchy.

Engel, David M., and Jaruwan S. Engel. 2010. *Tort, Custom and Karma: Globalization and Legal Consciousness in Thailand*. Stanford, CA: Stanford University Press.

Gledhill, John. 1997. "Liberalism, Socio-Economic Rights and the Politics of Identity: From Moral Economy To Indigenous Rights." In *Human Rights, Culture and Context: Anthropological Perspectives*, edited by Richard A. Wilson, 70–110. London: Pluto Press.

Goodale, Mark. 2009. *Surrendering to Utopia: An Anthropology of Human Rights*. Stanford, CA: Stanford University Press.

Goodale, Mark, and Sally Engle Merry. 2009. *The Practice of Human Rights: Tracking Law between the Global and the Local*. Cambridge: Cambridge University Press.

Government of Thailand 1997. *Constitution of the Kingdom of Thailand 1997*. Election Commission of Thailand. Accessed at http://www.ect.go.th/english/laws/constitutioneng.html.

Haberkorn, Tyrell. 2011a. "Dispossessing Law: Arbitrary Detention in Southern Thailand." In *Accumulating Insecurity: Violence and Dispossession in the Making of Everyday Life*, edited by Shelly Feldman, Charles Geisler, and Gayatri A. Menon, 122–40. Athens, GA: University of Georgia Press.

————. 2011b. "The Unbearable Lightness of Justice: Review of *Tort, Custom and Karma: Globalization and Legal Consciousness in Thailand*." Accessed at http://asiapacific.anu.edu.au/newmandala/2011/06/15/review-of-tort-custom-and-karma -tlcnmrev-xxiv/.

Harrison, Rachel. 2007. "Somewhere Over the Rainbow: Global Projections, Local Allusions in 'Tears of the Black Tiger' [Fathalaijone]." *Inter-Asia Cultural Studies* 8 (2): 194–210.

Harrison, Rachel, and Peter A. Jackson, eds. 2010. *The Ambiguous Allure of the West: Traces of the Colonial in Thailand*. Hong Kong: Hong Kong University Press.

Hayami, Yoko. 2000. "Challenges to Community Rights in the Hill Forests: State Policy and Local Contradictions. A Karen Case." *Tai Culture: International Review on Tai Cultural Studies* (Special Issue on Community Rights in Thailand and Southeast Asia) 5 (2): 104–31.

————. 2006. "Redefining 'Otherness' from Northern Thailand. Introduction: Notes Towards Debating Multiculturalism in Thailand and Beyond." *Southeast Asian Studies* 44 (2): 283–94.

Ignatieff, Michael. 2001. *Human Rights as Politics and Idolatry*. Princeton, NJ: Princeton University Press.

Kasian Tejapira. 1997. "The Story of Three Songs: Illuminations on the Cultural Politics of Thai Cultural Citizenship." *Journal of Behavioral and Social Sciences* 1: 105–28.

Keyes, Charles F. 2008. "Ethnicity and the Nation-States of Thailand and Vietnam." In *Challenging the Limits: Indigenous Peoples of the Mekong Region*, edited by Prasit Leepreecha, Don McCaskill, and Kwanchewan Buadaeng, 13–53. Chiang Mai: Mekong Press.

Kukathas, Chandran. 1992. "Are There Any Cultural Rights?" *Political Theory* 20: 105–39.

Kymlicka, Will. 2004. *Culturally Responsive Policies*. Background Paper for UNDP Human Development Report. New York: UNDP, Human Development Report Office. Accessed at http://hdr.undp.org/en/reports/global/hdr2004/papers/HDR2004_Will_Kymlicka.pdf

Levitt, Peggy, and Sally Engle Merry. 2009. "Vernacularization on the Ground: Local Uses of Global Women's Rights in Peru, China, India and the United States." *Global Networks* 9 (4): 441–61.

Logan, William S. 2007. "Closing Pandora's Box: Human Rights Conundrums in Cultural Heritage Protection." In Silverman and Ruggles 2007, 33–52.

Loos, Tamara. 2006. *Subject Siam: Family, Law, and Colonial Modernity in Thailand.* Ithaca, NY: Cornell University Press.

Meijknecht, Anna, and Byung Sook de Vries. 2010. "Is There a Place for Minorities' and Indigenous Peoples' Rights within ASEAN?: Asian Values, ASEAN Values and the Protection of Southeast Asian Minorities and Indigenous Peoples." *International Journal on Minority and Group Rights* 17: 75–110.

Merry, Sally Engle. 2006. *Human Rights and Gender Violence: Translating International Law into Local Justice.* Chicago: University of Chicago Press.

Missingham, Bruce D. 2003. *The Assembly of the Poor: From Local Struggles to National Protest.* Chiang Mai: Silkworm Books.

Munger, Frank. 2006/7. "Culture, Power, and Law: Thinking about the Anthropology of Rights in Thailand in an Era of Globalization. *New York Law School Law Review* 51: 818–38.

Nidhi Eoseewong. 2003. "The Thai Cultural Constitution." *Kyoto Review of Southeast Asia* 3. Accessed at http://kyotoreview.cseas.kyoto-u.ac.jp/issue/issue2/index. html.

Pinkaew Laungaramsri. 2003. "Ethnicity and the Politics of Ethnic Classification in Thailand." In *Ethnicity in Asia,* edited by Colin Mackerras, 157–73. London: Routledge.

Prasit Leepreecha, Don McCaskill, and Kwanchewan Buadaeng, eds. 2008. *Challenging the Limits: Indigenous Peoples of the Mekong Region.* Chiang Mai: Mekong Press.

Rajagopal, Balakrishnan. 2010. *International Law from Below: Development, Social Movements and Third World Resistance.* Cambridge: Cambridge University Press.

Reynolds, Craig, ed. 1993. *National Identity and Its Defenders: Thailand, 1939–1989.* Chiang Mai: Silkworm Books.

Saneh Chamarik. 2006. *Thai Human Rights in Global Perspective.* Bangkok: Thailand Research Fund.

Shaheed, Farida. 2010. "Report of the Independent Expert in the Field of Cultural Rights, Ms. Farida Shaheed, Submitted Pursuant to Resolution 10/23 of the Human Rights Council." UN General Assembly, Human Rights Council, 14th Session, March. Accessed at http://www.awid.org/Library/Report-of-the-independent-expert-in-the-field-of-cultural-rights-Ms.-Farida-Shaheed-submitted-pursuant-to-resolution-10-23-of-the-Human-Rights-Council.

Silverman, Helaine, ed. 2011. *Contested Cultural Heritage: Religion, Nationalism, Erasure and Exclusion in a Global World.* New York: Springer.

———. n.d. "Cultural Rights, Human Rights, and Heritage." Unpublished manuscript.

Silverman, Helaine, and Fairchild Ruggles, eds. 2007. *Cultural Heritage and Human Rights.* New York: Springer.

Sinnott, Megan. 2011. "The Language of Rights, Deviance, and Pleasure: Organizational Responses to Discourses of Same-Sexuality and Transgenderism in Thailand." In *Queer Bangkok: 21st Century Markets, Media, and Rights*, edited by Peter A. Jackson, 205–28. Chiang Mai: Silkworm Books.

Stamatopolou, Elsa. 2004. "Why Cultural Rights Now?" *Human Rights Initiative Program (1994–2005)*. Accessed at http://www.carnegiecouncil.org/resources/transcripts/5006.html.

Streckfuss, David. 2011. *Truth on Trial in Thailand: Defamation, Treason, and Lese-Majeste*. New York: Routledge.

Suchat Wongsinnak. 2009. "Legal Consciousness, Human Rights, and the Thai War on Drugs." PhD diss., University of Florida.

Tamthai, Mark, and Somkiat Boonchoo. 2009. "National Security Policies on the Southern Border Provinces, 1974–2003." In *Imagined Land? The State and Southern Violence in Thailand*, edited by Chaiwat Satha-Anand, 17–44. Tokyo: Research Institute for Languages and Cultures of Asia and Africa.

Tanabe, Shigeharu. 2008. "Imagined and Imagining Communities." In *Imagining Communities in Thailand*, edited by Shigeharu Tanabe, 1–20. Chiang Mai: Mekong Press.

Thanapol Limapichart. 2011. "The Prescription of Good Books: The Formation of the Discourse and Cultural Authority of Literature in Modern Thailand (1860s–1950s)." PhD diss., University of Wisconsin, Madison.

Thanet Aphornsuvan. 2001. "*Sitthi* in Thai Thought." *Tai Culture: International Review on Tai Cultural Studies* 6 (1&2): 273–89.

Thongchai Winichakul. 2000. "The Others Within: Travel and Ethno-spatial Differentiation of Siamese Subjects, 1885–1910." In *Civility and Savagery: Social Identity in the Tai States*, edited by Andrew Turton, 38–62. Richmond: Curzon.

Turner, Bryan. 2006. *Vulnerability and Human Rights*. University Park: Pennsylvania State University Press.

UNHCR [United Nations High Commission on Refugees] Thailand. 2010. "Statistical Snapshot of Thailand." Accessed at http://www.unhcr.org/cgi-bin/texis/vtx/page?page=49e489646.

Vail, Peter. 2006. "Can a Language of a Million Speakers Be Endangered?: Language Shift and Apathy among Northern Khmer Speakers in Thailand." *International Journal of the Sociology of Language* 178: 135–47.

Walker, Andrew. 2001. "The 'Karen Consensus,' Ethnic Politics, and Resource-Use Legitimacy in Northern Thailand." *Asian Ethnicity* 2 (2): 145–62.

———. 2009. *Tai Lands and Thailand: Community and the State in Southeast Asia*. Singapore: National University of Singapore Press.

Wilson, Richard A. 1997. "Human Rights, Culture and Context: An Introduction." In *Human Rights, Culture and Context: Anthropological Perspectives*, edited by Richard A. Wilson, 1–27. London: Pluto Press.

———. 2004. "A Response to Elsa Stamatopoulou's Paper 'Why Cultural Rights Now?'" Accessed at http://www.carnegiecouncil.org/studio/transcripts/5084. html.

Woodiwiss, Anthony. 2005. *Human Rights: Key Ideas*. New York: Routledge.

2

A Rights-Based Approach to Cultural Heritage Management at the Phanom Rung Historical Park in Northeast Thailand

―――∞∞∞――

Alexandra Denes and Tiamsoon Sirisrisak

Introduction

An important development in the field of cultural heritage in recent years has been its growing, explicit linkage to human rights. Legislative instruments have been promulgated and campaigns launched that advocate for the rights of individuals and communities to participate fully in the enjoyment, use, and interpretation of their cultural heritage.[1] As Farida Shaheed, an independent expert in the field of cultural rights at the Office of the UN Human Rights Commissioner in Geneva, has written (2011, 7), the growing international support for cultural heritage as a human right signifies that

> . . . a shift has taken place from the preservation/safeguard of cultural heritage as such, based on its outstanding value for humanity, to the protection of cultural heritage as being of crucial value for individuals and communities in relation to their cultural identity.

In keeping with these international trends, official heritage sectors in many countries have begun to endorse legislation that promotes a rights-based approach to heritage management. For instance, the 1990 US Native American Graves Protection and Repatriation Act (NAGPRA) requires federally funded agencies and institutions to repatriate human remains and cultural objects requested by their Native American descendant communities. At the Ngorongo World Heritage site in Tanzania, the Maasai have come to play an integral role in the management of the conservation area (Chirikure et al. 2010). And in Australia, archaeological projects attend to local indigenous interests in heritage (see, for example, Greer 2010).

In Thailand—the focus of this chapter—there also are signs that the pendulum is swinging towards participatory heritage management and recognition of cultural rights. Indeed, the rights of communities to manage their own cultural and natural resources are stipulated in Section 65 of the 2007 Constitution:

> Persons so assembling as to be a traditional community shall have the right to conserve or restore their customs, local knowledge, arts or good culture of their community and of the nation and participate in management, maintenance, preservation and exploitation of natural resources and environment in a balanced and sustainable manner and persistently.

Community rights and responsibilities to manage cultural heritage resources are also stipulated in Section 7 of the ICOMOS-Thailand "Draft Charter for Preservation and Management of Monuments and Cultural Heritage," which addresses the importance of community stakeholder engagement, and specifies that the heritage sector must respect the beliefs, values, and cultural practices of local communities. A Cabinet resolution passed on 3 August 2010 recognizes the rights of some 300,000 indigenous Karen to maintain their cultural identity and traditional forest-based livelihoods in special "cultural zones." Policy areas covered by the resolution include ethnic identity and culture, resource management, citizenship rights, the transfer of cultural heritage, and education.

While these new directions at the level of policy are encouraging, in practice, the turn to a more rights-based approach to heritage management is still at a very early stage in Thailand, and faces a host of challenges. Drawing on field research at one of Thailand's preeminent national heritage sites—the Phanom Rung Historical Park in Buriram province—this paper identifies some of the core obstacles to a rights-based, participatory heritage management in the Thai context, and proposes some actions that can be taken around those obstacles.

Context and Background:
The Khmer Sanctuaries in Buriram Province

Located in Thailand's northeastern region, Buriram province is situated in the Mun River Basin, on the southern end of the Khorat Plateau, bordering Cambodia to the south. With the rise of the Khmer empire centered at Angkor beginning in the ninth century, the earlier Mon-Dvaravati culture of the Mun Valley was gradually eclipsed by Khmer civilization and the Hindu-Brahman cult of the god-king, or *devaraja*, a highly ritualized mode of statecraft that centered on the construction of monumental temples symbolizing the Hindu cosmos wherein the king was the divine universal ruler and living manifestation of the Hindu god Shiva (Chandler 2000; Freeman 1998).

Following the collapse of Angkor in the fifteenth century, the Khmer temples in the northeast of Thailand lost their original function and meaning as sites for the ritual legitimation of a ruler's divine power. Nevertheless, while construction of new temples and associated buildings ceased after the fall of Angkor, they were never completely abandoned. As the Thai historian Srisaksa Vallibhotama has argued (1989), local populations in the northeast— including the indigenous ethnic Khmer and Kui, as well as subsequent settler populations of Lao and Thai—continued to modify, repair, rebuild, and reuse the Khmer structures, which suggests the temples' reincorporation into local beliefs and a continuation of religious practice, albeit not in the context of a state cult.

> We can think of this kind of renovation [*kan som saem*] as a kind of revival of "dead" religious architecture. However, it was not necessary for this revival to restore the original beliefs and practices associated with the site. Rather, it was the belief systems of the living that would be instilled in the edifice. This is because the people of this region shared the conviction that it was not necessary to destroy ancient religious sanctuaries, as it was possible to transform them. (Srisaksa 1989, 46; our translation)

Byrne (2009), Byrne and Barnes (1995), Edwards (2008), Karlström (2005), and Thompson (1997) have all made similar observations about the transformation of religious architecture and artifacts in Thailand, Lao PDR, and Cambodia through renovation and repurposing by successive populations. Within the syncretic religious paradigm of popular Buddhism, which combines Theravada Buddhism with Hindu-Brahmanism and animism, the remains of historical religious structures are not regarded as archaeological sites belonging to the past. Rather, they are regarded as sites of potent spiritual power[2] that can be harnessed through propitiation, veneration, and renovation. As Byrne writes (1995, 274) with regards to the Buddhist stupa, "even as a ruin, there is always the possibility of a stupa or temple being reactivated." Similarly, Thompson (1997, 23) notes that in the post-Angkorian period, Khmer monarchs and other pilgrims "reappropriated" and incorporated the sacred space of the Angkorian sanctuaries into their own local sects of ancestor worship and Theravada Buddhism.

David Engel, a legal scholar of Thailand, brings to the fore another important dimension of the adaptive potential of archaeological remains (2009). He observes that a traditional belief in guardian spirits inhabiting specific geographical loci such as trees, mountains, and rocks is a sociocultural construct found throughout Thailand and much of Southeast Asia. The spirits of place inscribed in the landscape are symbols of the community, and the collective identity associated with these loci is regularly reaffirmed through ritual propitiation, mediumship rites, and offerings. Tutelary spirits of place offered protection and were invoked to negotiate one's luck and fate, identify the causes of illness and injury, and mediate conflicts and determine compensation in the case of violations of social norms.

In our fieldwork we found evidence of this adaptive reincorporation of the ancient Khmer sanctuaries into living local beliefs and practices associated with both Buddhism and the tutelary spirits of place at the sites that are the focus of this study: Prasat Phanom Rung and Prasat Mueang Tam.

Phanom Rung and Mueang Tam:
Mythic Landscapes and Places of Pilgrimage

Prasat Phanom Rung lies on a dramatically and strategically situated site on the summit of an extinct volcano, four hundred meters above sea level overlooking the Dong Rek mountain range to the southeast. Built of laterite and sandstone during the tenth to thirteenth centuries, the Hindu shrine is dedicated to the deity Shiva, and symbolizes his heavenly abode, Mount

Kailash. Phanom Rung was connected to another nearby Saivite temple called Mueang Tam, meaning "lower city," because of its position vis-à-vis the hilltop sanctuary. Located eight kilometers southeast of Phanom Rung in Prakhon Chai district, the Prasat Mueang Tam sanctuary is linked to Phanom Rung by the ancient "royal road," which stretched from Phimai, another great Khmer sanctuary (in present-day Nakhon Ratchasima) to Angkor.

The communities that today live in the vicinity of the Phanom Rung and Mueang Tam sanctuaries are predominantly ethnic Khmer and ethnic Lao, with a sprinkling of Thai Khorat and ethnic Kui. Ethnic Khmer of this region are known as Khmer Leu, or "Northern Khmer"—an appellation that refers to the Khmer who live north of the Dong Rek mountain range, which forms a natural boundary between Thailand and Cambodia. Historians have suggested that some of the ethnic Khmer populations living near the sites may be the descendants of the Khmer-speaking peoples who would have lived in the vicinity of the sanctuaries at the height of the Khmer empire, and who stayed on in the region following the empire's collapse (Srisaksa 1989). This idea is supported by royal archives from the kingdom of Ayutthaya, which make reference to "the forest Khmer" (*khamen pa dong*) living in the area of present-day Buriram, who were a tribute-paying principality under the authority of Phimai and Nakhon Ratchasima. Other Khmer villages around the sites were settled by later waves of Khmer migrants, who moved into Buriram from Surin and Sisaket in the eighteenth to nineteenth centuries to flee war between Cambodia and Thailand during the reign of King Taksin (1767–82) and seek new territories for rice cultivation (Paitoon 1984).

The first wave of Lao settlers could have come to the region as early as the sixteenth century, when the Lao kingdom of Lan Xang made major inroads into the Khorat Plateau and Mun River Valley, in what is now northeastern Thailand. Later waves of Lao settlement due to war and forced migration came in the eighteenth century.[3]

The authors conducted fieldwork in Buriram from October 2010 to June 2012. Through interviews with twenty-two residents living near Phanom Rung and Mueang Tam, focus group meetings, and cultural mapping, we learned that these ancient sites are an important part of local beliefs and ritual practices among both the Khmer and Lao communities. (fig. 2.1) For instance, before the road was built up to Phanom Rung in 1968, and prior to its restoration by the Fine Arts Department (FAD) and declaration as a

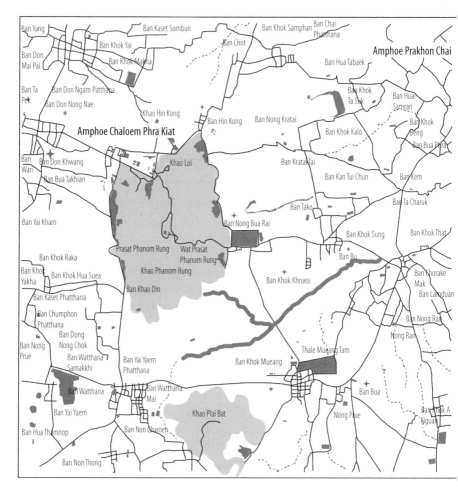

Figure 2.1. Phanom Rung map with surrounding villages.
Stars indicate villages where interviews were conducted.

historical park by the government in 1998, villagers from across the region would come for an annual pilgrimage, which they called *prapheni duean ha sip ha kham*, or the festival of the waxing moon during the fifth month of the lunar calendar, which falls in the month of April in the solar calendar. One informant, Mr. Tia, said that every year the villages around Phanom Rung would ready themselves to welcome their ethnic Khmer "kin" (*phi nong*) who traveled by oxcart from as far away as Surin province to participate. During this annual festival, pilgrims would climb the path up the mountain to Phanom Rung to pay respects to the tutelary spirits and deities of the sanctuary (*sen wai chao thi lae thepphachao*), to ask for their benevolent protection, and to ensure sufficient rain and fertility of the soil in the coming year. The sanctuary was a place for asking for good luck and good fortune, and for repaying the deities who fulfilled one's wishes (*bon lae kae bon*). Villagers used to come to pay respects to the spirits of place with flowers and incense, and some would also put gold leaf on the sanctuary structures. There was also a belief that disrespectful acts or violations of the site could lead to misfortune, such as illness and flooding, and Mr. Tia added that those who took rocks away from the site would fall ill and would have to return them.

Another informant was Phra Bandit, a sixty-one-year-old ethnic Khmer monk at the Wat Sahamit Narueman monastery in Khok Sung village. Prior to entering the monkhood he had served as a restoration worker at Phanom Rung from 1971 to 1988. Phra Bandit told us that prior to restoration, local villagers used to organize the annual pilgrimage to Phanom Rung every year in April. He said that another important reason why villagers traveled by foot up the mountain was to give alms to the monks at the forest monastery on the grounds of the Phanom Rung sanctuary and to pay respects to the image of the Buddha's footprint (*roi phra phutthabat*) (fig. 2.2). The monk who established the monastery in the 1930s was named Luang Pu Plian—a wandering monk (*phra thudong*) from Surin. The area was heavily forested, and there was no road up to the site at the time. Phra Bandit speculated that before the establishment of the monastery, local people would rarely climb the mountain, because it was so heavily forested and there were all kinds of snakes and wild animals. Phra Bandit maintained that people in this region have always known about the sanctuaries even though they were rarely visited. In the past, there were villagers who could recount lengthy stories about the

Figure 2.2. Archival photo of Prang Noi housing the Buddha's footprint, from Prince Damrong's visit to Phanom Rung, 1929. Courtesy of National Archives.

temple—such as the legend of Nang Oraphim and Thao Pachit—but these storytellers are all gone now.

Many of the local informants we interviewed in the region of Phanom Rung gave similar accounts of the beliefs and practices surrounding the site, which centered on pilgrimage to seek protection from tutelary spirits of place, paying alms at the forest monastery, and worshipping the Buddha's footprint. While it is impossible to ascertain how long these beliefs and practices have been in existence, we know from the historical record that the worship of the Buddha's footprint has been taking place for at least one hundred years (Aymonier 1999 [1901], Phumjit 1986).

The syncretic integration of spirit worship and Theravada Buddhism is typical of popular Buddhism in Thailand, which recognizes spirits as being part of Buddhist cosmology and the cycle of karmic causation (Tambiah 1975). This also confirms that Khmer temples were not abandoned after the fall of the Angkorian kingdom; rather, their functions and meanings were transformed through their integration into local beliefs and practices associated with animism and Theravada Buddhism.

Another related point has to do with how Theravada Buddhism was vernacularized through its inscription in the local cultural landscape. After the fall of Angkor, Theravada Buddhism became the ascendant religion in present-day Thailand and many neighboring countries. The Buddhist teachings were conveyed by monks who studied, taught, and preached Pali texts, such as the Jataka tales, which recount the previous lives of the Buddha. Through their oral transmission, the Jataka tales were often modified and localized to reflect attributes of the storytellers and their audiences and features of the local landscape. This process of vernacularization was evident in the legend of Oraphim and Pachit, an epic love story featuring the Buddha in a past life that takes place against the backdrop of the Angkorian sanctuaries in the northeast, including Phimai, Phanom Rung and Mueang Tam. In the version found in the northeast of Thailand, the protagonist, Thao Pachit, is a virtuous prince related to Khmer royalty, who traveled to Phanom Rung to study with a famous ascetic. According to the tale, Thao Pachit is responsible for renovating Phanom Rung, as well as constructing the sanctuary of Mueang Tam for the birth of his future wife, Oraphim. What is most striking is that events and places in the legend are linked to place names across Buriram and Nakhon Ratchasima, clearly indicating the centrality of this story and the sanctuaries to the identity of the local populace.[4]

The sanctuary of Mueang Tam also evoked a strong sense of connection among villagers in the past. An informant told us of a range of ritual practices performed there to appease the spirits and ask for their protection. For instance, there was a ritual called *tham bun tak bat prasat*, or making merit at the sanctuary, which was performed every year around May for the well-being and health of the community. One headman of Khok Mueang village, Mr. Prasit, referred to these as rites of offering (*phithi buang suang*) and worship of the spirits (*sen wai*) and said that failure to perform them could lead to misfortunes and poor agricultural yields. Indeed, the ancient site of Mueang Tam was like a central community-meeting place (*sala klang ban*), but after restoration, community members lost their role as primary custodians when the FAD came to manage the site.[5]

We also encountered beliefs in the tutelary spirits of the Khmer ruins at Nong Bua Lai village—a predominantly ethnic Khmer community located to the east of Phanom Rung. There the headman recounted how his election as headman had been foretold by a spirit medium of the Kuti Ruesi *arokayasala* (hospital). He explained that his village had many problems, including drug use among youth and internal factionalism; however, since becoming headman, he had successfully restored unity to the village, in part through organizing *buang suang* rites at the *arokayasala*.

To summarize, we found that the original function of the sites had been transformed through the agency of local ethnic Khmer, Lao, and Thai populations, who adapted the sites following the expansion of Theravada Buddhism in the post-Angkorian period. It is noteworthy that local populations adapted a Buddhist Jataka story to reflect their own cultural and historical landscape—turning a Buddhist legend into a vehicle of cultural "memory" about the Khmer empire in present-day northeastern Thailand. In this sense, Theravada Buddhism did not completely erase the earlier Khmer culture; rather, elements of local Khmer culture were integrated into post-Angkorian Buddhist practice and the cultural landscape.

"Discovery" and Restoration:
From Site of Pilgrimage to National Heritage

As Siam struggled to maintain its independence against the expanding European powers in Southeast Asia in the late nineteenth and early twentieth centuries, its ruling monarchs sought to establish their equality with European colonizers by proving their own civility, or *siwilai* (Thongchai 2000). The disciplines of history and archaeology were crucial tools in this endeavor, as they were a means for the ruling elite to harness the authority of the past while substantiating their grasp of Western scientific rationalism, hence legitimating their rule (Peleggi 2002).

One figure who played a prominent role in constructing Siam's official history and national heritage during this period was Prince Damrong—a prominent statesman during the early years of Siam's modernization. In 1929, Prince Damrong visited the northeastern provinces of Siam, making his way to the Phanom Rung sanctuary by elephant (fig. 2.3).[6] A few years after this visit, in 1935, Phanom Rung was declared a national historic site in the *Government Gazette* No. 52, Chapter 75.

During the decades of the 1930s through the 1950s, the sanctuaries and communities near Phanom Rung were little affected by its national heritage status, and local practices of worship and pilgrimage at the site reportedly continued. The situation began to change in the 1960s, when the FAD launched the restoration of Phanom Rung and Phimai under the supervision of two French experts, Bernard P. Groslier and Pierre Pichard, working for UNESCO.

In his 1972 survey report and restoration plan, Pichard described the history, grandeur, and monumentality of Phanom Rung, and the value it would have for cultural tourism—while noting the FAD's lack of interest in the site. To Pichard, the value of the site and the rationale for its restoration did not derive from the place of Khmer heritage within the Thai past or its significance to local populations. Rather, the value of the site was its import as a monumental vestige of the ancient Khmer empire, which would attract "enlightened" cultural tourists. Importantly, Pichard acknowledged that Phanom Rung was a living Buddhist site, and he remarked upon the existence of a Buddhist monastery located on the hill near the sanctuary where local villagers regularly paid alms to the resident monks. Pichard regarded the existence of the monastery in a positive light, stating that "it prevents the site

Figure 2.3. Prince Damrong's visit to Phanom Rung, 1929. Courtesy of National Archives.

from becoming a deserted spot or a mere museum" (1972, 32). He nonetheless recommended the relocation of the monastery so as to preserve the visual integrity of the monument.

As it was explained to us by the present abbot of the Phanom Rung monastery, which is now situated at the base of the sanctuary, the relocation of the monastery in the early 1970s marked the beginning of enduring tensions between local villagers and the FAD. What to the conservation experts might have seemed like a relatively minor move from the hilltop to the base of the sanctuary for the sake of preserving the aesthetic quality and visual integrity of the site, the abbot described as a violation of local beliefs and Buddhist values. Recounting the incident of a car accident that left a FAD staff member badly injured, he went so far as to suggest that some FAD staff members had suffered negative karmic consequences from their actions as a result. Several other informants confirmed the abbot's view that the relocation of the monastery was something that local people were unhappy about.

From 1971 to 1988, the FAD—together with local villagers hired as laborers—restored Phanom Rung using the technique of anastylosis. Several former laborers whom we interviewed reported that local communities continued to practice their annual pilgrimage ritual over the course of the restoration. Upon completion in 1988, the Phanom Rung Historical Park was officially opened. The opening of the park coincided with another important event—the repatriation of the Phra Narai (Vishnu) lintel (fig. 2.4). The lintel, which depicts a creation myth featuring the Hindu god Vishnu asleep on the serpent Ananta, was stolen from the Phanom Rung sanctuary in the early 1960s, and eventually made its way to the Art Institute of Chicago. With the imminent opening of the park, the Thai public rallied to demand the return of the lintel. They were joined by the Thai rock band Carabao, which wrote a song featuring the lyrics, "Take back your Michael Jackson, and give us back our Phra Narai!" In December 1988, the lintel was returned to Thailand.

This longstanding and ultimately successful campaign to repatriate a piece of Thailand's Khmer heritage marked a turning point in Thai public awareness about Phanom Rung and the place of Khmer heritage in the national imaginary (Keyes 1991). When the park opened its gates in 1988, it was inundated with visitors, most of whom came to see the famed lintel. As Mr. Suchart, a local resident employed as a security guard at the park, explained,

Figure 2.4. Narai lintel. Courtesy of Alexandra Denes.

With the return of the Narai lintel in 1988, the annual festival began, and the flood of visitors began, too. We can thank Aed Carabao for this. . . . Thais now understand the value of the *prasat hin* (stone sanctuaries) and the *thap lang* (lintel), whereas before they didn't care at all.

Cultural Tourism and Heritage Management: Development of the "Phanom Rung Historical Park Master Plan"

Upon completion of the restoration in 1988, the Phanom Rung Historical Park was officially opened. In 1989 the annual Phanom Rung festival began, bringing with it a dramatic increase in domestic tourism. Organized by the Provincial Cultural Council and the Provincial Administrative Organization, the cultural pageantry and iconography on display at this state-sponsored event offered a stylized performance of the imagined past, when Phanom Rung was the center of a powerful local kingdom connected to the Angkorean empire, replacing the syncretic Buddhist and animist beliefs of the local residents with an ostensibly "authentic" procession of the "vehicles of the gods" (*khabuan hae thep phahana*) and Hindu-Brahman rituals invoking the power and protection of the Hindu deity Shiva, thus symbolically restoring the sanctuary to its original function (fig. 2.5).

Many local informants reported that they lost a sense of connection to the site and their own traditions as a result of the shift in the site's status and the state sponsorship of the festival. Mr. Suchart explained that the festival organizers had moved the dates of the annual pilgrimage in April to the weekend for the convenience of tourists, so that the event no longer fell on the auspicious dates as determined by the Buddhist lunar calendar. The whole event became more of a festival organized for tourists than a ritual, and many elders no longer wanted to participate. Suchart went on to say that now that the site was "state-owned" (*khong luang*), it no longer belonged to the community. The growth of tourism did bring some benefits, however, and the monk, Phra Bandit, explained that many villagers from his community—Bu village—were able to make a living selling souvenirs at the sanctuary.

Figure 2.5. Cultural pageantry. Courtesy of Tiamsoon Sirisrisak.

Although the local people were not personally invited to attend the 1989 festival, they were still free to join the event. As tourism increased in 1991, the festival was elaborated to include a *son et lumière* performance, and a ticketing system was introduced. As a result, most of the local people could not afford to attend the event and were thus excluded from participating. It was at this point that the local people said they almost completely lost their sense of ritual custodianship of the site.

In the 1990s, Phanom Rung (along with the Phimai Historical Park) became the centerpiece of a cultural tourism campaign focused on promoting Thailand's Khmer heritage, and thirty more sanctuaries—including Mueang Tam—were restored by the FAD during that decade (Peleggi 2002, 50). In 2003, the FAD commissioned the preparation and publication of a "Master Plan for the Conservation and Development of Phanom Rung Historic Park," with the primary objective of putting forward a proposal for a UNESCO World Heritage nomination (FAD 2005, 3). The Phanom Rung Historical Park master plan includes a total of eight historic properties—two sanctuaries (Phanom Rung and Mueang Tam), two *arokayasala* (Kuti Ruesi Khok Mueang and Kuti Ruesi Nong Bua Lai), two *dharmasala* (Prasat Ban Bu and Prasat Plai Bat), and two *barai* reservoirs (Barai Nong Bua Lai and Barai Mueang Tam)— within a designated management area of 280 square kilometers, covering sixty-six villages across six subdistricts.

The stated aim of the plan is to lay the groundwork for promoting cultural tourism (and eventually World Heritage tourism), which is presented as a potential engine of sustainable development and improved quality of life for poor local residents who are predominantly employed in the agricultural sector. The plan includes a range of propositions for how local residents could benefit from cultural tourism, including the sale of high-quality local products and handicrafts, as well as hosting village homestays.

With respect to how the plan represents local residents and their role in the management of the historic park, the plan recognizes communities as key partners and explicitly refers to the 1997 Constitution's setting out of the rights of local communities to practice, conserve, and revive their cultural traditions, arts, and local wisdom (Article 46), and the rights of communities to participate in the management of natural resources for community benefit (Article 56). It also refers to the decentralization policy and the important role of local government agencies such as the Tambon Administration

Organization (TAO) in representing community interests in the management of cultural heritage resources for collective benefit (FAD 2005, 127).

And yet, it soon becomes clear that the plan presents a very specific and narrow interpretation of "community rights" and "participation," circumscribed by the notion that local communities need to be educated about the value of heritage sites and informed about the various roles they can play in heritage conservation. This heritage conservation education campaign is presented as the necessary first step for preparing the local populace to participate in management and decision-making. Nowhere in the plan is there any mention of collective rights that might be granted to local communities in recognition of their identity as cultural custodians of the sites; nor is there any mention of the role that the sites have played as "sacred centers" of belief and customary legal practice.

Indeed, if fully implemented, the management plan would have significant implications for the villages within the designated historic park. In one section of the plan, entitled "Relocation Plan for Affected Communities," the plan proposes that residents now living within the historic boundaries of several heritage properties would be relocated elsewhere. In the case of Bua Lai village, in Chorakhe Mak subdistrict, the boundary enclosing the ancient Bua Lai reservoir and the Kuti Ruesi Bua Rai *arokayasala* presently encompasses a total of 115 households, six of which "obstruct the view" between the *arokayasala* structure and the reservoir. Another fifty-nine households are located in the buffer zone. The plan's author notes that care must be taken when initiating the resettlement of residents within the historic property, given that Bua Rai village is quite an old community (FAD 2005, 143). Apart from the proposed resettlement, the plan also expects residents to adhere to land use control measures that limit population density, restrict the building of new commercial structures, and protect and restore "green zones" in residential areas (151).

From our interviews with FAD park officers and local residents, we found that, in fact, few of the recommendations in the 2003 Master Plan had been implemented. Moreover, the FAD recognized that the plan would have to be revised in order to reflect more of the needs and interests of community stakeholders and to meet World Heritage management plan requirements. We also learned that the Phanom Rung Historical Park director did not support the proposal to relocate all residents now residing within the historic zones;

rather, he hoped to work with residents to control land use and relocate only those households that obstructed the view of the sanctuaries (as in the case of the six households in Bua Rai village.) Nevertheless, from our interviews with the headmen at Bua Rai village and Khok Mueang village, we learned that local residents were under the impression that they might be relocated at some point in the near future, particularly if the FAD moved forward with the World Heritage nomination.

Finally, we learned that the FAD's rationalized master plan for the management of the Phanom Rung Park not only downplayed the local histories and values of the sites to nearby residents,[7] but it also failed to acknowledge the meaning of the Khmer sites to another group of key stakeholders—politicians.

Khmer Heritage and Magico-Politics:
Harnessing the Power of the Gods

Concurrent with the FAD's efforts to rationalize and streamline the management of the Phanom Rung Historic Park in the bid for World Heritage status, another group of key stakeholders was endeavoring to harness the growing visibility and magical potency of the Khmer sanctuaries. Beginning in the 2000s, local politicians began to organize and sponsor elaborate Brahmanic rituals aimed at invoking the power and protection of the Hindu gods and tutelary spirits of place. As Pasuk and Baker (2008) have discussed, astrology (*horasat*) and magical supernaturalism (*saiyasat*) have long played an important role in Thai politics, and in spite of twentieth-century efforts at religious reform, these domains of belief and practice have continued to serve as widely accepted symbolic expressions and instruments of political power. Whereas astrology endows politicians with the powers of prediction, magical supernaturalism provides them with the ritual and material means to augment their power and influence people and events. *Saiyasat* is not one singular or unified field of religious knowledge or expertise; rather it represents an eclectic assortment of beliefs and practices deriving from ancient Vedic texts (particularly the fourth Veda, or Atharvaveda), Buddhist asceticism, Hinduism, and animism. At its core, *saiyasat* is about invoking gods and spirits and using magical objects and spells to intervene in the world of the living (fig. 2.6).

Figure 2.6. Brahman rites at Phanom Rung. Courtesy of Tiamsoon Sirisrisak.

We have already seen from the earlier section of this chapter that local populations in the vicinity of the sanctuaries considered the sites to be "sacred centers" (Engel 2009) inhabited by guardian spirits of place, and in this sense, the sanctuaries were already inscribed with magical supernaturalism. However, what happened from the 1990s onwards was what might be thought of as the "reactivation" (Byrne and Barnes 1995) of the sites' Hindu-Brahman supernatural aspects, in part via the state-sponsored reinvention of ritual practices and the reinterpretation of architectural layouts and iconography.

In the case of Phanom Rung, the governor and the Buriram Provincial Administrative Office played a leading role in spearheading the reinvention of Brahmanic rituals and pageants to propitiate the site's Hindu deities—particularly Shiva. Astrologers were consulted, and Brahman priests were invited from Bangkok to organize and lead the rites following Vedic traditions. This reinvention and revival of Brahmanic rituals had the effect of raising the status of the deities associated with the sanctuary and subordinating local tutelary spirits to the Hindu gods. Moreover, this reinvention and "upgrading" of ritual practices from relatively simple rites and offerings to a sumptuous feast accompanied by highly structured Brahmanic rites reflected the changed symbolic status of the site, from a local "sacred center" for local populations to a site of regional and national significance. For instance, the annual pageant and procession of "vehicles of the gods" (*khabuan hae thep phahana*)—also spearheaded and organized by the Provincial Administrative Office—is a reinvented tradition that is ostensibly based on stone inscriptions as well as sculpture and iconography at Phanom Rung.[8] In addition to being a cultural spectacle aimed at tourists, the pageant is described as an act of propitiation, wherein the animal vehicles of the gods (*phahana*) are offered to the Hindu deities.

Similarly, at Mueang Tam sanctuary, local politicians played a leading role in the reinvention of annual Brahman rites invoking the protection of Hindu gods. At the TAO of Chorakhe Mak subdistrict, we met with two informants: Ms. Jiraporn Pianprakhon, the permanent secretary of the TAO, and Ms. Napha Iamsiri, the deputy mayor of the TAO, both ethnic Khmer. Jiraporn and Napha confirmed the importance of the sanctuary to the cultural identity of the residents of Chorakhe Mak, and said that the local people were the heirs and rightful custodians of the site. This historical and cultural connection was expressed in many ways, including *buang suang* rituals held at the site, as well as the legend of Oraphim and Pachit, described earlier. Indeed, as an ethnic Khmer herself, Jiraporn felt very strongly about maintaining the ritual traditions associated with the site, and since 2002, in her role as the permanent secretary, she had taken a leading role in the revival and elaboration of the annual *buang suang* ceremony held on April 2, to honor Crown Princess Maha Chakri Sirindhorn's birthday. Whereas the traditional *buang suang* ceremonies at the sanctuary were fairly small rituals organized by ethnic Khmer villagers in one of the oldest Khmer villages in the area (Village 6 of Khok Mueang village, discussed above), the ritual organized by the TAO of Chorakhe Mak was a far more elaborate and formal affair involving the entire Prakhonchai district, as well as Brahman priests, traditional folk *kantruem* musicians, and *apsara* dancers. Generous funds to hold the annual event were provided by the TAO, and participating subdistrict community leaders would bring objects for offerings (for instance, *baisi*, or banana-leaf offerings) as well as provide funds in support.

On April 2, 2011, we had the opportunity to attend the *buang suang* rites at Mueang Tam organized by the TAO. The event, which was held in a clearing under a tree some thirty feet from the eastern doorway of the sanctuary, was attended by approximately eighty local residents and a dozen representatives from local and central government agencies, all dressed in white. At the center of a half-circle of chairs and facing the temple was the offering table, which featured the golden mask of a hermit (*ruesi*)[9] at its center, surrounded by fruits, traditional sweets, and banana-leaf *baisi* offerings. The vice-governor of Buriram province and the director of the Phanom Rung Historical Park both gave brief opening statements emphasizing the value and importance of Khmer heritage for educational purposes, national identity-building, and tourism. Then the Brahman priest began the rite, chanting in Khmer to call the deities and spirits of place to attend the ritual and partake of the offerings that were laid before them by the devotees. Toward the end of the chanting, attendees were invited to place incense in the offerings of fruits and banana-leaf *baisri*. The hosts had also arranged a musical troupe of traditional *kantruem* performers and dancers to perform the *apsara* dance for the deities and spirits of place. While those in attendance were placing incense in the offerings, a middle-aged woman entered into what appeared to be a spontaneous state of trance. When the *apsara* dancers began to perform, the possessed woman joined them, moving in slow, graceful movements before the offering table. Then the host of the event asked her name and what level of heaven she came from, whether she was pleased with the *buang suang* ritual, and whether it had been done "correctly." The woman nodded, and confirmed that everything had been done according to the gods' desires and wishes. With tears of joy on her face, the spirit expressed her sense of happiness and well-being at joining the world of the living to receive this offering. The woman was then invited to sit in a place of honor to the right of the offering table. After the rite was finished, a long line formed in front of her, and she proceeded to bless those in attendance by placing her hand upon their heads. The Brahman priest then invited the spirit to return home to her place in heaven, and after apparently regaining consciousness, the woman told the eager onlookers her real name, and the nearby village where she came from. The rite was concluded with the hosts inviting the guests to take home the offerings, which would bring them good luck and well-being.

There are several important points to be made about how these state-sponsored Brahmanic rites, cultural performances, and pageants augment political power, symbolically reproduce and legitimate social hierarchies, and subsume the local within the nation-state. First, the ceremonies and cultural events associated with the sanctuaries have clearly become stages for demonstrating political prowess and social connections, inasmuch as both local and central government representatives are invited to participate. Second, sponsorship of these cultural events is a means for politicians to symbolically raise their own status through invocation and affiliation with the Hindu pantheon, while simultaneously encompassing the guardian spirits of their local constituencies. This is because officially sponsored Brahmanic rites do not displace local tutelary spirit beliefs, but rather co-opt and subordinate them to higher Hindu deities, who can offer yet a higher level of benevolent protection (*athan*). And third, in addition to supernatural protection, these ceremonies and events offer local residents an imagined past as the heirs of Thailand's Khmer heritage. This is exemplified by the annual procession of vehicles of the gods (*thep phahana*) up the *naga* causeway at Phanom Rung, for which the Provincial Administrative Office recruits hundreds of local residents of all ages to perform the roles of ancient foot soldiers, courtiers, Brahmans, *apsara* dancers, and Khmer kings and queens (fig. 2.7). In this elaborate staging of an imagined past, local residents are encouraged to identify with the grandeur of ancient Khmer civilization, albeit well within the boundaries of the Thai nation. For instance, Mr. Somphon, a forty-two-year-old ethnic Khmer resident of Chaloemprakiat who was recruited to play the role of a soldier, said that he felt proud to do this for the province and the nation, and also suspected that it meant that he had been a soldier in a past life.

We maintain that the revival of Brahman rites and the reinvention of cultural traditions by local politicians and government offices can be interpreted as a reactivation (Byrne 2009) of the latent, supernatural powers associated with ancient Khmer sites for present political purposes. However, through our fieldwork, we found that the perception of this process of political appropriation and "reactivation" of the sites was not monolithic. Some local informants saw these recent developments in a positive light, inasmuch as they described the "spirits of place" as being very powerful, and thus entitled to bountiful offerings and elaborate rituals and pageantry. Yet other local residents

Figure 2.7. Cultural pageantry, soldiers, and princesses. Courtesy of Tiamsoon Sirisrisak.

we spoke with described these rites and pageants as a waste of resources, inauthentic, and politically motivated.

However, the most visible and outspoken critic of these reinvented rites and cultural events has been the Fine Arts Department. Given the FAD's intellectual and technical grounding in conservation principles and scientific archaeology, it generally views these syncretic rites and cultural events not only as distortions of the sanctuaries' historical value and significance, but also as a potential threat to their physical fabric (for instance, through the use of ritual paraphernalia such as candles, powder, and gold leaf). While the FAD has long endeavored to maintain control over the interpretation of the site, powerful political figures were able to use their influence to gain access to the sites for ritual purposes.

Tensions between the FAD and the political sponsors of Brahman rites reached a head on May 19, 2008, when the Phanom Rung sanctuary was vandalized. Nineteen pieces of statuary—including a *nandin* bull, *naga* serpents, *sing* lions and a guardian figure—were damaged. Suspecting that the vandalism was linked to a superstitious ritual, local villagers invited a *ruesi* to interpret the meaning and motive behind the desecration. The *ruesi* told them that the act was black magic intended to scare away Phanom Rung's protective spirits. Evidence soon surfaced that prior to the vandalism, the ethnic Khmer politician and native of Buriram, Newin Chidchob, had been permitted to invite ritual specialists to perform Brahmanic rites at the Phanom Rung sanctuary in order to ward off bad luck and augment the power of former Prime Minister Thaksin Shinawatra. Many speculated that the desecration was the result of black magic rites intended to negate the power of Newin's earlier Brahmanic rites (Pasuk and Baker 2008).

Following the vandalism, lax rules regarding public use and access to the Khmer sanctuaries became an issue that the FAD was expected to solve. Mr. Montri Thanapattraapornchai was sent by the FAD to be the new head of the historical park. One of the first things he did was to introduce a new system of regulations for requesting permission to use the historic park area, including for ritual practices, which requires the applicant to fill in a form declaring the purpose, materials, and procedures of the ritual thirty days in advance. The new regulations prompted many complaints by the local government and the local people who had previously used the sites for a range of purposes, including cultural events and ritual activities. One example given by the TAO of Chorakhe Mak was the Loi Krathong festival in November 2009, when the historic park declined their request to use the ancient *barai*, as they had failed to submit an application in time. Apart from prompting a closer surveillance and control of ritual activities, the vandalism also led to a much tighter monitoring of land use by residents and government offices within the historic park. All in all, the FAD's efforts to increase supervision and management of the park following the events of 2008 have led to heightened tensions and conflicts with local stakeholders, who, in principle, are supposed to be the FAD's equal partners in heritage management.

Conclusions

Our fieldwork revealed that local residents living in the vicinity of the Angkorian-era sanctuaries in Phanom Rung Historical Park used to regard the ancient ruins as the abodes of protective, tutelary spirits. With the sanctuaries' incorporation into Thai national heritage beginning in the early twentieth century, these values were eclipsed by modern scientific narratives and conservationist principles, which continue to valorize national narratives and the "historical truth" over local cultural values associated with heritage—particularly those values that might be regarded as premodern and superstitious (Byrne 2009). Thailand's heritage authorities, such as the FAD, continue to adhere to a narrow and rigid interpretation of scientific archaeology, in spite of the international campaigns led by ICOMOS and IUCN and national legislation we mentioned in our introduction (see note 1).

A second issue has to do with how the sanctuaries in the Phanom Rung Historical Park have become stages for the ritualized performance of political prowess. Like other countries in Asia, Thailand is a hierarchical society in which authority is strongly correlated with social status, and power is often concentrated in the hands of influential, charismatic individuals, particularly politicians. As we have seen in the case of Phanom Rung, for many political figures, the staging of rituals and cultural pageants at the sanctuaries is a source of legitimacy and a symbolic expression of authority. Even though politicians appeal to local identity and claim to represent the ethnically diverse populace, these ritual events are organized in a top-down rather than a participatory manner, thus reinforcing established social hierarchies. These complex contextual realities lead to an important dilemma at the heart of this study; namely, how can rights-based approaches to heritage that advocate more democratic, participatory processes be implemented in contexts where social hierarchies are the norm?

This brings us back to one of the central questions of this research project: what rights should local residents living in Phanom Rung Historical Park have in the use, management, and interpretation of this national, and possibly soon-to-be World Heritage site? As our research discovered, local populations have inscribed the Angkorian-era Khmer sanctuaries with complex meanings, values, and narratives that are part of the people's history and identity. In keeping with Section 65 of the Thai Constitution, as well as international cultural rights instruments and proclamations that recognize the right to culture as fundamental to human dignity, we maintain that the Thai state agencies involved in heritage management should acknowledge these populations as the bearers of a corpus of traditional knowledge and practices associated with the sanctuaries, and consider supporting initiatives to safeguard these community-based practices. For instance, state agencies such as the FAD could provide financial support for organizing village rituals, and could also work with local stakeholders to research, document, and transmit this knowledge to the next generation (for instance, through the school curriculum, local museums, or community learning centers). Furthermore, we propose that state agencies involved in the management of Phanom Rung Historical Park must do more to ensure that local populations are actively involved in the management process, including issues pertaining to land use, tourism planning, and the use of the sites for rituals and cultural events.

Setting aside these general prescriptions and recommendations for the moment, however, what we have learned from field research in Buriram is that the idea of rights—much less cultural rights—remains an elusive concept in the Thai context. While we certainly found what might be termed "rights consciousness" among local residents, who expressed a sense of injustice about the loss of their sacred landscapes and restricted land use within the park, this sense of injustice had not been overtly mobilized in any way into rights-claiming behavior. Based on our observations, we argue that this is because the notion of rights carries very little weight when set within the context of the state's rationalized, bureaucratic hierarchy, on the one hand, and the symbolic performances of political influence, on the other.

Indeed, as we discovered through our field research, local meanings and values associated with the sites have largely been subsumed by two groups of powerful stakeholders—the FAD and politicians. With their training in scientific archaeology and a mandate to protect and conserve Thailand's national heritage, the FAD see themselves as the official arbiters and gatekeepers of heritage management and interpretation. At Phanom Rung Historical Park in particular, their fundamental role is to educate the general public about the sites' religious symbolism, historical value, and significance, and linkage to the ancient civilization of Angkor. The FAD's rationalizing impulse is heightened further by the prospect of UNESCO World Heritage status, not only because management plans are a requirement in the World Heritage nomination process, but also because the anticipated visitors to World Heritage sites are generally not religious pilgrims, but rather knowledge-seeking cultural tourists, such as Pichard (1971) described above. It is for this reason of preventing the distortion or misrepresentation of historical facts that the FAD historical park officers assert their authority to monitor and censor inappropriate local interpretations of the sites, in spite of the Thai state's constitutional enshrinement of the rights of traditional communities to practice their cultures. As we have seen, this has led to the marginalization of local beliefs and practices considered "legendary" or superstitious.

On the other hand, running against this rationalizing impulse, we have also seen how politicians have "reactivated" the supernatural aspects of the Khmer sites since the early 1990s, using the heritage sites as platforms for the performance of their power and prowess through the staging of Brahmanic rituals and elaborate cultural pageants. What is striking about these political uses of the sites is how they co-opt vernacular concepts of "sacred centers" (Engel 2009), inasmuch as the sponsors invoke the supernatural protection of Hindu deities that encompass and subsume the local tutelary spirits of place. Local residents are invited to take part in these ritual events; however, this mode of participation is a passive one that lends power and legitimacy to the political sponsors—who are cast as benevolent patrons—rather than one that empowers local populations to interpret and represent their own cultures in ways that are meaningful and beneficial to their communities.

Given these two extremes—the FAD's rationalizing impulse, on the one hand, and the political use of the sites for harnessing supernatural prowess, on the other—how then might genuine participation be realized? In the absence of community-led mobilization to demand the cultural rights that are guaranteed in the 2007 Constitution, who might take the lead in advocating for the rights of local culture-bearers? The authors tentatively propose that the FAD could potentially play a much more vital and active role in mediating the divergent stakeholder interests in the Phanom Rung Historical Park than they have up to this point. However, the FAD must first understand that their role in supporting the realization of cultural rights is not just a matter of informing and educating the local residents about "heritage values." It entails creating an arena for local residents and stakeholders to engage in dialogue about the local meanings, traditional beliefs, and practices associated with the sites, as well as heritage management and land use issues. Indeed, this is an initiative that was already started by the former director of the historical park, Mr. Montri, who spearheaded the establishment of a Mueang Tam Committee comprised of village headmen and other community leaders, with the office of the head of the historical park as the secretariat. The objective of the committee was to support community participation in the management and use of the historical park. One successful outcome of the committee that should be mentioned was the decision regarding the use of the land near the *barai* reservoir, which had been a longstanding source of conflict between the FAD and the local people. Mr. Montri agreed to allow the local residents to use the historic property for productive purposes under the condition that it had to be for communal benefit. After a long discussion, the committee came up with a proposal to use the land as a community garden where everyone was entitled to grow agricultural products for personal consumption. Montri also worked with the committee to launch a tree-planting project around the Mueang Tam sanctuary, with saplings donated from another government authority. Since there was no budget for the labor for this activity, Montri permitted the local people to catch fish in the *barai* (which is usually prohibited) for consumption during the working day. Now local residents are happy with their new communal gardens, and the longstanding tensions over conflicts of interest between FAD and the communities around Mueang Tam have been partially mitigated.

Following the appointment of a new director to the historical park in February 2011, however, the Mueang Tam committee activities ceased. We still maintain, though, that the model of the Mueang Tam committee could be applied throughout the historical park and could go further in supporting community engagement in all aspects of heritage management. For instance, working with schools, monasteries, and possibly the TAOs, the FAD could initiate a community-based research project on the intangible cultural values, meanings, oral narratives, and practices associated with the sanctuaries. In addition to providing an invaluable record of intangible aspects of Khmer heritage, the findings for this research would offer a baseline for understanding how the meanings of the sanctuaries have changed as a result of their incorporation into national heritage and political pageantry. Both the research process and the findings would give communities an opportunity to consider what aspects of their traditional practices they should endeavor to protect and maintain—for instance, the role that rituals for tutelary spirits can play in the resolution of conflicts.

The community committee model could also possibly offer leverage for counterbalancing the influence of politicians over the sites. If community committees had a genuine voice in issues of use and management, this could extend to how the sites should be used for ritual purposes and cultural events.

Over the course of our fieldwork, several local residents told us that they felt that the use of the sanctuaries for elaborate, politically motivated rituals and cultural events was not only inappropriate, but also a waste of taxpayer resources. One headman in Mueang Tam told us that not only was the *buang suang* ritual a questionable use of TAO funds, but it was also labor-intensive, requiring the volunteer labor of local residents.

In a genuinely participatory process, these kinds of local concerns and grievances about the use and management of the heritage park would be brought to the table for discussion and debate, and local residents would have a voice in the decision-making process. It is our hope that the critique and suggestions offered in this chapter can serve as a starting point for dialogue between the different stakeholders involved in the management and interpretation of the Phanom Rung Historical Park.

Notes

1. The International Council on Monuments and Sites' (ICOMOS) "Ename Charter for the Interpretation and Presentation of Cultural Heritage Sites" is an example of such a legal instrument, and the International Union for Conservation of Nature's (IUCN) "Theme on Indigenous Peoples and Local Communities, Equity and Protected Areas" is a characteristic campaign.

2. Byrne (2009) refers to this potency as the "magical supernatural."

3. Later waves of Lao settlement came in the early eighteenth century, when the Lao king of Champasak sent a Lao noble with thousands of Lao *phrai* (registered persons) to settle on the right side of the Mekong. During the late eighteenth century, yet more Lao from across the Mekong migrated to the Khorat Plateau to flee the Siamese King Taksin's attacks on Champasak and Vientiane. Then, starting in 1831, after suppressing the rebellion of the Lao king Chao Anu of Vientiane, the Siamese launched a campaign to repopulate the northeast by relocating more than 30,000 Lao from the right bank to the Khorat Plateau (Paitoon 1984).

4. The authors are indebted to Rungsima Kullapat for sharing her knowledge about the legend of Pachit Oraphim and its place within the cultural memory of the residents of Nakhon Ratchasima and Buriram provinces. Her forthcoming doctoral dissertation, "Living Heritage through Literature: The Development of a Cultural Route from Phimai to Angkor," features extensive research findings on the Pachit Oraphim legend.

5. Seidenfaden (1932, 96) reported seeing a Buddha image within the central tower of the Mueang Tam sanctuary that had been placed there by villagers in place of the original statue, which was moved to the Bua village spirit shrine. This suggests that beliefs relating to the site date to at least as early as the 1930s.

6. Photographs taken during this trip featured the reclining Vishnu lintel and were later used as evidence to reclaim the lintel from the Art Institute of Chicago in 1988 (Subhadradis 1989).

7. Cultural sites nominated to the World Heritage List must manifest one or more criteria of "Outstanding Universal Value." Criterion VI specifically states that a site must "be directly or tangibly associated with events or living traditions, with ideas, or with beliefs, [or] with artistic and literary works of outstanding universal significance." Since the local histories and value of the Phanom Rung sites to local residents meet the requirements of Criterion VI, and other UNESCO criteria seem to be fulfilled, the bid for World Heritage List inscription should ultimately be successful.

8. Interview with Mr. Jirasak, the head of the Buriram Cultural Council.

9. The figure of the hermit, or *ruesi*, is linked to Hinduism, and symbolizes renunciation as well as the Vedic teachings.

References

Aymonier, Etienne. 1999 [1901]. *Khmer Heritage in Thailand*. Translated by Walter E. J. Tips. Bangkok: White Lotus Press.

Byrne, Denis. 2009. "Archaeology and the Fortress of Rationality." In *Cosmopolitan Archaeologies*, 68–88. Durham, NC: Duke University Press.

Byrne, Denis, and Gina L. Barnes. 1995. "Buddhist Stupa and Thai social practice." *World Archaeology* 27 (2): 266–81.

Chakrabarty, Dipesh. 2007. *Provincializing Europe: Postcolonial Thought and Historical Difference*. Princeton, NJ: Princeton University Press.

Chandler, David. 2000. *A History of Cambodia*. Third edition. Boulder, CO: Westview Press.

Chirikure, Shadreck, Munyaradzi Manyanga, Webber Ndoro, and Gilbert Pwiti. 2010. "Unfulfilled promises? Heritage Management and Community Participation at Some of Africa's Cultural Heritage Sites." *International Journal of Heritage Studies* 16 (1): 30–44.

Coedès, Georges. 1986. *Angkor*. Oxford: Oxford University Press.

Edwards, Penny. 2008. *Cambodge: The Cultivation of a Nation, 1860–1945*. Honolulu: University of Hawaii Press.

Engel, David M. 2009. "Landscapes of the Law: Injury, Remedy, and Social Change in Thailand." *Law and Society Review* 43 (1): 61–94.

FAD [Fine Arts Department]. 2005. *Phaen maebot khrongkan anurak lae phatthana Mueang Phanom Rung* [Master plan for the preservation and development of Phanom Rung]. Buriram: Winai Publishers.

Freeman, Michael. 1998. *Khmer Temples in Thailand and Laos*. Bangkok: River Books.

Greer, Shelley. 2010. "Heritage and Empowerment: Community-based Indigenous Cultural Heritage in Northern Australia." *International Journal of Heritage Studies* 16 (1/2): 45–58.

Karlström, Anna. 2005. "Spiritual Materiality: Heritage Preservation in a Buddhist World?" *Journal of Social Archaeology* 5 (3): 338–55.

Keyes, Charles. 1991. "The Case of the Purloined Lintel." In *National Identity and Its Defenders*, edited by Craig Reynolds, 261–92. Clayton, Victoria: Centre of Southeast Asian Studies, Monash University.

Langfield, Michele, William Logan, and Mairead Nic Craith. 2009. *Cultural Diversity, Heritage and Human Rights: Intersections in Theory and Practice*. London: Routledge.

Niyada Laosunthorn. 1995. *Panyat chadok prawat lae khwam samkhan thi mi to wannakam thai* [Pannasa Jataka: Its genesis and significance to Thai poetical works]. Bangkok: Mae Kham Fang.

Meskel, Lynn, ed. 2009. *Cosmopolitan Archaeologies*. Durham, NC: Duke University Press.

Paitoon Mikusol. 1984. "Social and Cultural History of Northeastern Thailand, 1868–1910: A Case Study of the HuaMueang Khamen Paadong (Surin, Sangkha, and Khukhan)." PhD diss., University of Washington.

Pasuk Phongpaichit, and Chris Baker. 2008. "The Spirits, the Stars, and Thai Politics." Unpublished lecture delivered 2 December, Siam Society, Bangkok. Accessed at http://pioneer.netserv.chula.ac.th/~ppasuk/spiritsstarspolitics.pdf.

Peleggi, Maurizio. 2002. *Lords of Things: The Fashioning of the Siamese Monarchy's Modern Image*. Honolulu: University of Hawaii Press.

Phumjit Ruangdej. 1986. *Prapheni khuen khao phanom rung changwat buriram* [The Phanom Rung pilgrimage, Buriram]. Buriram: Art and Cultural Centre of Buriram Teacher's College.

Pichard, Pierre. 1972. *Restoration of a Khmer Temple in Thailand*. Paris: UNESCO.

Rasmi Shoocongdej. 2007. "The Impact of Colonialism and Nationalism in the Archaeology of Thailand." In *Selective Remembrances: Archaeology in the Construction, Commemoration, and Consecration of National Pasts*, edited by Philip L. Kohl, Mara Kozelsky, and Nachman Ben-Yahuda, 379–400. Chicago: University of Chicago Press.

Seidenfaden, Erik. 1932. A Siamese Account of the Construction of the Temple on Khao Phanom Rung. *Journal of the Siam Society* 25: 83–108

———. 1952. "The Kui People of Cambodia and Siam." *Journal of the Siam Society* 39: 144–180.

Shaheed, Farida. 2011. "Report of the Independent Expert in the Field of Cultural Rights, Farida Shaheed, United Nations, March 21." Accessed at: http://daccess-dds-ny.un.org/doc/UNDOC/GEN/G11/122/04/PDF/G1112204.pdf?OpenElement.

Silverman, Helaine. 2011a. "Border Wars: The Ongoing Temple Dispute between Thailand and Cambodia and UNESCO's World Heritage List." *International Journal of Heritage Studies* 17 (1): 1–21.

———, ed. 2011b. *Contested Cultural Heritage: Religion, Nationalism, Erasure, and Exclusion in a Global World*. New York: Springer.

Smitthi Siribhadra, Elizabeth Moore, and Michael Freeman. 2001. *Palaces of the Gods: Khmer Art and Architecture in Thailand*. Bangkok: River Books.

Srisaksa Vallibhotama. 1989. "Sisaket: Sisaket khet khamen padong" [Sisaket: The area of the 'backward Cambodians'], *Mueang Boran* 15 (4): 27–50.

Subhadradis Diskul, M. C. 1989. "Stolen Art Objects Returned to Thailand," *SPAFA Digest* 10 (2): 8–12.

Tambiah, S. J. 1975. *Buddhism and the Spirit Cults in North-east Thailand*. Cambridge: Cambridge University Press.

Thompson, Ashley. 1997. "Changing Perspectives: Cambodia after Angkor." In *Sculpture of Angkor and Ancient Cambodia: Millennium of Glory*, edited by Helen Ibbitson Jessup and Thierry Zephir, 22–32. Washington: National Gallery of Art.

Thongchai Winichakul. 2000. "The Quest for 'Siwilai': A Geographical Discourse of Civilizational Thinking in the Late Nineteenth and Early Twentieth-Century Siam." *Journal of Asian Studies* 59 (3): 528–49.

Wolf, Eric R. 2010. *Europe and the People Without History*. Berkeley: University of California Press.

3

Conserving Bangkok's Premier Heritage District: Ambitious Plans and Ambiguous Rights

K. C. Ho and Pornpan Chinnapong

Rights and the City

The city is a product of our everyday practices. We recognize this fact when we shift our attention to questions about what the city means and, more importantly, whom cities are for (Friedmann 2000; Lepofsky and Fraser 2003). Marxist philosopher Henri Lefebvre wrote of the opposition between exchange value (and its capitalist "utilizers") and use value (and its community "users"), the production of surplus value versus nonproductive "enjoyment" of lived user spaces, and the fundamental contradiction between the two uses and two groups (1991, 356–62). Given these fundamental tensions, Lefebvre warned of the danger that "urban space tends to be sliced up, degraded, and eventually destroyed by this contradictory process" (359).

When Lefebvre argued for the rights of all groups to the city, he saw the issue as being more than just a narrow focus on consumption rights. The right to urban space ultimately implies the right to participate in urban life (through having a place in the city) and as Fincher and Iveson (2008, 9) point out, "to use and shape the city as an equal." The issue of social justice for all groups becomes more compelling when rights are associated with the rights to urban space.

Thus, for Lefebvre and others who have followed in his footsteps, the right to the city implies a city for all, where uses and their consequences for the built environment of the city are determined not just by dominant economic interests whose rights are enshrined through exchange value, but by an equally important urban population segment whose use value is equally important. The use value is tied closely to efforts at place-making. As Lepofsky and Fraser (2003, 128) suggest, "place-making is participation in both the production of meaning and the means of production of a locale."

The production of meaning and the right of a community to determine its way of life are two issues that open up the discourse on rights from individual to community, from the economic to the cultural, and from the tangible to the intangible. This shift to the community, the cultural, and the intangible takes center stage in heritage development. Heritage conservation is a common facet of today's urban development and is embarked upon for a variety of reasons, including the strengthening of local identity, economic development, tourism, and the overall improvement of aesthetics and quality of life (De Frantz 2005). The implementation of conservation projects may create conflicts, however, between state authorities and local communities. The latter's perspectives may differ from the state's, and they may lack a voice in the development process (Hampton 2005).

The issue is often more complex than participation in the planning and implementation processes. Heritage development often involves more than the conservation of the physical site and involves communities and their ways of life, bringing into the deliberation the issue of cultural rights. Cultural rights, as Farida Shaheed observed (2010), refers to the right to have access to, participate in, and contribute to the cultural life of the group. For the community, the notion of intangible cultural heritage is, as Logan (2007, 50) terms it, "living heritage embodied in people." Heritage is a community attribute since its vibrancy depends on shared practices around an identity, and ties between generations, households, and families. And, as the notion of cultural rights is developed in relation to indigenous peoples, Gilbert (2010, 39) observes that "the notion of cultural heritage for indigenous people is tied to the notion of territory" because their traditional practices are intricately linked to the natural world.

In this volume on culture and rights in Thailand, the contribution of our chapter aims to show the complexity of the cultural rights issue within the context of the city.

The first complexity is naturally concerned with the type of city. Bangkok is the historic capital of Thailand, and this status brings with it the role of the capital city as the cultural heart of the nation and associated issues involving rights and representation. The second complexity of urban centers concerns the group. Cities have high residential mobility, and the notion of territorial communities does not neatly fit with cultural communities as captured by the definitions of Shaheed (2010) and Logan (2007), where communities in a particular place are neatly congruous with communities of practice. Third, while it is possible to find evidence of cultural practices unique to a particular community within a city, the association of a set of social and economic practices with a particular group is complicated by the availability of mass education, higher inter-generational social mobility, and the enlarged labor market in the city. Fourth, in contrast to non-urban locations, market-based and high-density urban land-use systems displace people and activities, thus making it even more difficult to argue for a link between cultural practices and locality. These complexities create hybrid pairings and incomplete sets: heritage claims based on practices tied to place but that are not necessarily tied to the groups who originated those practices, and community rights claims that are not necessarily linked to cultural rights.

The fifth complexity is contained in Doreen Massey's notion (1995) of "sedimentation" in the city. History as produced by the interconnected processes of human activity has the ability to embed itself in places as layers. As Massey (116) remarks, "the layers of history which are sedimented over time are not just economic; there are also cultural, political and ideological strata, layers which also have their local specificities." The deep sedimentation in historical districts in the city then becomes a source of conflict over the cultural rights of groups tied to these localities and heritage preservation.

We use two cases to highlight these complexities: Tha Tian and Fort Mahakan are found in the Rattanakosin heritage district of old Bangkok. The former represents the early river commerce that thrived historically in the royal district, and the latter was where the court officials settled. To the extent that the current plans of the Bangkok Metropolitan Authority (BMA) to develop a heritage district express a dominant state view, the implementation of the plans may have the unintended effect of eradicating elements of local cultural heritage and may impose a single vision rather than a more diverse one, in effect erasing important physical elements and memories of the old city.

Communities are generally conceived of as groups sharing an assemblage of beliefs and practices, a common language, ethnicity, and religion. A community based on identity is not necessarily conterminous with a community based on residence. Thus, our two sites incorporate resident groups that lack any of the primordial, ascribed traits that normally make distinctive cultural communities. Moreover, our two communities face the shared fate of being powerless either because they are renters (Tha Tian) or squatters (Mahakan). It is important to note that the stories of Tha Tian and Mahakan are not simply examples of the urban poor being resettled or evicted, as happens widely around the world. What is unusual in our cases is that both groups are using heritage claims in their attempt to stay where they are. They argue that their activities are significant in Rattanakosin's history. They claim that their local histories and practices matter and should be preserved alongside more prestigious royal and religious narratives of the place.

These claims are important to analyze from a cultural rights framework. As we will show in this chapter, the claims by the Mahakan and Tha Tian communities fall short of a more rigorous measure of cultural rights as claims made by groups. They nevertheless matter from a broader community rights agenda. Fostering a rights culture within the context of the city should involve securing government support of a rights framework and instilling in public authorities the necessity of treating people with fairness and dignity (Butler 2005). This leads to the broadening of the work of city government beyond its housekeeping (public works) and entrepreneurial functions (working with businesses to improve economic competitiveness) to include a community function (working with groups to improve their neighborhoods). The active operation of the community function should lead to a stakeholding approach where community groups exercise their right to govern, not only in common areas such as public security and the improvement of amenities, but also in terms of what Brown (2009, 146) calls "community curation"— the active involvement of a community in preserving and representing its own history. The result would be a convivial city that is open to differences and where a dynamic governance system enables the participation of citizens from different walks of life and a range of ways of life enshrined in vibrant neighborhoods.

Introducing Rattanakosin Heritage District

Rattanakosin Island is Bangkok's historic royal district where King Rama I built his new capital in 1782. Like many pre-industrial cities, Bangkok was built as a fortified city. Small and compact, the inner city area was encircled by protective walls, forts, and canals dug on the east side. The great Chao Phraya River curved around from the northwest to the south. The boundary of the walled old-city core demarcates what is presently known as Rattanakosin Island. The design of the city followed a cosmological concept based on the previous capital of Ayutthaya, with the Grand Palace and the Temple of the Emerald Buddha forming the key elements of the city center (Pornpan Boonchuen and Ho 2006).

While Rattanakosin was the area of the king's palace and thus has many royal components, it should not be seen only in terms of its royal character. Sanam Luang, in the heart of Rattanakosin Island, for example, was originally an exclusive royal ground in the early Bangkok period (1782–1851), which hosted royal ceremonies and events. But it evolved to become a place for public celebrations and exhibitions from 1851 to 1925. With the institution of the constitutional monarchy in 1932, Sanam Luang eventually became a public, civic space. Its status as a civic space is also tied to its proximity to Ratchadamnoen Avenue and the Democracy Monument (Pornpan Chinnapong 2008). As a large, open space, it has often been used as a staging area for mass political demonstrations, with crowds then marching down Ratchadamnoen Avenue. Thus, as Thailand's political modernization process developed, new civic elements also flourished alongside the cultural heritage stemming from Rattanakosin's royal past.

The effort to redevelop and conserve Rattanakosin was launched in 1982 in conjunction with Bangkok's bicentennial celebrations. The BMA issued administrative regulations on building code controls for the inner and outer zones of Rattanakosin precinct in 1985 and in 1987, respectively (BMA 1985, 1987). The main objectives of the BMA building code controls, especially for the inner zone (see fig. 3.1), are to preserve historic sites and heritage, to prevent traffic congestion, and to maintain order in the area. Thus, in Area 1 of Inner Rattanakosin, where the two sites we studied are located, it is prohibited to construct row houses, shop-houses, factories, commercial buildings, or public buildings of any kind—except religious-related buildings

Figure 3.1. Map of Rattanakosin Island. It is encircled by the Chao Phraya River on the west and Khlong Lot (inner canal) on the east. This is referred to as Inner Rattanakosin. Outer Rattanakosin extends futher east until it is encircled by Khlong Ong Ang and Khlong Banglamphu. Adapted from Google maps.

or government buildings—that are higher than existing structures or exceed sixteen meters in height. In accordance with the building code control, in 1994 the Committee for Krung Rattanakosin Project, formulated a Master Plan for Conservation and Development of Krung Rattanakosin, which was approved by the cabinet in 1997.

An associated development includes the relocation of a number of government ministries out of Rattanakosin and the adaptive reuse of these buildings. One example is the conversion of the former Ministry of Commerce building to become the Museum of Siam. The state-driven Master Plan focuses heavily on heritage linked with Rattanakosin's royal activities and buildings and attempts to create more open space and public parks especially along waterfront areas (Synchron Group 1994).

The Rattanakosin Master Plan represents a bold and ambitious attempt at preserving officially recognized heritage.[1] With the focus on the royal history associated with the area, the main objective of the Rattanakosin plan is to strengthen the cultural power of the capital city through showcasing Thailand's culture to locals and tourists. Compared to other cities, capital cities have the added role of representing the culture of the whole nation. As Logan (2009, 19) points out, "it continues to be critically important for the sense of nationhood to create a capital worthy of the nation." This ideological project results in the mobilization of the capital city's landscape to this end. For example, Leitner and Kang (1999) show the many ways in which the nationalist ideology is inscribed into the landscape of Taipei. Hershkovitz (1993) shows how the built heritage of Beijing, and the meanings associated with it, were appropriated to shore up the political and cultural power of the capital city.

Referring to Thailand, Reynolds (1991, 8) points out that the promotion of a national culture reflects the interests of the dominant ethnic group, the Thai-speaking people of the central plains, and has the unintended effect of "masking cultural and ethnic heterogeneity in the name of national uniformity." This has clearly been the case for the palaces, museums, and temples of Rattanakosin. Is there still room in Rattanakosin, then, for the community-level versions of heritage that Tha Tian and Fort Mahakan represent? What exactly is the "content" of this community voice? The two communities under study clearly want to stay on and practice their way of life. In what ways do their claims concur with or depart from our understanding of cultural rights?

Saving, Redeveloping, and Living in Rattanakosin: Different Visions, Contrasting Claims

We argue that from a rights approach to cultural heritage, if Rattanakosin is to be developed as the cultural heart of Bangkok, then conservation practices should allow for a process that balances national heritage with living community traditions, thus ensuring a living, vibrant place that contains a mix of people, activities, and buildings.

Our proposition is immediately challenged by the realities of Tha Tian and Mahakan. In terms of ownership, control, and claims, Tha Tian represents the more complex of the two cases. Bounded by Soi Tha Rong Mo, Maharat Road, Chakrabongse Villa, and the Chao Phraya River, Tha Tian comprises four parcels of land (see fig. 3.2). The parcel of land around Tha Tian market, seen at the top of figure 3.2, is owned by the Crown Property Bureau. This consists of a group of shop-houses surrounded by a market hall that houses dried seafood sellers. Fishermen who come in and out by boat took over this market area from a group of fruit sellers, who moved out to Pak Khlong Market some thirty years ago, and they deal in dried seafood. The condition for their takeover was that they were to be responsible for security and fire safety. The second and the fourth parcel are in the hands of a fragmented group of property owners. The third parcel, encompassing Soi Pratu Nokyung (Peacock Gate), is owned by Wat Pho (Temple of the Reclining Buddha), and the residents in this parcel are in one way or another connected to that temple.

By contrast, Mahakan is a smaller site on a narrow strip of land next to Fort Mahakan (see fig. 3.1). Flushed with success in restoring the Fort Sumen site,[2] the BMA has set its sights on restoring Fort Mahakan and redeveloping the surrounding area into a park. The history of the conflict with local citizens that this plan engendered has been well documented by scholars and filmmakers (see, for example, Herzfeld 2003 and 2006; Bristol 2010; and for two video documentaries, Aphiwat 2003; Skiotis 2004). The point in including this case is not to repeat the history of the conflict but rather to analyze the nature of the community's local heritage claims within a cultural rights framework. Fionn Skiotis of the Centre on Housing Rights and Evictions concluded his documentary (2004) by predicting that "eviction in the near future now appears likely," but the Mahakan community has persisted and has, with external support, refined its heritage claims. Tha Tian's negotiations, by

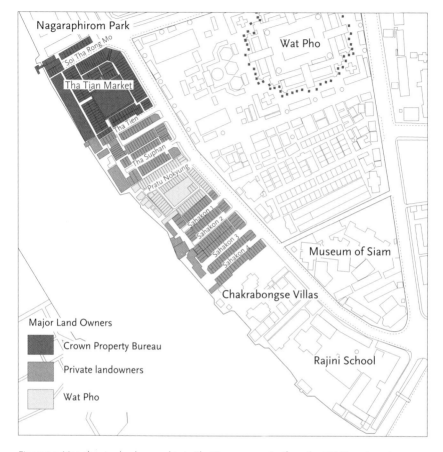

Figure 3.2. Map showing land ownership in Tha Tian community (from the BMA Department of City Planning, 1998; reproduced from Napat Settachai, "Global Tourism and Community Life: Toward a Responsible Tourism Framework," PhD diss., University of Hawaii, 2008, 194). Nagaraphirom Park, completed in March 2010, occupies the site by the river adjacent to Tha Tian Market. In the process, the row of shophouses on the north side of Soi Tha Rong Mo was removed and the land incorporated as part of the park

contrast, are more recent and make use of the claim that the community's livelihoods are closely tied to the history of commerce in the area. In the following section, we examine how these claims are evaluated, supported, and challenged by a set of actors with diverse interests and viewpoints.

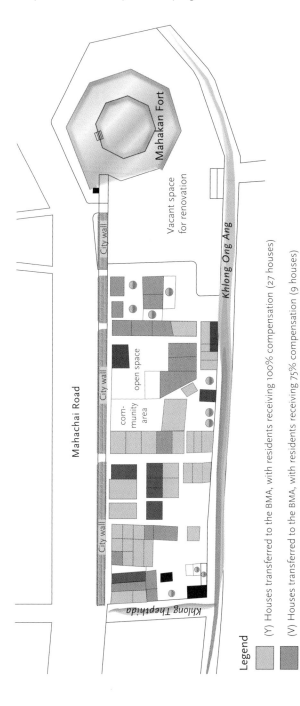

Figure 3.3: BMA survey map of land ownership and compensation

Legend

(Y) Houses transferred to the BMA, with residents receiving 100% compensation (27 houses)

(V) Houses transferred to the BMA, with residents receiving 75% compensation (9 houses)

(B) No agreement with the BMA, with residents receiving 75% compensation (18 houses)

(P) Houses transferred to the BMA for dismantling and rebuilding, with residents receiving 100% compensation (2 houses)

Three Major Players

Bangkok Metropolitan Authority

The BMA is responsible for managing the historic district in accordance with the guidelines drawn up in the Master Plan. The BMA moved forward with a plan to turn the Fort Mahakan area into a park and proceeded to buy the land from the owners (see fig. 3.3 for map specifying the portion of compensation given to the house owners). Sakchai Boonma, director of the Land Acquisition Division, Public Works Department, BMA, told us the history of the compensation scheme, which actually began in 1960 with the purchase of the first parcel of land. However, the plan to turn Mahakan into a park could not be implemented because some residents refused to move out, and the situation remains unresolved to this day.

With regard to the Tha Tian market area, Sakchai Boonma explained that the Rattanakosin Master Plan intends to keep only the buildings belonging to the Crown Property Bureau (CPB) in the U-shape next to Soi Tha Rong Mo (see fig. 3.2). With the exception of Chakrabongse Palace and Rajini School, the other buildings in the area fronting the river will be demolished in order to create an open space and park. The Land Readjustment and Urban Renewal Division cannot carry out its role in any development until the land is vacated, however. Mr. Settaya, the director of the Land Readjustment Urban Renewal Division, extolled the great potential of the development of Tha Tian and Tha Chang (the pier just north of Tha Tian), given their proximity to major attractions such as the Grand Palace and Wat Pho.

Crown Property Bureau

As the major landowner in Rattanakosin, the CPB has worked closely with BMA to maintain the "atmosphere of the place," respect the feelings of the people, and incorporate the conceptual visions of the planners.[3] The CPB thinks that the tenants' participation in restoration is important because they will feel more secure and more responsible. In both the Phra Athit and the Na Phra Lan projects, CPB underwrote the temporary relocation costs, developed a co-payment scheme for the renovation, and agreed on the uniform façade of both projects.

Kemtat Visavayodhin, director of the Conservation Projects Department, Crown Property Bureau, pointed to CPB's involvement in the Nagaraphirom Park project as an example of its commitment to the redevelopment of Tha Tian. There were initially protests from the tenants of the market against the building of the park, but the director pointed out that after the park was built, those protesters became regular users of the park. According to the director, the opening of the park in December 2010 was an important event to let the community know about CPB's efforts and what he called its "corporate social responsibility" in heritage management.

The CPB has plans to get rid of the dried seafood market at Tha Tian and in its place to provide a lawn where sellers of Thai handicrafts can ply their wares to tourists. With regard to the slum dwellers, Kemtat cited the response of Queen Sirikit when she was asked about the issue of slum clearance. She replied that since the CPB are not experts on the matter, they should seek the advice of knowledgeable persons. Thus, based on the advice of experts, CPB will move in a legal, dignified way, seeking to promote the welfare of the public.

Wat Pho

Like the CPB, Wat Pho is a major landlord in Tha Tian. The total land owned by the temple is about 3.3 *rai* (1.304 acres). From the reign of King Rama I to the reign of King Rama IV, the riverfront area accommodated a pavilion to tie boats used by the monks on their alms rounds, a pavilion for robe-dying, a pavilion for food distribution, and the houses of boatmen who served the royal family. The current assistant abbot, Phra Ratchawethi, observed that the Tha Tian market is not as active as it was thirty to forty years ago, when it was the destination for transportation of goods via river and canals. In recent years, more restaurants and shops have opened up in the Tha Tian area to serve tourist activities around Wat Pho. Wat Pho itself has become one of the most important tourist destinations of Rattanakosin Island, and in 2009 it was included in the UNESCO Memory of the World Program.

The temple wants to redevelop the land it owns for tourism. According to the assistant abbot, Phra Ratchawethi,

At present, what is important is tourism. But we don't focus much on business. We focus more on [opening up] the vista and views [of the riverfront] for people. Business we cannot really handle. Most [of the redevelopment plan] is about opening up the view. . . . The first point is the riverfront view. Secondly, we want to make connections between the tourism activities at the group of temples on the opposite side of the river—Wat Arun, Wat Rakhang, and Wat Kalaya—with Wat Pho and Wat Phra Kaeo on this side. There's a high potential of connecting people taking the boat from the piers on the opposite riverbank to here.[4]

The assistant abbot thinks that an open vista is important for sightseeing and for a new river node to connect both sides of the river. Asked if the Wat Pho redevelopment plan will improve the worship experience for Buddhists, he replied that the plan focuses on benefits for both tourists and local people.[5] The assistant abbot elaborated on the plans, saying that some conservation will be done, along with the building of two new pavilions with piers (see fig. 3.4) creating space for tourist souvenir shops, a tourist service center, an upper-deck viewing area, and a meeting hall on the second floor. The plan called for "the removal of the unpleasant structures encroaching the river and two rows of wooden shophouses on the river bank" and the building of a park. Figure 3.2 shows the planned urban design scheme in Rattanakosin and the Chao Phraya riverfront. The assistant abbot said in the interview that the urban design scheme is from the proposal submitted by Wat Pho. The riverfront urban design scheme, following the guidelines from the Rattanakosin Committee, has more open space set back in the form of a park. Wat Pho's plan, which we were shown at the interview (but were not given a copy of), involves two pavilions stretching to the edge of the river. Wat Pho will reimburse relocated residents by allowing them to set up business or vending activities, such as providing Thai massage. On the whole, few people will be affected, but the residents in the adjacent neighborhood are worried, the assistant abbot acknowledged. Two or three years ago, there was a meeting between Wat Pho and the community who live on the temple's property to inform them that Wat Pho will not renew the residents' leases, and so the community should already be prepared for the changes.

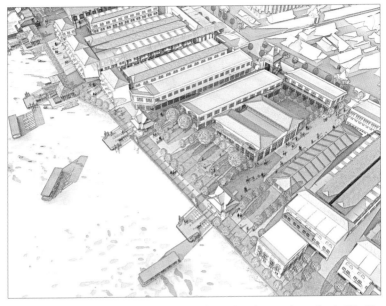

Figure 3.4. Rattanakosin and Chao Phraya riverfront urban design scheme for the Wat Pho area (with two new pavilions with piers, and Pratu Nokyung in the background). Weeraphan Shinawatra, ed., *Rattanakosin and Chao Phraya River Front*, Bangkok: Plus Press, 2009, 82.

Minority Voices

Community Leaders and Residents

The Tha Tian community chairman, Kriangkrai Olarnphansakul, has lived in Tha Tian for fifty years. He rents shop-houses on CPB property and runs a wholesale business that sells animal feed and transports them to other provinces. Of the land parcel owned by Wat Pho, the Tha Tian community chairman said that Wat Pho developed a redevelopment plan for the temple's property among the Tha Tian community. This area is denoted as the site bordering Soi Pratu Nokyung in figure 3.2. Wat Pho has rented out the buildings in this area to residents and small businesses. According to Uncle Yuu, a resident in his eighties, he feels a strong attachment to the place, but if he had to move, he could move in with his daughter or son who live in the suburbs. His granddaughter, however, likes Tha Tian because she says "there are many people [in her family and in the neighborhood area], so it's better to stay at [the Tha Tian] house."[6]

On the third plot, which belongs to private owners, there has been little development. We interviewed several owners in this area, two of whom are old residents who have developed new businesses in the area. For example, Yui Naowarat,[7] the daughter of a longtime resident, created a small café selling pastries and drinks alongside their wholesale business supplying kitchenware. The family stays on the third floor of the shop house. When asked about changes in the neighborhood, she said that when she was growing up in this area, there were a lot more children in the neighborhood. Many families with grown-up children have moved to the suburbs. This account of inter-generational changes extends to the nature of business. Since transportation by big trucks is no longer allowed in the Rattankosin area, Yui said, "many wholesale businesses have closed, because some families have moved their businesses out. There is less wholesale activity in Tha Tian . . . , and more tourist-related business."

Although the Tha Tian neighborhood comprises three land parcels with different owners, our interviews indicated that the community is well organized. Somchai and Petchara, a couple who have stayed in a shop-house on Soi 4 (Soi Pansuk) with their children and Somchai's mother for more than thirty years, told us that "on every *soi*, there are alarm buttons installed for fire alarm and burglar alarm. There are also loudspeakers to broadcast any community announcements. Announcements are made on such occasions as the Songkran festival, New Year's, Chinese holidays, or for various other community events. There are vigilant volunteers riding bicycle watching every *soi*."

The Fort Mahakan community also showed evidence of community organization, but after a ten-year history of consolidation in the face of a relocation threat.[8] During this period, the community received help from nongovernmental organizations (NGOs), particularly the Community Organizations Development Institute (CODI).[9] In 1999, the community set up a "community-saving group" to motivate members to fight for housing rights. The residents managed to convert into useful sites several of the houses that had been vacated by other residents who had accepted the BMA offer of financial compensation and alternative premises.[10] The remaining households, who manufacture and trade in fireworks, now dry their wares on concrete roofs where the threat of fire is minimized. There is a playground for the children, a laundry yard, and community spaces with places to sit and chat. There is also a modest library documenting the history of the place, a community structure for gatherings that they designated a "community learning center," and a place for Thai massage. The community leaders told me that they made sure that any unoccupied sites were given some function, so that new squatters would not move in. At the edge of the community, where a metal wall was built to fence off the fort structure from the community, and near the site of the boat landing, was a huge pile of rubbish. Community leaders told me that this was left by vagrants and other users of the park. They said that villagers are vigilant against various intruders. Our walk through the community indicated a well-organized and clean neighborhood.

Community Support from NGOs and Academic Experts

Askew (2002, 148) observed that in Thai slum settlements "the existence of strong, weak, united or divided communities is tied to the circumstances and settlement histories, but the more important question . . . is how the slums (as social formations) and slum dwellers (as agents) have incorporated the ideas and methods and language introduced by NGOs." We saw in the case of the Mahakan community how CODI was important in helping organize the community. Suk, a community leader, highlighted the close association with CODI and other NGOs and how he, as a community leader was part of an important set of NGO networks:

> In 1999, we got together. . . . This time we had CODI. Staff from CODI asked what we needed and we told them our problems. . . . After that, in 1999, we set up a community savings group as a tool in motivating people in the community to fight for housing rights at Fort Mahakan. CODI was among the people who helped bring together communities who were in trouble with housing. . . . Now we are in the network of NGOs, such as Four Region Slum Network that works throughout the whole country, Assembly of the Poor, and the Urban Poor Community Organization. . . .

I myself am a member of an NGO. I was trained and shared experiences among groups of people in other organizations.[11]

Tawatchai, another Mahakan leader, also mentioned the importance of academics who contributed their time and expertise to the community:

There were several academics from different institutes and universities . . . [who] inspired us to present to society our local identity and self-capital (organization), which differed from the other evicted communities in the past. This was to support our proposal to stay. And if we stay, what can we do for society and for Bangkok?[12]

The Tha Tian community is also tied to similar academic and NGO networks. We were invited to a community mobilization event organized by the King Mongkut Institute of Technology for a Chinatown precinct that was likely to be affected by the building of a new subway line. The Tha Tian residents' community chairman Kriangkrai Olarnphansakul was one of the five members of the panel discussion, the other four coming from other communities and NGOs. After the contributions from the panelists, the first question from the floor was directed at the Tha Tian chairman on how to organize and mobilize the community.[13] Here was clear evidence of how communities work with academics and NGOs to share best practices to solve common problems.

Aside from community forums, academics are also involved in undertaking the research necessary to advance the community's claims. Chatri Prakitnontakarn, a lecturer at Silpakorn University Faculty of Architecture, is a key member of the team that produced a study of Fort Mahakan (SURDI 2006) as part of an agreement between then BMA Governor Apirak Kosayodhin, the rector of Silpakorn University, and Mahakan community leaders to show the BMA's good intentions in fostering community participation. The research team helped to clarify and strengthen the importance of the ancient teak houses to the community. The research team also raised the issue of cultural identity and the importance of the community's intangible cultural heritage, such as its birdcage manufacture, potteries, gold smelting, and *like*, a performing arts form.[14] Chatri told us in an interview that one focus of the research team is captured in Professor Srisak Vallibhotama's description of the Fort Mahakan community as "the community at the edge of the city wall" (*chumchon chan kamphaeng phra nakhon*). He said that the unique feature of the Mahakan community is that it represents an old community that has no fences at the periphery of the royal city with its fort and wall, and along the *khlong,* or canal. This is unique and is a history worth retelling.[15] The Silpakorn study team also proposed a solution to the present conflict between the BMA and the community. This would allow the residents to stay at the present site on the condition that they are willing to undertake activities that also have historical value.[16] In addition, every household would have to play a caretaker role by taking turns at neighborhood watch duty and upkeep of the neighborhood— on a voluntary basis, without payment. Mahakan would be open to the public, and four museum exhibits would be set up displaying birdcage manufacture, gold smelting, cockfighting, and pottery making.

Cultural Heritage and Rights

Our presentation of the major players and minor voices above reveals their varying visions and expectations. The three major players share considerable power in terms of their legal authority as agents of resettlement and redevelopment (BMA) and as legal landlords (Crown Property Bureau and Wat Pho) with rights to redevelop the area in accordance with the broad guidelines laid down in the Rattanakosin Master Plan. These three players also share a consensus on what is to be conserved and redeveloped in accordance with the plan, on what constitutes officially sanctioned heritage, on the need for more public parks, and on the importance of Rattanakosin for Thailand's tourism industry. They thus represent dominant economic interests in pushing for a redevelopment scheme that, in their view, can best deploy tangible heritage to serve nation-building goals and simultaneously attract tourists.

At the other end of the spectrum are the minor voices of the community leaders and residents at both Mahakan and Tha Tian who want to keep their way of life as craftsmen, small-business owners, and as residents. While their interests are clear, do their claims carry any weight as cultural rights claims?

The claim of cultural rights becomes a compelling argument when the focus is on a community of practitioners whose assemblage of beliefs and practices tied to a particular locality is under threat. Cultural rights become important when they are exercised by individuals in choosing to be involved in the cultural life of the group. When the community of practitioners is actively involved in perpetuating this cultural life, the result is a flourishing of cultural diversity in society (Shaheed 2010, 6, 7; Logan 2007, 49). Ignorance about, or the deliberate neglect of, cultural rights results in the bleeding away of minority cultures, a loss that Meskell (2002, 564, quoted in Silverman and Ruggles 2007, 5) describes as a "crime which affects multiple generations, erasing cultural memory and severing links with the past that are integral to forging and maintaining modern identities."

Set in the context of the city, the Tha Tian and Mahakan claims clearly fall short of an ideal cultural rights claim in which an indigenous or minority group's place-based cultural way of life is being threatened. For Tha Tian, an economic livelihood was placed at risk when CPB decided to evict the dried seafood merchants. The merchants' claim that the trade is tied to the history of river commerce may be a place-based form of heritage or cultural claim, but it is not a cultural rights issue since the activity was not originally practiced by or distinctive to this group of merchants alone.

Mahakan residents' claims are similar. There are several features that have heritage merit: birdcage-making may be a place-based heritage claim that Mahakan can legitimately make; some of the teak houses are worth preserving for their links to court officials; other houses are related to the origins of the *like* dance drama; and certainly the Mahakan site represents an example of an old Thai community with teak houses, unfenced and adjacent to a canal. However, these are disparate elements, and the residents at Mahakan cannot lay any claim to being the descendants of the earlier residents or practitioners. These may be group claims to particular ways of life—that is, intangible heritage claims in which cultural or economic activities have a demonstrated tie to the history of a place (Tha Tian as a commerce node; birdcage-making in the Mahakan area, as the Rattanakosin Exhibition Hall notes). However, the urban context promotes both inter-generational and residential mobility and both forms of mobility work to weaken cultural rights claims.

Without the compelling power of cultural rights, the most likely positive scenario for the future is a community rights entitlement for Mahakan in which the group becomes the collective caretakers of the site in exchange for the right to stay. If the Tha Tian chairman has his way, the positive scenario for his community will be a renovated seafood market that is capable of meeting tourists' and locals' needs. However, in contrast to Mahakan's negotiation with BMA, Tha Tian seafood merchants will have to deal with CPB and Wat Pho as landlords, and the more likely outcome will be the eviction of the merchants and a renovated but re-designated market hall with a new group of merchants catering primarily to tourists.

We should, however, still see value in Tha Tian and Mahakan as place-based communities. Both the Tha Tian and Mahakan communities have successfully leveraged the help provided by NGOs and academics. In the process, as Askew suggests (2008, 148), they have "incorporated [their] ideals and methods and language." In the case of the Mahakan community, we saw how community leaders like Suk and Tawatchai have not just acknowledged the contributions of these outside supporters, but have adopted their suggestions: (a) to organize the residents to improve the community; (b) to gain public support for the plight of the community; and (c) to accept the proposed caretaker solution as an alternative to resettlement.

In the video documentary produced by the Centre on Housing Rights and Eviction (Skiotis 2003), Mahakan community leader Tawatchai clearly articulated the language of NGOs when he framed his community objectives in terms of preservation and linked the struggles of his community to Thai national heritage:

> In my view, this community is an ancient one. The community has tried to preserve the old houses, the sacred tree, and our way of life here; and so we should come together and talk about preserving it, because it's not just our community heritage, but part of Thai national heritage. I believe people from other countries will understand this point about preserving national heritage. Heritage is part of our history, which will be remembered in the future if we preserve it now.

A heritage conservation approach that takes into account community interests and histories has merit for several reasons. From the viewpoint of history and heritage, places have both national and local elements in history-making. The character of a place is also a result of a sedimentation or layering process in which activities and buildings from different periods are superimposed. An approach that recognizes this diversity allows for a more attractive and accurate portrayal of heritage sites. These community-based efforts within the heritage district of Rattanakosin may be taken to reflect community curation, a space to allow for the voice of the communities living in Rattanakosin to be heard. Such an approach allows everyday practices that are part of a larger cultural stock to be framed as local heritage, as Mahakan community leader Tawatchai argues. And, as Silpakorn lecturer Chatri suggested, this approach can be elaborated to involve members of the community as caretakers and curators of the site. From a governance viewpoint, the recognition of a community and its active involvement in the heritage production process allows for active place-making that ultimately results in a more vibrant city.

Notes

1. The plan is, after all, related to an attempt to relocate government ministries from Rattanakosin to a new government area, Chaeng Watthana; the creation of river vistas through the creation of parks such as Fort Sumen; and a strict control of building activities, especially in Inner Rattanakosin.

2. At the Fort Sumen site, located on Phra Athit Road, was a sugar warehouse that was acquired and redeveloped into a park along with the restoration of the fort. Opened in December 1999 to commemorate the king's birthday, the site was important in opening up to the public the view and access to the Chao Phraya River and in providing green spaces in a very built-up central area. The restoration was also important in its efforts to keep existing trees on the site.

3. Interview with Kemtat Visavayodhin, Director of Conservation Project Department, Crown Property Bureau, 17 November 2010.

4. Interview with Phra Ratchawethi (Surapon Chitayano), assistant abbot, Wat Phra Chetuphon Vimolmangklararm Rajwaramahaviharn (Wat Pho), 17 November 2010.

5. The economic concerns of the abbot may be traced to the shift away from traditional sources of economic support for temple upkeep. Reynolds (1979), for example, showed how temples in Thailand could no longer depend on royal land and labor endowments for their maintenance, which thus required abbots to become increasingly concerned about the economic upkeep of the temples under their charge. Referring to abbots, Reynolds (1979, 225) remarked that "world renunciation, for some of these men, did not mean indifference toward the economic circumstances of their monasteries. . . . Indeed, it was 'world renunciation' which made the monasteries

situation so precarious." Thus, the assistant abbot's concern is economic in the sense that the renovations are likely to increase tourism-related revenues to the temple, but his concern was also religious and cultural in that the plan will strengthen the experience of Rattanakosin for locals, too.

6. Interview with Uncle Yuu and Ink, his granddaughter, 11 June 2011.

7. Interview with Yui Naowarat, 11 June 2011.

8. For an account of the confrontations, see Herzfeld (2003).

9. This information is based on an earlier field trip conducted in February 2009, when co-author K. C. Ho met with three Mahakan community leaders. After interviewing them, one of the leaders took him on a tour of the Mahakan community. The project "Rattanakosin as a Cultural District" was funded by the National University of Singapore, with a research license from the National Research Council of Thailand (project number 2008/064).

10. Writing about the Fort Mahakan community and their community spaces, Herzfeld (2006, 140–41) observes that for the Mahakan community (and for the urban poor in general) community spaces are of great importance in facilitating social interaction. Residents therefore treated community spaces as intimate places to relax and talk while at the same time respected them as communal amenities.

11. Interview with Suk, 25 February 2009.

12. Interview with Tawatchai during a tour of the Sirindhorn Anthropology Centre group, 23 June 2010.

13. Notes of meeting, 13 November 2010.

14. *Like* drama is a traditional Thai performing art. According to the community leaders interviewed on 25 February 2009 (cf. SURDI 2006), a *like* drama troupe who performed for King Rama IV was based in the Mahakan community.

15. Interview with Chatri Prakitnontakarn, 18 November 2010.

16. This recommendation is found in chapters 6 and 7 of SURDI 2006. According to our interview with community leader Tawatchai on 23 June 2010, the community adopted SURDI's recommendation as a condition for staying on the Mahakan site and included it in their proposal to BMA.

References

Aphiwat Seangpatthasima, dir. 2003. *Behind the Wall.* DVD documentary. Bangkok.

Askew, Marc. 2002. *Bangkok: Place, Practice and Representation.* London: Routledge.

BMA [Bangkok Metropolitan Administration]. 1985. *Kho banyat krungthep maha nakhon rueang kamnot boriwen ham ko sang datplaeng chai rue plianplaeng kan chai akhan bang chanit rue bang praphet phai nai boriwen krung rattanakosin chan nai nai thongthi khwaeng phra borom maha ratchawang khet phra nakhon krungthep maha nakhon pho so 2528* [Regulation of 1985 on areas with prohibitions on construction, modification, use, or changes of use of some types or categories of buildings within the inner Krung Rattanakosin sub-area in Phra Ratchawang subdistrict, Phra Nakhon district, Bangkok Metropolitan Area]. Bangkok: BMA.

————. 1987. *Kho banyat krungthep maha nakhon rueang kamnot boriwen ham ko sang datplaeng chai rue plianplaeng kan chai akhan bang chanit rue bang praphet phai nai thongthi khwaeng chana songkhram, khwaeng talat yot, khwaeng san chao pho suea, khwaeng bowonniwet, khwaeng sao ching cha, khwaeng samranrat, lae khwaeng wang burapaphirom, khet phra nakhon krungthep maha nakhon pho so 2530* [Regulation of 1987 on areas with prohibitions on construction, modification, uses, or changes of use of some types or categories of buildings within the Outer Krung Rattanakosin sub-area in subdistricts of Chana Songkhram, Talat Yot, Chao Pho Suea Shrine, Bowonniwet, Sao Ching Cha, Samranrat, and Wang Burapaphirom of Phra Nakhon district, Bangkok Metropolitan Area]. Bangkok: BMA.

Bristol, Graeme. 2010. "Rendered Invisible: Urban Planning, Cultural Heritage and Human Rights." In *Cultural Diversity, Heritage and Human Rights: Intersections in Theory and Practice*, edited by Michele Langfield, William Logan, and Mairead Nic Craith, 117–34. London: Routledge.

Brown, Michael F. 2009. "Exhibiting Indigenous Heritage in the Age of Cultural Property." In *Whose Culture? The Promise of Museums and the Debate over Antiquities*, edited by James Cuno, 145–55. Princeton, NJ: Princeton University Press.

Butler, Frances. 2005. "Building a Human Rights Culture." In *Human Rights in the Community: Rights as Agents for Change*, edited by Colin Harvey, 69–73. Oxford: Hart Publishing.

De Frantz, Monika. 2005. "From Cultural Regeneration to Discursive Governance: Constructing the Flagship of 'Museumquartier' Vienna as a Plural Symbol of Change." *International Journal of Urban and Regional Research* 29 (1): 50–66.

Fincher, Ruth, and Kurt Iveson. 2008. *Planning and Diversity in the City: Redistribution, Recognition and Encounter*. New York: Palgrave.

Friedmann, John. 2000. "The Good City: In Defense of Utopian Thinking." *International Journal of Urban and Regional Research* 24 (2): 460–72.

Gilbert, Jérémie. 2010. "Custodians of the Land: Indigenous Peoples, Human Rights and Cultural Integrity." In *Cultural Diversity, Heritage and Human Rights: Intersections in Theory and Practice*, edited by Michele Langfield, William Logan, and Máiréad Nic Craith, 31–43. London: Routledge.

Hampton, Mark P. 2005. "Heritage, Local Communities and Economic Development." *Annals of Tourism Research* 32 (3): 735–59.

Hershkovitz, L. 1993. "Tianamen Square and the Politics of Place." *Political Geography* 12 (5): 395–420.

Herzfeld, Michael. 2003. "Pom Mahakan: Humanity and Order in the Historic Center of Bangkok." *Thailand Human Rights Journal* 1: 101–19.

———. 2006. "Spatial Cleansing." *Journal of Material Culture* 11 (1–2): 127–49.

Lefebvre, Henri. 1991. *The Social Production of Urban Space*. Translated by D. Nicholson-Smith. Oxford: Blackwell.

Leitner, H., and P. Kang. 1999. "Contested Urban Landscapes of Nationalism: The Case of Taipei." *Cultural Geographies* 6 (2): 214–33.

Lepofsky, Jonathan, and James C. Fraser. 2003. "Building Community Citizens: Claiming the Right to Place-Making in the City." *Urban Studies* 40 (1): 127–42.

Logan, William S. 2007. "Closing Pandora's Box: Human Rights Conundrums in Cultural Heritage Protection." In Silverman and Ruggles 2007, 33–52.

———. 2009. "Hanoi: Representing Power in and Of the Nation." *City* 13 (1): 87–94.

Massey, Doreen. 1995. *Spatial Divisions of Labour: Social Structures and the Geography of Production*. 2nd ed. New York: Routledge.

Meskell, Lynn. 2002. "Negative Heritage and Past Mastering in Archaeology" *Anthropological Quarterly* 75 (3): 557–74.

Napat Settachai. 2008. "Global Tourism and Community Life: Toward a Responsible Tourism Framework." PhD diss., University of Hawaii.

Pornpan Boonchuen, and K. C. Ho. 2006. "Bangkok as Capital and Emergent World City." In *Capital Cities in Asia-Pacific: Primacy and Diversity*, edited by Kong Chong Ho and Michael Hsiao Hsin-Huang, 119–138. Taipei: Center for Asia-Pacific Studies.

Pornpan Chinnapong. 2008. "Bangkok's Sanam Luang (The Royal Ground): From a Historic Plaza to a Civic Space." In *Globalization, the City and Civil Society in Pacific Asia Cities*, edited by Mike Douglass, K. C. Ho, and Giok Ling Ooi, 254–67. London: Routledge.

Reynolds, Craig J. 1979. "Monastery Lands and Labour Endowments in Thailand: Some Effects of Social and Economic Change, 1868 to 1910." *Journal of the Economic and Social History of the Orient* 22 (2): 190–227.

———. 2002. "Introduction: National Identity and Its Defenders." In *National Identity and Its Defenders: Thailand, 1939–1989*, edited by Craig J. Reynolds, 1–32. Chiang Mai, Thailand: Silkworm Books.

Shaheed, Farida. 2010. "Report of the Independent Expert in the Field of Cultural Rights, Ms. Farida Shaheed, Submitted Pursuant to Resolution 10/23 of the Human Rights Council." UN General Assembly, Human Rights Council, 14th Session, March. Accessed at http://www2.ohchr.org/english/bodies/hrcouncil/docs/14session/A.HRC.14.36_en.pdf.

Silverman, Helaine, and D. Fairchild Ruggles, eds. 2007. *Cultural Heritage and Human Rights*. New York: Springer.

———. 2007a. "Cultural Heritage and Human Rights Protection." In Silverman and Ruggles 2007, 4–22.

Skiotis, Fionn, dir. 2003. *Pom mahakan: People of the Fort*. DVD documentary. Geneva: Centre on Housing Rights and Evictions.

SURDI [Silpakorn University Research and Development Institute]. 2006. *Khrongkan wichai phue chat tham phaen maebot phuea kan anurak lae phatthana: Chumchon ban mai boran pom mahakan* [Research project of a model scheme for preservation and development of "ancient wooden houses in mahakan Fort community". Final Report submitted to Bureau of City Planning, Bangkok Metropolitan Administration. Bangkok: Silpakorn University.

Synchron Group. 1995. *Phaen maebot phuea kan anurak lae phatthana krung rattanakosin* [Rattanakosin conservation and development master plan]. Final report submitted to Office of the Natural and Environment Policy and Planning. Bangkok: Phimphan kan phim.

Weeraphan Shinawatra, ed. 2009. *Rattanakosin and Chao Phraya River Front*. Bangkok: Plus Press.

4

Rights Claims and the Strategic Use of Culture to Protect Human Rights: The Community Forest Movement in Thailand

———— ∞∞∞ ————

Bencharat Sae Chua

"We don't care about the Community Forest Bill anymore. With or without it, we would still take care of our forest anyway." This is the typical response that villagers taking part in the movement for a Community Forest Bill would often give me when I asked what their next steps were in the movement's campaign. The Community Forest Act that the National Legislative Assembly passed in 2007 was ruled invalid by the Constitutional Court in November 2009 on the technical grounds that it was passed with an insufficient quorum of the legislature. This put the attempt to get legal recognition of communities' rights to access and manage local forests on hold once again, as had often happened in the previous two decades: Various drafts of the bill had gone through five Cabinet meetings, three parliamentary deliberations, and three public hearings. The view quoted above fits well with the community forest movement's claim that local communities' customary practices in forest stewardship give them the rights to stay in protected forests. However, the assertion does not outweigh the fact that currently, probably more than one million people are considered in violation of the law for living on state-designated protected forestland. The goal of the movement is to secure those people's rights to live on and exploit the land and forests for their survival, not for them to be allowed to protect the forest.

In this chapter I will examine the context in which the community forest movement's environmental discourse on forest protection has developed. I will relate this to what is considered the movement's strategic rights frame, the limits of which are the focus of this chapter. The environmental discourse and the forest stewardship identity the movement has constructed for its members powerfully challenge the Thai state's claim to centrally control the country's forests. The movement asserts that control over the forest belongs to local communities since the communities possess traditional knowledge of how to live in harmony with their forest environment. I will argue in this paper, however, that by focusing on environmental legitimacy—that is, by using an "environmentalist framing"—the movement has chosen to limit itself within the scope of the state's definition of permitted forest use. This forces the movement to avoid discussion of farmland issues for fear of their perceived association with forest encroachment. As a consequence, the movement cannot address the essential needs of its members: access to forestland for viable commercial agriculture.

While this chapter studies the community forest movement in Thailand in general, it specifically focuses on the northeastern region, despite the fact that the movement's stronghold is among ethnic minority communities in the northern region. In the northeast, the reality of extensive commercial agriculture, including within the state-designated protected forests, and of relatively new village settlements underline the need to extend the movement's discourse beyond legitimacy based on traditional subsistence agricultural practices. A study of the community forest movement members in the northeast also keeps issues of land rights in focus and avoids these issues being obscured by the related problems of legal citizenship and ethnic discrimination faced by many ethnic communities in the northern forests. The limit of the community forest movement's ability to address villagers' livelihood issues will therefore become more apparent. Moreover, I opt to focus on the situation of communities within protected forests to explore the struggle in cases where the state's policies, if fully implemented, imply total deprivation of communities' livelihood rights. Therefore, I do not consider here the situation of communities outside the protected forest who need access to forest resources, or communities fighting against businesses that encroach on and destroy their forests, both of which also constitute key elements of the community forest movement.

The first part of the chapter introduces the state's forest-related policies and their impacts on the livelihood rights of the communities. I contend that the conflict over forests should not be seen simply as a result of the state's environmental conservation policy, but should be analyzed as the state's attempt to control territory and resources within them. The chapter then elaborates on how the community forest movement strategically frames the legitimacy of communities' rights to manage forests with the argument that the communities possess environmentally friendly "traditional" cultures. In order to deal with the implications of the state's forest control for the rights of communities and the movement's use of an environmentalist discourse, I integrate into the analysis the experiences of two villages in the northeast that joined the community forest movement.

I spent about two weeks each in Nong Tio village in the Noen Nam Lot National Park, Yasothon province, and in Khok Sombun village in the Pha Din Wildlife Sanctuary, Sakon Nakhon province, in August, November, and December 2010, observing their forest use and, in the case of Khok Sombun, the community's struggle against an ongoing relocation effort.[1] In addition, after Khok Sombun's relocation was completed, I briefly visited Khok Sombun villagers at the relocation site in July 2011 and in February 2012. With the experiences of the two villages in mind, I discuss in the last section how the community forest movement's self-limiting claim may affect the land tenure and livelihoods rights of farmers living in the forest.

Control of Forests and Forest People

With the establishment of the Royal Forestry Department (RFD) in 1896, all land that had not been legally acquired by individuals was deemed forestland and claimed by the central Thai state.[2] Through the RFD, the Thai state could exercise power over the forests, which covered most of the country, the people living within those forests, and the forest resources previously controlled by local lords (Vandergeest and Peluso 1995, 408). The central Thai state started to manage the forest in order to extract benefits from forest products, such as from teak concessions given to private companies. When forest conservation was later added to the national agenda in the 1980s, human activities were excluded from forest territory, leaving the state with sole authority over forests.

The Thai state's forest conservation policy should not be seen as being driven purely by environmental concerns. In arguing this, I borrow from Peluso and Vandegeest's analysis (2001) of the "political forest" and their earlier discussion of territorialization of land and forest in Thailand (Vandergeest and Peluso 1995). They see the demarcation of protected forest in Thailand as part of an internal territorialization process initiated by the Thai state, not only to address environmental concerns but also for security and administrative purposes. In this process, the state defined the geographic boundaries within the country to control people and access to natural resources within each boundary. In addition to identifying and mapping villages to facilitate local administration, other territorial mechanisms included territorialization of forest. The forest territorialization techniques involved using scientific knowledge to zone and map territorial areas into different classes of forest and then defining what could be done within each category of forest. Through this process, a "political forest," or "territories that have been legislated, zoned, mapped, and classified as permanent forest and managed by professional, 'scientific' government agencies" (Peluso and Vandergeest 2011, 588), was developed. The enacted land and forest laws govern the "political forest" by defining the scope of legal forest use. In a "political forest," previously common forest-related practices were criminalized through enforcement by state forestry institutions—in the Thai case, the Royal Forestry Department and the forest police (tamruat pa mai). The disciplining methods used in controlling the forest forced "the population to think about and act towards 'the forest' in specific ways," as defined and approved by the state (Peluso and Vandergeest 2001, 764).

The Royal Forestry Department started to demarcate forests into different categories from the 1930s. A series of laws, including the Protection and Reservation of Forests Act (1938),[3] the Wildlife Reservation and Protection Act (1960)[4] and the National Park Act (1961), prescribe permitted activities in each category. What these laws have in common are provisions prohibiting occupation of and farming in the forest and regulatory limits on people's access to forest products. The forest territorialization process accelerated from 1985, when the Cabinet approved the National Forest Policy Committee's proposal to aim for a total forest cover of 40 percent of the country's area, with 25 percent as commercial forest and the other 15 percent as conservation forest.[5] The National Forest Policy Committee identified forest encroachment for farming as the main cause of deforestation (NFPC 1988). The policy therefore prohibits any use of 1A-level watershed areas—the category of the most fertile forest—except for special purposes permitted by the state. The conservation policy marked a turn away from the state's previous approach—which had lasted until the mid-1980s[6] and had encouraged community settlement in the forest to increase farming productivity—and away from the even earlier commercially dominated forest policy that promoted commercial plantation and logging concessions. After severe floods in which logs destroyed houses in southern Thailand in 1988, the Thai government came under public pressure to protect the forest and decided to cancel all logging concessions.

When the National Forest Policy was formulated in 1985, the forest cover area in Thailand was 112,937,500 *rai*[7] (34.8 percent) with 30,656,250 *rai* (9.4 percent) as protected forest (NFPC 1988). To meet the aim of having conservation forest cover 15 percent of the country, the RFD rapidly demarcated more and more forest as protected areas and promoted reforestation programs. It defined the protected forest (*pa anurak*; hereinafter "protected forest" or "protected areas") as comprising national parks, wildlife sanctuaries, non-hunting areas, protected mangroves, and areas the Cabinet designated to be reserved as watersheds or for other purposes. During 1990–1991, for example, fourteen new national parks were demarcated adding 4,240,625 *rai* to the national forest area. Eight other national parks were extended (totally 369,872 *rai*) and forty new parks (11,607,206 *rai*) were being planned (RFD 1993a, 219). By the end of 1990, the RFD had already met its target.[8] However, the trend continued after the seventh National Economic and Social Development Plan (1992–1996) raised the threshold for conservation forest cover to 25 percent of the country's land. In 2010, there were 123 national parks covering 37,700,068 *rai* and fifty-eight wildlife sanctuaries with 23,077,106 *rai*. Combined with other kinds of protected forest, the total area of protected forests was 64,881,185 *rai* (National Parks, Wildlife, and Plants Conservation Department 2010). The forest demarcation relied mainly on satellite images of forest cover and scientific criteria defining the forest—for example, land with more than a thirty-five-degree grade would be considered a watershed area. There was limited actual land surveying before the forest boundaries were drawn on the map.

With such rapid forest expansion beyond actual existing forests, many protected forest demarcations were imposed upon areas already occupied and farmed by local communities. Since the National Park Act 1961 (Article 16) and the Wildlife Reservation and Protection Act, 1992 (Article 38) prohibit human settlement and activities in their respective forests, communities settled before the demarcation of protected forests were turned into "squatters" on state land. There has been no thorough survey of forestland occupation and, therefore, there are still no definite numbers for people living in the forest. The estimated numbers of people "illegally" living in the protected area given by different sources differ widely. In 1998, the National Park and Wildlife Reserve Section in the RFD reported about 140,000 people living in the protected forest and around 177,900 farming on forestland but residing outside it (cited in Sayamol et al. 2002, 248). In 2001, the Operational Center to Solve Land and Forest Problems, also under the RFD, put the number much higher, with 460,000 households "living in, farming, and utilizing" the forest reserves (cited in Thailand Community Forest Network 2003).

Forest Conservation and Eviction

One of the methods used to enforce protected forest laws and the National Forest Policy was the eviction of communities from protected forests, mostly without providing adequate compensation or effective measures for resettlement. Massive evictions of the communities from Khlong Lan National Park, Kampaeng Phet province in 1985, of Hmong ethnic communities from Thung Yai-Naresuan Wildlife Sanctuary in 1988, of Karen ethnic communities from Huai Kha Kheng Wildlife Sanctuary in 1990–1991, and of several ethnic groups from Doi Luang National Park in 1994 are notorious cases of eviction in the north. The Land Distribution Program for the Poor Living in Degraded National Forest Reserves in Northeast Thailand in 1991, which will be discussed further below, was another large-scale, forced relocation of communities from the protected forest.

Walker and Farrelly (2008) have argued that subsequent campaign materials and published writings about the situation in the 1980s by community forest advocates tend to evoke the "specter of eviction" to support their claims against eviction, although not many cases of forced eviction actually took place. They argue that actual eviction from protected forest during the 1980s–1990s was relatively low compared to the 1960s–1970s, when many communities were evicted for "security" reasons to cut off support for a Communist insurgency. I would argue, however, that both the security and environmental justifications of eviction should be seen from the forest territorialization perspective. As will be shown in the case studies below, in cases where no eviction took place, limitations on activities allowed in the protected forest, especially on farming activities and village development, were imposed upon forest communities and harshly affected their livelihood rights. In effect, the state's goal of forcing people to accept what they can or cannot do in the forest was also achieved, even without having to resort to actual evictions.

Besides the enforcement of forest laws, the exclusion of local communities from access to forests also occurred as the result of other forest management schemes. Examples include the Forest Village Program (*khrongkan muban pa mai*) approved by the Cabinet on 29 April 1976, many royal projects related to forest conservation, and the New Forest Village Program approved by the Cabinet on 27 July 2004. The Forest Village Program was the main model for all these programs. During the period of the Communist insurgency in the 1970s and 1980s, the Forest Village Program was introduced to "rehabilitate degraded forest" and to improve the quality of life in areas occupied by the Communists (Amnuay 1993, 2). In those areas, the Communist Prevention and Suppression Command ran the Forest Village Program,[9] while the RFD was mainly in charge of the Program outside the Communist-influenced areas. The Program involved relocation of villagers from watersheds in the Reserved Forests and their resettlement in other areas of the forest with usufructuary license (*nangsue sitthi thamkin*). Each household would receive up to fifteen *rai* of land and support for basic needs. The villages were to work on forest conservation activities, either in reforestation, community forest management, or agroforestry (Amnuay 1993, 2). The "New Forest Village Program" was designed about three decades later on the same model. It was set up as the queen's royal project in honor of her seventy-second birthday (*khrongkan muban pa mai phaen mai tham naeo phraratchadamri chaloem phrakiat 72 phansa maharachini*). The Program planned to manage or relocate 10,866 villages that were settled in or bordering on national parks, wildlife sanctuaries, and reserved forests. When a pilot project was launched in Huai Pla Lot village in Taksin Maharat National Park, Tak province, each household was told to limit the area they farmed to two *rai*. The authorities then claimed the villagers had given the remaining farmland back to the state (*Prachatai*, 31 July 2005), implying that Huai Pal Lot village had invaded state land, even though the villagers had lived there from before the demarcation of the national park.

Some of the projects claimed to promote the idea of "humans living in coexistence with the forest" (*khon yu ruam kap pa dai*), despite involving attempts to relocate communities from the forest. Such contradictory claims were especially evident in forest-related royal projects which arguably follow the principle of "human living in coexistence with the forest in a sustainable way" (*khon yu ruam kap pa yang yang yuen*). Among sixty-five royal projects in which the RFD was involved in 1992, for example, twelve projects included the resettlement of local communities of 3,080 households under the model of the Forest Village (RFD 1993b). More recently, the website of the Department of National Parks, Wildlife and Conservation, the department now in charge of protected forests,[10] lists eighty-one royal projects in which it is involved.[11] Among these, twenty-one projects clearly stated that they relocate local communities or their farmland out of the forest area using the Forest Village model. Details on impacts from these projects, however, are not widely available. Royal projects are those initiated by the king or the queen or those inspired by their ideas. Each project is run by various government agencies and mainly funded and monitored by the Office of the Royal Development Projects Board. Being a "royal project" provides de facto protection from criticism, as the aura of the king and the laws protecting the monarchy from criticism are informally extended to the royal projects. The experience of Khok Sombun village described below sheds some light on what has happened to those affected by royal projects and also on communities in protected forests in general.

Khok Sombun was a small village of approximately seventy households in Pha Din Wildlife Sanctuary, Sakon Nakhon province. People from various provinces had used Don Pha Din forest for farming and pastoral purposes since the 1950s, and some had started to settle in the area that was later called Khok Sombun village from the mid-1970s. In 1980, the government designated Don Pha Din forest as the "Pha Din Wildlife Sanctuary." Since then, the RFD had limited forest use by Khok Sombun villagers and those others who farmed in the forest. Several villagers were arrested for cutting down trees or using certain types of small tractors on their farms. As in many villages within protected forests, Khok Sombun did not have electricity and did not receive any development support from the state, because the village was not included in the official census. Khok Sombun villagers had their names registered as residents of another, official village. There was a school in the village, but with only two teachers teaching all six primary classes. It took about thirty minutes by motorbike along a hilly, ten-kilometer-long gravel road to get to the nearest paved road. From there it was a short drive to the nearest market. In the rainy season, the gravel road was sometimes accessible only by four-wheel-drive vehicles.

The Sakon Nakhon authorities constantly tried to relocate the people of Khok Sombun, whose struggle led them to join several peasant organizations and networks, including the Small Scale Farmers Assembly of Isan,[12] Assembly of Isan Farmers for Land Rights and Improvement of Natural Resources, and the Assembly of the Poor. Through these organizations, Khok Sombun villagers became part of the community forest movement demanding their rights to stay in protected areas. The initial phase of relocation during the 1990s was ineffective, partly because many villagers refused to move and partly because the compensation scheme was launched in a highly corrupt manner. Part of the land allocated as compensation was given to outsiders who had connections with local authorities. Besides, the compensation land was already occupied by people from other local villages. While some Khok Sombun villagers agreed to move to the resettlement area, only a small number of them have managed to survive on that resettlement site to the present. The poorly built four-by-four meter cement houses that the authorities built for the relocated villagers are now largely abandoned.

After Princess Sirindhorn visited a royal project near the relocation site in early 2009 and asked the Sakon Nakhon governor and the commanding general of the Second Army Area (Northeastern Region) to relocate Khok Sombun out of the forest,[13] the relocation plan resumed vigorously. The Sakon Nakhon provincial authority acquired another piece of land in Dong Sue village, some twenty kilometers away from Khok Sombun, and allotted it as a new resettlement site. Sixty houses, on one-half *rai* each, were built along an asphalt road. They stood awaiting occupancy by the Khok Sombun villagers. The fact that this resettlement scheme was now designated as part of the "Huai Nam Din Development Royal Project," whose operations covered the relocation area, was now made clear by the authorities. Several privy councillors, the personal advisors to the king, visited the new resettlement site a couple of times in 2010. Some villagers were wary when I told them that activists had been trying to urge journalists to report about the potential eviction in mid-2010. "It may be difficult (for them to report about us), because this is a project of His Highness,"[14] an elderly woman warned me, despite her strong words of criticism against the project. Some villagers decided to resettle to this new site. As compensation, each household was promised six pigs, five cows, and vocational training. They also received another 2.5 *rai* of land each for farming, which the villagers claimed was not enough even to grow rice for household consumption.[15] Besides, the land was poorly irrigated.

In August 2010, the authorities started to put more pressure on the villagers who still insisted on staying in Khok Sombun. The authorities threatened to arrest them if they refused to "voluntarily" relocate.[16] During the week before a deadline set for early November 2010, troops from different units, including soldiers, police, Border Patrol Police, and Defense Volunteer Units (*O So*), were deployed in the village. About forty villagers, among them ten children, insisted on staying in the village even after the deadline. *O So* units then took fortnightly shifts with twenty armed personnel who were stationed in the village up until April 2011. In June 2011, all the households in Khok Sombun finally moved out after another visit from soldiers from the Internal Security Operations Command (ISOC), Northeast Regiment, who gave an ultimatum claiming that Princess Sirindhorn was about to visit the area soon. In fact, however, there was no royal visit. The military helped the villagers to dismantle their houses and transported them to the relocation area. A few days later, the military tore down a wooden bridge that allowed vehicles to cross a stream to get to Khok Sombun to prevent the villagers from getting back, despite the promise to allow the villagers to tend their farms until harvesting time. The military and the RFD reforested the former farmland and the forest near Khok Sombun by clearing the land and planting new trees.

Since the authorities did not prepare enough houses to accommodate every Khok Sombun household, some families from this last group of villagers were put in abandoned RFD offices a few kilometers from the main relocation area. There was no electricity or running water at this site. Eight months had gone by when I last visited them in February 2012, and the authorities had built four more houses at this ad hoc site and allocated farmland nearby. Those groups of villagers who were relocated in June 2011 were allowed to go back to Khok Sombun to harvest agricultural products from their farm for one last time. But with no rice grown the previous year, since they could not transplant the rice during the eviction in 2011, they were worried about how to survive once their rice stocks were depleted. There was still no electricity or water for the four households. In the main relocation area, tap water mostly runs only a few days a week. The villagers had to collect drinking water from a natural spring in another village.

Nong Tio village experienced similar attempts at relocation by authorities, but they managed to negotiate with local forestry officials, and they still remain in the forest. The village was formed in the 1950s after people migrated to settle in the area of what is today Nong Tio in Dan Prao Forest. In 1962, then Prime Minister Field Marshal Sarit Thanarat ordered the villagers of Nong Tio to leave their land to cut off support for the Communist insurgency.[17] A few years later, in 1965, the same year that Dan Prao Forest was declared National Reserved Forest, the villagers moved back to Nong Tio and made their homes around different capillary water sources in the area. Now being in Reserved Forest, the villagers' agricultural practices were deemed illegal, and they had to take turns watching out for each other when working the land to avoid being arrested.[18]

During the military rule in 1991, Nong Tio was relocated again, this time by the "Land Distribution Program for the Poor Living in Degraded National Forest Reserves in Northeast Thailand" (abbreviated in Thai as *Kho Cho Ko*). The program aimed to relocate farmers living in protected forest by allocating land for them elsewhere. After moving the farmers out, the protected forest would then be rehabilitated by planting eucalyptus. Nong Tio was among the first few communities to be violently evicted from the forest. As with the first relocation of Khok Sombun, most of the villagers were allotted a piece of farmland already occupied by other farmers in the resettlement sites. Thus, the Nong Tio villagers could not engage in farming. The villagers then joined the anti-*Kho Cho Ko* movement together with other affected communities and staged a mass demonstration in Nakhon Ratchasima province in mid-1992.[19]

When *Kho Cho Ko* was cancelled after demonstrations by the people victimized by it, and after the change from military regime to an interim civilian one, some Nong Tio villagers returned to their village in the end of 1992. However, they found that the area had been demarcated that year as part of Noen Nam Lot National Park, so once again no community was allowed to settle there. The villagers insisted that they should be able to go back to the area by referring to the Cabinet Resolution that revoked the *Kho Cho Ko* and allowed people to return to protected areas for "temporary" residence.[20] In the first few years back, the villagers were not allowed to farm. They had to take turns plowing the land, while other villagers stood watch to prevent RFD officers from approaching and arresting any farmers caught at work. Because the village lacked official status, it received no development support from the government. Several development projects from some nongovernmental organizations (NGOs) were also stalled: for example, no backhoe was allowed in the village to help dig wells, and cattle some NGOs had donated for livelihood support were not permitted in the national park.

The stories from Nong Tio, Khok Sombun, and other communities who have settled in protected forest reveal how the Thai state has used disciplinary methods to force local villagers to accept the state's authority over forestland. In this process, the forest is defined as a state-controlled area that must be free from human activities, and farming is depicted as one of the main causes of deforestation and therefore to be prohibited in forests. As Peluso and Vandeergeest (2001, 764) have pointed out, the political process of defining state forests has "redefined the basic terrain on which future struggles over the roles of states in managing and imagining nature would be played out."

By using a discourse of environmentalism and claiming to protect the nation's forests, the state has drawn support from the general public. The state then uses this support to legitimize its territorialization of forest and to deafen the public to the voices of the evicted communities. The power of the state's discourse is evident from the experience of the community forest movement's advocacy for a Community Forest Bill that would recognize local communities' rights in managing the forest. During the two decades of the Community Forest Bill drafting process, the central debate centered on whether communities should be allowed to manage community forests in protected areas that are deemed ecologically sensitive. Public discussion on the issue and parliamentary debates on the draft bill manifested two different approaches to environmentalism. On one side were the "dark greens" or "greens" who argued for pristine forest protection. On the other side, the community forest movement drew support from the "red-greens" or "light greens," who prioritized the rights of the community in accessing the forest (see Forsyth 2007 and Kristoffersen 2005 on the various "green" approaches and debates). It is upon this terrain of struggle that the Thai community forest movement has framed its campaign to draw support from the public and to advocate for policy change. The next part of this chapter explores how the movement for the rights of the communities in accessing forest and forest resources constructed its argument within the scope of this debate.

Environmentalism as a Basis for Claiming Rights

At the entrance to the Noen Nam Lot National Park office, a signboard that reads "Conservation Farming Village,[21] Nong Tio Village" stands next to a National Park sign. A right turn from there leads to the premises of the Noen Nam Lot National Park office and its tourist facilities; going straight, visitors find themselves in Nong Tio village. It is ironic to see the signs side-by-side, since Article 16 (1) of the National Park Act prohibits "land occupation or possession" within the national park area.

After years of struggle for their rights to live in the forest, Nong Tio villagers finally came to a semi-official agreement with the Noen Nam Lot National Park authority and were allowed to stay on their land on the condition that they live in an environmentally friendly way. The villagers promised to adjust their farm to the so-called *wanakaset*[22] system by growing several species of plants together to approximate a natural forest. The villagers also vowed not to encroach upon more forestland for agriculture and gave an assurance that if any community member encroached upon the forest, the whole community would concede to being relocated (Nukaen et al. 2000, 62). To strengthen their stand, the Nong Tio villagers, with the encouragement of NGOs, redistributed the land among themselves. Those who previously had more than twenty-five *rai* before being evicted by *Kho Cho Ko* agreed to limit their land to twenty-five *rai,* while those who had less than twenty-five *rai* were allotted fifteen *rai* of land.[23] Anyone with more than fifteen but less than twenty-five *rai* would get the same amount of land they had had before. Since not all Nong Tio villagers chose to move back to the village, there was enough land within the area previously occupied by the Nong Tio people to be reallocated to everyone based on this 15–25 *rai* arrangement, and for some land to be used for communal facilities or spaces, such as a school, a temple, grazing grounds, and a cemetery. The village boundary was made known to the local Forestry Department officers, and it was later co-monitored to ensure that there was no further land encroachment.

Nong Tio villagers also demarcated two areas as community forest: one of 150 *rai* on a former school site, and the other of eighty *rai* near a temple at the northern fringe of the village. Several NGOs worked with the villagers to design community forest management systems and to promote sustainable agriculture. A committee was set up in charge of community forest management, and forest use regulations were drawn up to prevent the felling of trees and hunting in the community forest. The rules, however, allowed gathering of mushrooms, ants' eggs, yams, and herbal medicines from the forest.

What happened in Nong Tio was common among the communities joining the community forest movement. Khok Sombun villagers, for example, also adopted community forest management and 15–25 *rai* of land reallocation after a visit to Nong Tio in the early 2000s. As the two case studies show, however, the claim based on environmental legitimacy does not guarantee the rights to stay in the forest. It depends very much on the local context of each community. Also important is the strategic framing of the wider community forest movement, of which the local community forest practices should be seen as a part.

Over time, the communities that had been turned into squatters as a result of the state policy on protected forests formed networks at the regional and national levels to enhance their negotiating power with the state. This "community forest movement" works in close collaboration with NGOs and academics to advocate for community rights over forest management. The movement operates in various spheres, including at the level of national policy, launching public awareness campaigns, and mobilizing communities. The movement proposed a Community Forest Bill that would allow community forest management within protected areas. Policy advocacy also included the demand for revocation of existing forest laws that centralize forest management in the hands of the state and for a survey to prove that communities had settled in protected forest prior to the areas' being gazetted as protected areas.

The campaign for the Community Forest Bill was also an effort to advocate for community rights, which were enshrined in the 1997 and 2007 Constitutions. The so-called "People's Constitution" of 1997, which was a result of extensive public deliberation and advocacy from community rights supporters, had specific provisions guaranteeing community rights over management of natural resources in its Section 46, which provided that:

> Persons so assembling as to be a local traditional community shall have the right to conserve or restore their customs, local knowledge, arts or the good culture of their community and of the nation and participate in the management, maintenance, preservation, and exploitation of natural resources and the environment in a balanced fashion and sustainably *as provided by law* [emphasis added].

However, without a specific organic law detailing the nature of rights and defining communities as rights-holders, the provision in the 1997 Constitution could not be enforced. Research on the Thai court decisions in cases related to community rights and land management has shown that the Constitutional Court tended to dismiss cases filed on grounds of violation of Article 46 of the 1997 Constitution, because there was as yet no law to enforce that article (see Luckana 2011).

In order to attract public support, the community forest movement launched a public campaign targeting public perceptions of the relationship between communities and forest. In its framing strategy, the community forest movement constructed a new meaning of the human-forest relationship to counter that implied in the forest territorialization process. The campaign was part of the movement's "framing process" through which they attempted to "assign meaning to, and interpret, relevant events and conditions in ways that are intended to mobilize potential adherents and constituents, to garner bystander support, and to demobilize antagonists" (Snow and Benford 1998, 198). Framing processes can help social movements to tap existing culture, values, and beliefs and amplify them to strategically communicate with potential supporters and, in particular, those with a different, often dominant view (Benford and Snow 2000, 624). In the Thai community forest movement's strategy, the local communities are framed as having inherited traditional cultural practices that enable them to live in harmony with the forest. Therefore, the movement argues, the communities have legitimate rights to live in and manage protected forest. The Community Forest Bill drafted by activists and academics supporting the community forest movement in 1993, for example, claimed to "translate the livelihoods, traditions, and 'community forest ideology' of the villagers into law" (Community Forest Action Research Project 1993, 4). This framing directly targets and reverses the state's forest conservation argument as well as the prevailing public discourse. By elevating the community's rights and legitimacy, the forest is redefined as under the control of local communities, who, because of their traditional practices, can best look after it.

Among the examples of how cultural practices are reinterpreted with an environmentalist add-on value in the framing process is a reference to local beliefs in nature spirits. The villagers' respect for such spirits is assigned a new meaning by the suggestion that the practice encourages them to protect the natural resources related to those spirits and prohibits over-exploitation. As Saneh Chamarik, a leading academic advocating community's rights in forest management, puts it:

> The beliefs in the forest's sacred beings led to forest use traditions that are reverent to and appreciative of the forest and the sacred beings in it. Sacred forest and the beliefs about it are common; examples include *pu ta* forest and cemetery areas. . . . These beliefs have established and evolved into a moral basis for management and exploitation of natural resources in a way that is responsive to agricultural production patterns (Saneh and Yos 1993, 163; my translation).

In the northeast, a "sacred forest" is often related to the area where the shrines of the *pu ta*[24] are located; *pu ta* are the spirits of the elders who, it is believed, stand watch over the village. A local belief that killing animals or cutting down trees near the shrines are acts of disrespect is presented as evidence of an environmentally friendly tradition.

Another significant example can be found in the campaign to change the public's perception of ethnic groups in the north from being considered as "forest destroyers" to being considered "forest caretakers." In addition to academic research to show the environmentally friendly nature of the Karen ethnic group's rotational farming practices, certain cultural ceremonies were "performed" to support those claims. One of the key campaign activities was the "ordination" of fifty million trees in honor of the fiftieth year of the King's accession to the throne in 1996. The "tree ordination" ceremony, in which the yellow robes normally worn by Buddhist monks were wrapped around the trees, and religious or animist objects were placed in the forest symbolizing the trees' sacred status, was used to reinforce the claim that local communities have forest-friendly local traditions. The campaign thus drew upon religious values and symbols of national identity to increase the ethnic group's legitimacy and its claim for citizenship rights (Pinkaew 1999). In addition to the main ceremony held in 1996, tree ordinations were performed in many other communities thereafter, and not only among minority ethnic groups. In Khok Sombun, for example, an annual forest ordination ceremony was organized from 2004 when the authorities increased pressure on the villagers to relocate. The ceremony served both the aim of public communication and of promoting environmental conservation awareness among the villagers.

The designation of local forests as "community forests" (*pa chumchon*), as mentioned above, is another common practice among the movement's communities. The RFD promotes community forestry in reserved forests (*pa sa-nguan*) and other forests, but not in protected forests (Community Forest Management Unit 2011).[25] The villagers in the community forest movement usually allocate some area of the protected forest close to their residential area to be a *pa chumchon* under the village's management. Usually a village committee is set up in charge of community forest management and the community members draft rules regulating the use of the community forest. The *pa chumchon* is generally reserved for minimal local use and hunting is prohibited. The practice of *pa chumchon* serves both as the movement's framing tactic and as a way to claim back land from the state. The management of community forests helps communicate to the public that the communities are taking care of their forests. By claiming part of the officially protected forest to be a *pa chumchon* managed by community members, the villagers have attempted to deterritorialize the state's land and forest control (Tegbaru 1997). The villagers unilaterally "declare the *protected forest* of the community without regard for any state law governing that area" (Sayamol et al. 2002, 267; my translation, emphasis in original). In cases where the Department of National Parks, Wildlife, and Conservation allows the communities de facto rights to stay in protected forests, use and management of the village-proclaimed community forest are also permitted, although it is still illegal to collect forest products from the protected forest beyond the community's claimed area.

In both Nong Tio and Khok Sombun, although the villagers designated some areas as community forest, their actual use of the community forests is very limited. One of the two community forests in Nong Tio was well fenced and had a padlocked gate. It could only be accessed with the permission of the abbot of the temple of which the community forest is a part. The villagers of both villages gathered mushrooms and some vegetables from those community forests, while their main sources of food and income came from their farms and surrounding protected forests, or from small shops in the villages. In Nong Tio's case, the bamboo shoots gathered from the forest generated the main income for many families during the rainy season. Bamboo shoot collection had to be done discreetly, though, for it was illegal according to the National Park Act. The head of the Noen Nam Lot National Park explained to me that he allows the villagers to collect some bamboo shoots for sale, but just enough to earn a small income. He saw this as a reward for Nong Tio people's taking care of the forest. "If we do not allow them [the villagers] to exploit the forest, they will have no incentive to protect it," he explained.[26]

Forest, Land, and Livelihoods

The community forest movement's appropriation of an environmental discourse reflects how the state's forest territorialization strategy has set the parameters of the movement's claim. The state's territorializing of the forest by claiming to be preserving that forest has forced the movement to offer local communities as alternative forest protectors. In this process, the community forest movement draws heavily upon a communitarian view towards the state and local communities. The environmentalist frame of the community forest movement described above reflects the influence of the "community culture" (watthanatham chumchon) school of development, which has been dominant among Thai activists and social movements since the 1990s (Yukti 2005, 17).

According to Chatthip Nartsupha (1991, 133), who is the main proponent of the idea, the community culture school is an "anti-state and non-capitalist" ideology that promotes full autonomy for small communities in political, social, and economic areas and a reduced role for the state. In Chatthip's view, the community culture school of thought is anarchistic in nature as it aims for distribution of power from the state to popular, small-scale organizations. He also claims that denial of the state is the underlying ideology of every peasant protest revolt (135). The communitarians' view is that Thai communities, mainly rural ones, have distinct characteristics that need to be maintained and promoted. Their approach focuses on the self-reliance of communities by bringing back "the inner core of Thai beliefs, to organize villagers and village communities to resist the state's power, and to bargain with capitalism" (134). They see the community "as an ideal and normative goal, and at the same time as a dynamic process to achieve this goal" facing the state and the destructive effects its development policies have on the subsistence livelihoods of farmers (Kitahara 1996, 77).

The community culture school's influence on the community forest movement can be seen in the way the movement frames its environmentalist arguments. As discussed earlier, the movement refers to the communities' traditional knowledge and culture to assert that the communities can live in harmony with the forest. In such a discourse, local communities are portrayed as subsistent forest people. Walker (2004, 311–14) describes this as an "arborealization" process, in which upland livelihoods are recast as forest livelihoods. The discourse, he argues (313), becomes "overwhelmingly subsistence-oriented" in that it does not recognize commercial agriculture being practiced or the farmer's need for individual land tenure. This analysis applies to the communities in the northeast, like Khok Sombun and Nong Tio, as well. The villagers in both villages depended largely on rice grown for household consumption and derived incomes for other necessary expenses from farm production, mainly cassava and sugar cane, or from remittances from family members working in the city. The villagers could not survive from forest resources or farm products alone. In Nong Tio, easy road access and the presence of several village shops selling fresh and ready-cooked food also resulted in less dependence on forest use for everyday consumption.

The presumption that forest communities are subsistence-based and the construction of their identity as forest stewards posit villagers who live in the forest as forest-dwellers, but not as farmers. This leads to a strategic avoidance of the more politicized issue of land rights. Property rights over land are generally seen to link to commercial agriculture and are presumed to lead to further forest encroachment. In the strategic move of the community forest movement, the issue of the land tenure rights of farmers who live in the forest is deliberately avoided. As confirmed by several participants in the

Community Forest Bill advocacy campaign, the community forest movement decided as part of its strategy not to touch land rights issues. They believed that if land rights were incorporated in the movement's demands, it would lead to more objections to the Community Forest Bill.[27] Every draft of the Community Forest Bill proposed by the community forest movement prohibits land occupation, settlement, and farming within the community forest. Community forest activists always insist publicly that community forestry would not confer land rights on the communities. Literally speaking, therefore, even when the communities' rights to manage community forest are legally recognized, the presence of their residences and their farmland within protected forest still leaves them at risk of eviction. Pairoj Polpetch, a key lawyer-cum-activist who took part in the Community Forest Bill drafting process, explained that the movement hopes that if the communities are allowed a role in forestry conservation, it should automatically follow that they are allowed to stay in the forest.[28]

Evidence of the disconnect between the movement's discourse and villager expectations is provided by the way in which villagers have sometimes negotiated with authorities. As mentioned earlier, for the villagers of Khok Sombun and Nong Tio access to land for farming is no less important than access to the forest. When the provincial authorities gave them an ultimatum to relocate from the forest, Khok Sombun villagers gave priority to land compensation in their negotiations with the authorities. Issues of rights to manage the forest hardly figured. Their main demand was to "get in compensation land as good as what we have now"—that is, the same amount of land and of the same quality. Villagers were looking at some plots of degraded forestland to propose as an alternative resettlement site. They were also considering the area of farmland that would produce enough for their survival. A villager told me several times during my stay in Khok Sombun that, "We are farmers. We are the backbone of the country. We need farmland to survive." Some villagers also admitted that moving to the relocation site meant better opportunities for their children's education.

The constructed claim of forest-friendly "traditional practices" does not fit well with the history of the Nong Tio and Khok Sombun villagers. Both villages were relatively new, since the inhabitants of both villages had migrated from different provinces in the 1950s and 1970s respectively. In addition, the diverse ethnic backgrounds of the Khok Sombun villagers—Kha (or Bru), Lao, Phu Tai, and Yao—make the traditionalist claim less viable.

Communal Land Title: Communitarian Land Struggle

At the time I was preparing this chapter, the Thai community forest movement had almost disappeared from the political struggle at the national level. Movement activists attribute this to the exhaustion of the movement's members after two decades of struggling for the Community Forest Bill. After years of public debates on whether community settlement should be allowed in protected forests, the National Legislative Assembly (NLA) passed the Community Forest Act in late November 2007. The Act permitted the communities who had settled "inside" protected areas before the protected area demarcation and who had managed forests as community forests for at least ten years before the Act came into effect to request to manage community forests (Article 25). In effect, this excludes communities who settled "outside" demarcated protected forests who have also been taking care of and using the forest: this would mean approximately one thousand communities in the northern region alone (Buntoon 2007).[29] In addition, the Act requires the approved community forest area to be divided into two zones; namely, the conservation zone and the usufruct zone (Articles 18 and 26). Article 35 prohibits the cutting and collecting of woodlots in community forests inside the protected areas, and in conservation zones of the community forests outside the protected forest. This would prohibit the use of forest timber for consumption or for household needs, such as repairing houses. A group of NLA members submitted the Act to the Constitutional Court for review on the grounds that it potentially violates community rights guaranteed under Section 66 of the 2007 Constitution:

> Persons assembling as to be a community, local community or traditional local community shall have the right to conserve or restore their customs, local wisdom, arts or good culture of their community and of the nation and participate in the management, maintenance and exploitation of natural resources, the environment and biological diversity in a balanced and sustainable fashion.

Instead of ruling on the constitutionality of the Act, the Constitutional Court in late 2009 ended up declaring the Act void on the technical grounds of an insufficient NLA quorum when it was passed. Most of the activists who took part in the community forest movement whom I met in 2010 were unaware of the Court's decision.

It seems community forestry is off the agenda for some activists, and the issue of access to forests is being advocated through other campaigns or efforts instead. Some villagers in protected forests who were formerly part of the community forest movement have now joined the National Land Reform Network, which proposed the idea of communal land titles (*chanot chumchon*). The government approved their request in mid-2010. Under the communal land title scheme, a community in a land conflict with the state, including one in a protected forest, may propose to manage its land communally. The community, if the government approves, must take care of the natural resources within the community, and the land may not be sold. Nong Tio joined this network, and in April 2011 the Coordinating Body for Communal Land Titles under the Prime Minister's Office endorsed Nong Tio's request to manage their village land as communal land. Interestingly, all 107 households in Nong Tio were included in the request to manage the land communally, although the local activists and informal leaders in the village had told me earlier that only the families that agree with communal land management would be included. In addition, the selling and long-term leasing of land (for four to eight years) to outsiders were quite common in the village.

In practice it seems unlikely a communal land title would be granted in the protected area. After the launch of the communal land title scheme, the Department of National Parks (DNP) insisted on limiting forest use in the ecologically sensitive protected area. While allowing people to reside or farm in the protected area during the process of verifying whether each community had settled there before the demarcation of protected forest, the DNP stands firm on following the Cabinet Resolution dated 30 June 1998, which states that:

> In the case of sensitive areas where there is potential harm to the ecological system and in areas affecting the capacity to protect the protected forest as declared by laws and by Cabinet Resolutions, the Royal Forestry Department is to provide appropriate assistance to the villagers to find a new residential/farming area. The RFD may relocate the people out of

that forest to stay/farm in the appropriate area. . . . In the area the people moved out of, there will be a reforestation program.[30]

Such unfavorable and limiting conditions may not be what the communal land movement ultimately hopes for, but they are the best they have managed to negotiate so far.[31] Being in a very preliminary stage of implementation, it will be interesting to see how the movement for communal land titles will evolve in the struggle for farmers' livelihood rights, especially with the movement's underlying communitarian approach, which is so similar to the community forest movement.

Conclusion

The community forest movement in Thailand essentially aims to claim local communities' rights to have access to and to manage forest resources. The state's disciplining methods in its control of forests set the stage for this struggle. When faced with the violation of communities' rights to livelihoods by the state's forest territorialization and exclusion of human activities from forest areas in the name of forest protection, the movement countered with an inverted environmentalist discourse that authorizes community control. As Forsyth and Walker (2008, 54) observed, the community forest movement "has framed environmental policy and development in terms of legitimate communities engaged in forest conservation." In this process, the movement uses traditional practices relating to forests and other natural resources as cultural resources to resist the state. The forest communities have adopted and adapted certain practices to strengthen their environmentalist credentials, reversing the state's claims to be the sole authority when it comes to conservation. The movement claims that a local traditional community should have the right to stay in and manage the forest provided that such a community is competent at forest protection. The local communities, not the state, have inherent capacities to protect the forest. This discourse is powerful in claiming back both actual forest space and management power for local communities. The way the movement challenges the state's dominant environmental discourse represents "a resistance ideology dressed in conservationist terms" (Tegbaru 1997, 151).

If this strategy has resulted in some gains, it also entails some limits, however. The forest-stewardship identity the movement adopted as its frame has resulted in the avoidance of explicit discussion of land rights issues. The movement chooses to focus mainly on access to and management of forests, not on security of tenure for farms and residential land. As a consequence, the movement does not address the issue of the legality of settling and farming in the forest, and its environmental frame also leads to a self-limitation of forest use. The quotation with which I began this chapter and the experiences of the two villages studied clearly show this dilemma. The movement's framing strategy forces the movement to merely hope to get de facto rights for local communities to stay in the forest if they are allowed to manage the forest. The communities' rights to forest is thus largely left to negotiation at the local level. Eviction on the grounds of forest conservation and development, as experienced by Khok Sombun villagers, may take place at any time as long as villagers' rights to stay in protected forest is not legally guaranteed. As of July 2012, there is yet another attempt afoot to advocate for a Community Forest Act or other legal provisions specifically to address this issue.

The shift of focus from community forests to communal land use and control may address the limitation of the community forest movement I have identified in this chapter. However, the process of getting a communal land title requires approval from the relevant government agencies whose interests over that particular piece of land are in conflict with those of the villagers. Nong Tio, for example, needs permission from the Department of National Parks. In essence, this implies the acceptance of the principle that the land— or the forest in the case of land in protected areas—belongs to the state. As a result, the powerful discourse of deterritorializing forests and redefining state forests as community-controlled areas may lose momentum under the communal land movement.

Notes

1. The names used in this paper for the villages, villagers, and related locations, including the names of the protected forests, are pseudonyms to preserve the anonymity of the individuals interviewed.

2. The most detailed inclusive definition of "forest" can be found in the National Reserved Forest Act (1964), which replaced other forest-related laws: "'forest' means

land, including mountain, stream, swamp, canal, pond, creek, waterway, lake, island, and seashore that no one legally owns" (my translation).

3. Replaced by the National Reserved Forest Act (1964).

4. Replaced by the Wildlife Reservation and Protection Act (1992).

5. Cabinet Resolution, 3 December 1985.

6. For the history of policies encouraging forest encroachment for farming, see Saneh and Yos 1993.

7. 1 *rai* = 0.4 acre.

8. By December 1990, there were seventy-three national parks including those being prepared for demarcation. The area of the land-based parks totalled 20.52 million *rai* (6.4 percent of the country's land). There were thirty-four wildlife sanctuaries of 17.22 million *rai* (5.37 percent), Level 1 (1A and 1B) watershed areas outside the national parks, and wildlife sanctuaries totalling 21.44 million *rai* (6.69 percent). Altogether there were 59.18 million *rai* (18.46 percent) of protected areas. See Pairoj 1992.

9. After the 14 October 1973 uprising, the organization was renamed the Internal Security Operations Command (ISOC), but it retained the same mandate.

10. During the administration reform in 2002, the Department of National Parks, Wildlife and Conservation was formed to look after protected forests. The Royal Forestry Department has since then been in charge of commercial forests.

11. Accessed at http://www.dnp.go.th/rsd/project%2Darea/.

12. Isan refers to the northeastern region of Thailand.

13. The princess's order was referred to in a letter from the Internal Security Operations Commander (Second Region) to the Sakon Nakhon governor, with the subject, "The Monitoring of the Implementation of the Princess' Order," dated 16 March 2006, and with an attached report on the Khok Sombun case.

14. *Cha pha nak-khao ma ko at cha yak, phro ni pen khrongkan khong nueahua.*

15. The Khok Sombun villagers told me that two and a half *rai* of land may yield twenty to thirty sacks of rice per year depending on the irrigation, while a family of four (two adults and two children) consumed approximately fifty sacks of rice per year.

16. A notice from the Sakon Nakhon provincial governor, dated 20 August 2010, said "In honor of and in contribution to the merits of His Majesty the King and Her Majesty the Queen, the people whose names appeared in the survey list of the Pha Din Wildlife Sanctuary (attached) are required to inform the staff of the Pha Din Forest Protection Unit by 15 October 2010. Anyone who fails to inform the authorities will face legal prosecution" (my translation).

17. The forest around Nong Tio was close to several Communist Party of Thailand bases.

18. Interview with Amnat, 20 August 2010. In the early 1980s, Amnat's father was arrested for planting sugarcane on his land.

19. For details on *Kho Cho Ko* and the struggle against it, see Pye 2005 and Somchai 2006.

20. Cabinet Resolution dated 28 July 1992, Re: Solution to the Problems from the Implementation of the Land Distribution Program for the Poor Living in Degraded National Forest Reserves in Northeast Thailand. Despite allowing the communities to move back to their land, the Cabinet Resolution affirmed that "the area the villagers request to move back to is in protected forest. The authorities will temporarily allow the villagers to live in that area. There will be no land deed issued."

21. *"Muban kaset anurak."*

22. Literally the term comes from *wana* (forest) and *kaset* (agriculture). *Wanakaset* has been promoted as an alternative agriculture method, especially in the forest area. As of November 2010, only a couple of Khok Sombun households still practice *wanakaset*. Some villagers explained that their products did not fetch good prices.

23. This agreement came after long debates within the community. Some villagers used to have more than 200 *rai* before *Kho Cho Ko*. The villagers finally agreed to this arrangement seeing it as the only option that would allow them to stay on their land. An NGO worker who worked with Nong Tio villagers at the time recalled that the villagers were so desperate that they even proposed to live on six *rai* of land (interview with Sakda Tongchampa, 19 February 2012).

24. Literally, *pu ta*, or sometimes called *chao pu*, means "grandfather."

25. As of 29 February 2012, 8,406 villages had registered 7,756 community forests with the RFD. Among them, 3,644 forests are in the northeast (RFD 2011).

26. Interview with Prayad Chancharoen, head of Noen Nam Lot National Park, 13 December 2010.

27. Interview with Anan Ganjanaphan, 7 January 2011; interview with Pairoj Polpetch, 28 July 2011.

28. Interview with Pairoj Polpetch, 28 July 2011.

29. Buntoon was a member of the NLA's Community Forest Bill Committee and the director of the National Resources Strategic Project under the National Human Rights Commission.

30. Letter from the Department of National Parks to the heads of Protected Areas Management Offices, Re: "Restating the Solutions of Land Conflicts Inside the Protected Areas," dated 6 September 2010. In this letter, the DNP insisted on following the 31 March 1998 Cabinet Resolution and on "strictly enforcing the laws" in cases of "new forest encroachment, or extension of residential/farm land, or (acts that) destroy or affect forest protection or the environment." Note that the RFD's tasks in the 1998 resolution were transferred to the Department of National Parks in 2002.

31. Interview with Pramote Polpinyo, coordinator of the Land Reform Network, northeastern region, 19 February 2012.

References

Amnuay Kovanich. 1993. *Kan pa mai chumchon nai rabop muban pa mai* [Community forestry in a forest village system]. Bangkok: Faculty of Forestry, Kasetsart University.

Benford, Robert D., and David A. Snow. 2000. "Framing Processes and Social Movements: An Overview and Assessment." *Annual Review of Sociology* 26 (1): 611–39.

Buergin, Reiner. 2003. "Trapped in Environmental Discourses and Politics of Exclusion: Karen in the Thung Yai Naresuan Wildlife Sanctuary in the Context of Forest and Hill Tribe Policies in Thailand." In *Living at the Edge of Thai Society: The Karen in the Highlands of Northern Thailand*, edited by Claudio O. Delang, 42–63. London: RoutledgeCurzon.

Buntoon Settirote, 2007. "Pho ro bo pa chumchon chabap so no cho: sanyan antarai samrap kan mueang phak prachachon" [Community Forest Act, NLA version: a dangerous sign for the people sector's politics], *Matichon*, 2 December.

Chatthip Nartsupha. 1991. "The 'Community Culture' School of Thought." In *Thai Constructions of Knowledge*, edited by Andrew Turton and Chitakasem Manas, 118–41. London: School of Oriental and African Studies.

Community Forest Action Research Project [Khrongkan wichai choeng patibatkan pa chumchon]. 1993. "Rang phraratchabanyat pa chumchon (chabap prachachon)" [The community forest bill (people's version)]. Bangkok: Community Forest Action Research Project.

Community Forest Management Unit, Royal Forestry Department [Samnak chatkan pa chumchon, krom pa mai]. 2011. *Khumue kan patibat-ngan tam naeothang kan chattham khrongkan pa chumchon khong krom pa mai* [Manual on the Royal Forestry Department's community forest management framework]. Bangkok: Royal Forestry Department.

Forsyth, Tim. 2007. "Are Environmental Social Movements Socially Exclusive? An Historical Study from Thailand." *World Development* 35 (12): 2110–2130.

Forsyth, Tim, and Andrew Walker. 2008. *Forest Guardians, Forest Destroyers: The Politics of Environmental Knowledge in Northern Thailand*. Seattle: University of Washington Press.

Kitahara, Atsushi. 1996. *The Thai Rural Community Reconsidered: Historical Community Formation and Contemporary Development Movements*. Bangkok: Political Economy Centre, Faculty of Economics, Chulalongkorn University.

Krisda Boonchai. 2005. "Bot samruat phuenthi kan khlueanwai khong khabuankan pa mai yuk lang sampathan pho so 2532–2547" [Survey of space of the forest movement post-logging concession, 1989–2004]. In *Kanmueang pa mai thai yuk lang sampathan* [Thai forestry post-logging concession], edited by Sayamol Kraiyoonvong and Ponpana Kueycharoen, 237–77. Bangkok: Project for Ecological Recovery.

Kristoffersen, Stine Rendal. 2005. "Disputed Forests: The Role of Conflicting Environmental Values in the Policy-Making Process of the Community Forest Bill in Thailand." MA diss., Roskilde University.

Luckana Popromyen. 2011. "Rai-ngan wikhro kham phiphaksa thai nai khadi thi kiaokhong kap sitthi chumchon lae kan chatkan sapphayakon thidin." [Analysis of Thai court decisions in cases related to community rights and land management]. Unpublished manuscript.

NFPC [National Forest Policy Committee (Kana kammakan nayobai pa mai haeng chat)]. 1988. *Rai-ngan kan patibat-ngan khong khana kammakan nayobai pa mai haeng chat* [Annual operation report of the National Forest Policy Committee]. Bangkok: National Forest Policy Committee, Royal Forest Department.

National Parks, Wildlife, and Plants Conservation Department [Krom uthayan haeng chat satpa lae phan phuet]. 2010. *Statistical Data of National Parks, Wildlife and Plant Conservation 2553.* Accessed at http://www.dnp.go.th/statistics/2553/stat2553.asp.

Nukaen Jantasi, Pramote Polpinyo, Areewan Koosantie, Pranom Petchsamai, Wayamol Kraiyoonwong, and Pongthip Samranchi. 2000. *Sakkayaphap chumchon isan nai kan chatkan sapphayakon* [Northeastern communities' potential in natural resources management]. Bangkok: RRAFA.

Pairoj Suwannakon. 1999. "Nayobai pa mai" [Forest policy: Lecture notes for Thammasat University, December 1990]. In *Chiwit lae ngan anurak sapphayakon pa mai khong nai Pairoj Suwannakon, atibodi krom pa mai (po so 2532–2534)* [Life and forest conservation works of Pairoj Suwannakon, Royal Forestry Department's Director General (1989–1991)], edited by Royal Forestry Department [Krom pa mai], 273–91. Bangkok: Royal Forestry Department.

Peluso, Nancy Lee, and Peter Vandergeest. 2001. "Genealogies of the Political Forest and Customary Rights in Indonesia, Malaysia, and Thailand." *Journal of Asian Studies* 60 (3): 761–812.

———. 2011. "Political Ecologies of War and Forests: Counterinsurgencies and the Making of National Natures." *Annals of the Association of American Geographers* 101 (3): 587–608.

Pinkaew Laungaramsri. 1999. "Khabuankan pa chumchon lae kho thathai kan chatkan pa khong rat thai" [Community Forest Movement and the challenge to the Thai state's forest management]. In *Sam thotsawat pa chumchon: Thamklang khwam sapson khong sangkhom thai* [Three decades of community forest: amidst confusion of the Thai society], edited by Bunta Suebpradit and Achara Rakyutidham, 21–25. Chiang Mai: Kruakai pa chumchon pak nua.

————. 2003. "Constructing Marginality: The 'Hill Tribe' Karen and Their Shifting Locations within Thai State and Public Perspectives." In *Living at the Edge of Thai Society: The Karen in the Highlands of Northern Thailand*, edited by Claudio O. Delang, 21–42. London: RoutledgeCurzon.

Prachatai. 2005. "Muban pa mai phaen mai nai krasae khwam kangwonchai khong chumchon" [The new forest village program in the concern of the communities]. 31 July. Accessed at http://www.prachatai.com.

Prapart Pintoptaeng. 1988. *Kan mueang bon thong thanon: 99 wan samatcha khon chon lae prawattisat kan doen khabuan chumnum prathuang nai sangkhom thai* [Street politics: 99 days of the Assembly of the Poor and the history of protest in thailand]. Bangkok: Textbook Project, Krek University.

Pye, Oliver. 2005. *Khor Jor Kor: Forest Politics in Thailand*. Bangkok: White Lotus.

RFD [Royal Forestry Department (Krom pa mai)]. 1993a. *Kan pa mai pai tai kan nam khong Pairoj Suwannakon 1 tulakhom 2532–30 kanyayon 2534* [Forestry under the directorship of Pairoj Suwannakorn, 1 October 1989–30 September 1991]. Bangkok: Royal Forestry Department.

————. 1993b. *Sarup phon-ngan khrongkan phatthana pa mai an nueang ma chak phra rachadamri pi-ngoppraman 2535* [Summary of the royal forest development projects of the budget year 1992]. Bangkok: Royal Forestry Department.

————. 2011. "Kan khuen tabian pa chumchon [Community forest registration]." Accessed at http://www.forest.go.th/community_forest/index.php?option =com_content&view=article&id=371&Itemid=3073&lang=en.

Saneh Chamarik and Yos Santasombat, eds. 1993. *Pa chumchon nai prathet Thai: Naeo thang kan phatthana* [Community forest in Thailand: development proposal]. Bangkok: Local Development Institute.

Sayamol Kraiyoonvong, Achara Rakyuttitham, and Krisda Boonchai. 2002. "Khabuankan khruea khai klum kasettakon phak nuea phuea phithak sitthi chumchon nai kan chatkan sapphayakon thammachat lae kan thamrong attalak thang chatphan" [Northern Farmer Network's movement to protect community rights in management of natural resources and maintaining ethnic identity]. In *Withi chiwit withi su: khabuankan prachachon ruam samai* [Livelihoods and struggle: the contemporary people's movements], edited by Pasuk Phongpaichit, 241–91. Bangkok: Silkworm Books.

Snow, David A., and Robert D Benford. 1998. "Ideology, Frame Resonance, and Participant Mobilization." *International Social Movement Research* 1 (1): 197–217.

Tegbaru, Amere. 1997. *Forest, Farmers and the State*. Stockholm: Stockholm Studies in Social Anthropology.

Thailand Community Forest Network [Khruea khai pa chumchon haeng prathet thai], ed. 2003. *Pho ro bo pa chumchon: Chao ban khue khon raksa pa* [Community forest bill: it is the villagers who take care of the forest]. Bangkok: Thailand Community Forest Network.

Vandergeest, Peter, and Nancy Lee Peluso. 1995. "Territorialization and State Power in Thailand." *Theory and Society* 24 (3): 385–426.

Walker, Andrew. 2004. "Seeing Farmers for the Trees: Community Forestry and the Arborealisation of Agriculture in Northern Thailand." *Asia Pacific Viewpoint* 45 (3): 311–24.

Walker, Andrew, and Nicholas Farrelly. 2008. "Northern Thailand's Specter of Eviction," *Critical Asian Studies* 40 (3): 373–97.

Yukti Mukdavichit. 2005. *An "watthanatham chumchon": Wathasin lae kanmueang khong chat phan naeo watthanatham chumchon* [Reading "community culture": rhetoric and politics of ethnography's community culture approach]. Bangkok: Fah Diew Kan.

5

An Uneasy Engagement: Political Crisis and Human Rights Culture in Thailand, 1958 to 1988

—∞∞∞—

Tyrell Haberkorn

"No one shall be subjected to arbitrary arrest, detention or exile."
—Article 9, Universal Declaration of Human Rights

On 24 June 1932, Thailand (then Siam) underwent a transformation from an absolute to a constitutional monarchy. In the eighty years since then, there have been ten successful coups, seven failed coup attempts, twenty-seven prime ministers, and eighteen constitutions. Modern Thai political history is frequently periodized by these coups and changes in government and has had a decidedly muddled trajectory. Instead of charting a clear, linear path from more authoritarian to more democratic rule, which tends to be a fiction rather than a reality globally, Thailand has moved in a zigzag pattern across a range of different kinds of regimes with divergent allowances for dissent and varying relations between citizens and the state. Across these different regimes, democracy, the rule of law, and human rights have struggled to take hold against forms of repression including the shadow of absolutism, Cold War counterinsurgency, a powerful military and an array of other state security forces, and other myriad attempts of elites to retain control.[1]

In the immediate aftermath of the global devastation wrought by World War II, the United Nations was founded on 24 October 1945. On 10 December 1948, after several years of drafting, negotiation, and re-drafting, the fledgling

UN proclaimed the Universal Declaration of Human Rights (UDHR) (Waltz 2002). Comprised of thirty articles covering civil and political rights as well as economic, social, and cultural rights, the UDHR specifies the rights that must be protected in order to make the ideal condition in its preamble—"recognition of the inherent dignity and of the equal and inalienable rights of all members of the human family [as] the foundation of freedom, justice and peace in the world"—real and material in the lives of people around the globe. The UDHR was affirmed unanimously by forty-eight member states, including Thailand, which was in the midst of the series of regime changes that characterized the early post-absolute monarchy period.[2]

While it is not legally binding, the UDHR became the basis for the two later treaties which *are* legally binding for states that ratify them: the International Covenant on Civil and Political Rights (ICCPR) and the International Covenant on Economic, Social and Cultural Rights (ICESCR).[3] In addition, the UDHR became the set of ideas around which human rights coalesced during the first decades after its emergence. The contradiction and tension which marked this moment is well captured by Samuel Moyn in his recent book, *The Last Utopia: Human Rights in History*, in which he argues that "human rights were compelled to define the good life and offer a plan for bringing it about precisely when they were ill-equipped by the fact of their suprapolitical birth to do so" (2010, 214). Complicating matters, despite the fact that human rights were a powerful ideal precisely because they rested on "the claim that their source of authority transcended politics," human rights very quickly became a site of contestation for authority operative within both national and international politics (223). In many cases, and certainly in the case of Thailand, in the movement from being an ideal above politics to a set of politically contested ideas, the active manipulation and redefinition of human rights emerged as a key strategy of domestic rule and international diplomacy by the state.

The contours of this redefinition and manipulation can be clearly seen at the point of contact between the Thai state and the UN-outlined standards of human rights outlined in the UDHR in early human rights reporting. During their second session in 1945, the UN Economic and Social Council made a resolution asking the UN Secretary-General to arrange for "the compilation and publication of a yearbook on law and usage relating to human rights" throughout the world (UN 1947, ix). The inaugural UN *Human Rights Yearbook* was published in 1946 and it was published until 1988, first as yearly volumes and then as a biannual publication after 1973. After 1988, a new series of human rights reporting mechanisms specific to each relevant international human rights treaty began to be developed and used, as well as the recent adoption of the Universal Periodic Review (UPR) system.[4] The content in each yearbook included short reports prepared by member governments about relevant legislation, court decisions, and other developments related to human rights. The *Yearbook* is striking for its comprehensive, global content and yet also marked by the limitations necessarily placed on length and by the fact that the only source of information present was the state. Unlike today, when there can be an unlimited number of shadow reports and statements made by nongovernmental organizations that explicitly query and challenge official reports made by states at the Human Rights Council in Geneva, and also enter into the documentation record, the *Yearbook* did not contain any information contributed by parties other than states.

In this chapter, I examine Thailand's contributions, and the lacunae in the contributions, to the UN *Human Rights Yearbook* in order to examine the culture of human rights reporting practiced by the Thai state. By "culture," here I refer to the practices, values, and forms surrounding human rights reporting. The content of the reports sheds light on the Thai state's public assessment and self-representation of its practices vis-à-vis emergent human rights standards. While the precise authorship of each report varied, they were written by a combination of officials from the Ministy of Foreign Affairs, the Prime Minister's Office, and the Office of the Juridical Council. Simultaneously, the reporting by the state offers a site in which to think about the changing meanings of democracy and justice across a range of political regimes and crises. It would be too great a stretch to argue that these reports could be used to study the culture of human rights itself, but instead my aim is to think carefully and critically about human rights reporting as one aspect of this broader culture.

My examination is limited further to reporting about arbitrary detention,[5] protected in Article 9 of the UDHR (see epigraph) during two moments of regime crisis in Thailand: the regime of Sarit Thanarat (1958–1963) and the years immediately following the 6 October 1976 massacre (1976–1979).

These periods, in which the regimes were unequivocally dictatorial and unequivocal in their abrogation of the basic human rights of citizens, are ideal for examining what Michael Connors has identified as the always present tension between liberalism and authoritarianism in Thailand. For Connors, liberalism is characterized by the respect and protection of rights, strength of independent institutions, and broad support for political participation from a range of citizens; authoritarianism is instead marked not only by the absence of these, but also the active arbitrary use and abuse of power by state and military officials. Connors notes (2011, 106) that despite Thailand's affirmation of the UDHR, and the later ratification of the ICCPR, ICESCR, and many other instruments, "rights abuses have accelerated, driven by the twin pressures of capitalist and prebendal predatory practices over common resources and political impulses for monopolistic power over people and institutions. . . . Human rights in Thailand are like flotsam and jetsam, subject to the ebbs and flows of political circumstance."

The reason for focusing specifically on detention is that how a regime treats its most marginal groups, of which those arbitrarily detained is one, is a measure of its capability for rights violations. Manfred Nowak, former UN Special Rapporteur on Torture (2004–2010), highlighted the importance of examining conditions of prison and detention for two primary reasons. The first is that he notes that they are "one of the last taboos, even in so-called 'open societies'" (Nowak 2010, 5). The second is that he notes that, "As soon as they are behind bars, detainees lose most of their human rights and often are simply forgotten by the outside world. . . . The way . . . a society treats its detainees is one of the best indicators for its human rights culture in general" (Nowak 2010, 61–62). If conditions of detention can tell us about the human rights culture, then how a state reports detention, what is included and what is excluded, and how it is explained or justified, may be able to tell us both about the culture of human rights reporting and also the tensions among violence, democracy, and security that form the basis of the actions and justifications for rights violations.

Between Security and Human Rights During
the Regime of Sarit Thanarat

Field Marshal Sarit Thanarat came to power on 16 September 1957, after launching a coup against the Phibun Songkhram government. He carried out a coup against himself on 19 October 1958 in order to further concentrate power in his hands; at this time, he abrogated the 1952 Constitution and declared martial law. Until February 1959, Sarit ruled exclusively through executive order, at which point a temporary Constitutional charter was put in place that remained in use until 20 June 1968. Thak Chaloemtiarana, who characterized Sarit's regime as one of "despotic paternalism," argues that Sarit "believed that . . . modernization and progress must start by insuring that the nation's citizens are in the correct state of mind; in this approach, he resembled a father who, when attending to his children's upbringing (their 'development'), believes that this undertaking must begin with proper moral education" (2007, 121). Sarit practiced a form of justice he described as "absolutely decisive" (*det khat*), perhaps most embodied in Article 17, which privileged him to take any action he believed necessary for the nation and under which eleven persons were summarily executed during his regime.[6]

This kind of rule sits uneasily with principles of human rights, no matter how defined. This unease was reflected in Sarit's final Constitution Day address, on 10 December 1962. He began by noting that 10 December was both the date named by Rama VII as Constitution Day and the day named by the United Nations as Human Rights Day. Sarit devoted the remainder of his speech to justifying the delay in promulgating a new constitution. He cited his personal belief in the value of constitutions, and the need for a constitution that would guarantee national security and be appropriate to the specific conditions in Thailand, which he left unspecified. In the final third of his speech, Sarit addressed human rights directly and said that he believed in the dignity and equality of all humans, as the basis for freedom, justice, and peace in the world. While noting that he holds international standards of human rights to be of utmost importance, he then said, "I will not allow anyone to cite the Universal Declaration of Human Rights as a tool to destroy the unity and security of the homeland" (Sarit 1965, 842).[7] Sarit concluded his speech by pledging to fight with blood, sweat, and his life to preserve the independence, stability, and security of the Thai nation.

Reading the contributions of Thailand to the UN *Human Rights Yearbook* during the years of the Sarit regime, particularly with reference to arbitrary detention, the tension present in Sarit's speech is muted. Several years before Sarit came into power, in the *Yearbook* for 1955, a special supplementary volume was to be produced on Article 9. In a statement sent to the United Nations on 17 May 1956, the government noted that there was no arbitrary arrest, detention or exile in Thailand (UN 1959, 220). In the report for 1958, Sarit's first full year in office, the report forthrightly notes that the government has abrogated the Constitution, but also, foretelling Sarit's later speech, notes that the coup group announced early on "that its policy was to 'respect human rights as set forth in the Declaration of Human Rights'" (UN 1960, 217). The report mentions the arbitrary detention order enacted by Sarit, Decree 21, describing it as "one of the most important innovations," which aims "to stop the nefarious activities of persons who earn their living by illegal means or pestering honest people. A special procedure has been organized in order to detain such person for enquiry; but the detention cannot exceed 30 days without a decision having been reached by a special committee having the legal power to send incorrigible characters to vocational training reformatories" (UN 1960, 217). The full details of Decree 21, and Decree 43, issued several months later to modify it, and the range of powers they gave state officials, were not covered in this statement.

Decree 21 was issued several weeks after Sarit's second coup, and began by defining "hooligans" (*anthaphan*) as individuals who, either by their own actions or supporting others, "bully, persecute, coerce or harass and disturb the people." One example of a kind of hooligan who posed an economic danger to his fellow citizens was a gambling dealer. The decree noted that gambling dealers and other hooligans needed to be dealt with "for the happiness of the people and the progress of the homeland." Those suspected of being hooligans could be apprehended and detained for investigation; during the first thirty days of detention for investigation, the police or other arresting official did not have to bring the case to a court. However, after thirty days, if the arresting official wanted to extend the period of detention of the suspected hooligan, the case had to be sent to court and a detention order issued following the procedure of criminal law.[8]

In January 1959, Sarit issued Decree 43, which further specified the implementation of Decree 21. In this decree, the role of the court vanished.

Decree 43 designated a vast amount of power concerning detention and release of suspected hooligans to the Director of Police in Bangkok, and to provincial governors in all areas outside Bangkok. During the first thirty-day period of investigation, "If those individuals continue to have the habits and behavior of a hooligan, then [the provincial governors and director of police] have the power to order those individuals to go to an occupational training center."[9]

With the disappearance of the court, the Ministry of Interior was charged with establishing the training centers as well as a review committee or committees. To be clear, this meant that individuals suspected of being hooligans did not have the right to a court examination—and only needed to be judged a hooligan by the director of police or a provincial governor in order to be detained. Every three months, each case was to undergo review and a decision made whether or not it was appropriate to release or further detain each hooligan. No time limit was put on the length of detention. Those suspected of being hooligans were not guaranteed protection under the criminal code, yet could find themselves subject to it. Decree 43 placed suspected hooligans under the power of the investigating officials who detained them. Further, the decree specified that criminal law covering escape applied to them; if they tried to leave the center without permission, it was considered a legal offense.[10] Paradoxically, this meant that the only way for suspected hooligans to find themselves before a judge was to attempt escape. Citing one of Sarit's funeral books, Thak offers a yearly breakdown of the arrests and detentions between 1958 and 1963. In total, 7,539 people were arrested under Decree 21. Of that number, 2,743 were detained for thirty days only, while 4,738 were sent for further reform training (Thak 2007, 122, n51).

In the UN *Human Rights Yearbook for 1959*, the success at combatting the problems of hooliganism is noted, with the following description: "Hooliganism, which is one of the chronic diseases of society, has been severely suppressed. Attempts have similarly been made to provide the hooligans with a good education as well as vocational training. By and large, steps have been taken in the direction of creating a good moral basis for society" (UN 1961, 281). The content of the "vocational training" or an examination of what rights may have been violated during the process of the *severe* suppression of hooliganism is not described. What is noted, however, is that the drafting of the new Constitution had been delayed, because "the

Constituent Assembly took cognizance of a political truth that 'the people have to be prepared for democracy, a pearl which the people must first learn to appreciate.' The need to build up a cultural basis as a prerequisite to true democracy is generally recognized in this country" (UN 1961, 281). What about the leaders of the country? Might they also need to be prepared for democracy, given the evidence of their readiness to suspend due process suggested by Decrees 21 and 43? From the perspective of the present, the answer is a resounding yes; understanding how this could be conceived as a logical and legitimate stance in the early 1960s reveals a great deal about both the ideas of democracy within the Thai state and the international human rights world at the time. The ICCPR and ICESCR had not yet elaborated the provisions of the UDHR. The international and Thai domestic human rights movements had not yet started to catalog abuses, elaborating violations of provisions of the conventions and connecting these violations to the broader political contest. In turn, the challenge made by the human rights movement to democracy—primary among these being the idea that arbitrary detention, by default, contradicts the basic freedom and liberty constitutive of democracy—had not yet been made.

The entries for Thailand in the UN *Human Rights Yearbook for 1960–1962* are uneventful. They note ongoing progress on the Constitution and legislation related primarily to economic and cultural rights (UN 1962, 1964a, 1964b). They make no mention of either hooligans or Decrees 21 and 43. Yet in 1963, a summary of a Supreme Court decision related to a man detained as a hooligan is included. The summary notes that the decision limited the power of the state to detain people under Decrees 21 and 43 (UN 1965, 212). Upon close examination of the Supreme Court decision itself, the Court emerges as a strong protector of human rights.

On 3 August 1960, Mr. Yiem Phunman escaped from detention in Surin province, where he had been held in a vocational training center for hooligans in the compound of the Surin provincial police station. His detention had been ordered eight months earlier, by provincial order 582/2502, issued on 24 November 1960. He was arrested three days after his escape, on 6 August 1960, and punished for fleeing under Article 190 of the Criminal Code. Mr. Yiem confessed to the allegations made against him.

Yet despite his confession, the court of first instance found him innocent. Contra to the provisions of Decrees 21 and 43, which specify that the detention must be renewed every three months, after the initial order declaring him a hooligan in need of reform, there were no further provincial orders regarding Mr. Yiem. Therefore, since he fled from a detention that was itself illegal, he was not guilty of violating the law. The prosecutor appealed, citing the broad powers of detention granted to officials under Decrees 21 and 43. The Appeals Court ruled in favor of Mr. Yiem again, citing the illegal, arbitrary nature of his initial detention. The prosecutor then appealed to the Supreme Court, which ruled that, given that there was no additional order of renewal after the initial provincial order, the detention of Mr. Yiem had been illegal. The Supreme Court further affirmed that the order did not provide for unlimited detention, but for detention for vocational training of a specific category of person (Supreme Court decision no. 105/2506).

Although the Supreme Court decision did not explicitly rest on principles identified as human rights standards, it was a powerful defense of Article 9 and a sharp refutation of the Sarit regime's authoritarianism. Read over fifty years later, side by side with the UN *Human Rights Yearbook* entries from that era, it is also a powerful critique of the comments submitted by the Thai government on alleged "hooligans" and human rights more broadly.

6 October1976 and the Absence of Human Rights Reporting

Field Marshal Sarit Thanarat died on 8 December 1963. His death ushered in the regime of Thanom Kittikachorn, who, along with his son Narong Kittikachorn and Narong's father-in-law, Praphat Jarusathien, continued the repressive rule initiated by Sarit. While their government submitted reports which were included in the UN *Human Rights Yearbook*, they primarily reported the passage of legislation related to economic, social, and cultural rights, and left both the excessive use of Article 17, promulgated by Sarit but still in force, and violations of human rights carried out in the name of counterinsurgency unmentioned (United Nations 1967, 1968, 1969a, 1969b, 1970, 1971, 1973, 1974, 1975).

Yet the triumvirate of Thanom-Praphat-Narong was not immune to pressure from citizens who were fed up and frustrated by years of dictatorship. They were ousted at the culmination of a massive uprising that began with calls by students and citizens for an end to dictatorship and a truly democratic

Constitution in early October 1973 (Charnvit 2001).[11] The original small group of people who called for a Constitution were arrested under Article 17, but their arrest catalyzed many thousands of people to come out into the streets calling for their release and in support of their demands. After nearly a week of growing protests in Bangkok and most provinces throughout the country, the protests reached a critical point on 13–14 October 1973. After sustained conflict, including attacks on protesters by state security forces, on the evening of 14 October 1973, the king asked the three dictators to leave the country and appointed Sanya Thammasak, then the rector of Thammasat University, as the interim prime minister. The next three years were an extraordinary period of political openness in which many members of society who had been excluded from politics, including farmers and workers, began to organize and demand their rights (Morell and Chai-anan 1981; Haberkorn 2011). The violent excesses of counterinsurgency of the prior regime began to be exposed and critiqued. Decrees 21 and 43 were repealed, with a note appended to the nullification law that they "contain articles that are inappropriate and not in line with a democratic regime."[12]

This radical regime shift was reflected in the form and content of the reports submitted to the UN for the *Human Rights Yearbook*. The introduction for the report for 1973–1974 noted, "Considerable changes have taken place since 14 October 1973. Much legislation that previously restricted the rights and freedom of the people has been repealed or amended. There is movement at all levels, both in rural and in urban areas, towards improved government administration and wider participation of individuals in government affairs" (UN 1977, 198). The report details the actions that had been taken, including making trials fair by removing them from military courts, bolstering access to property rights and fair rents, upholding freedom of the press, repealing laws constricting freedom of assembly and association, supporting the right to livelihood and health, bolstering of workers' rights, and making the right to a fair education universal (UN 1977, 198–203).

But this period of open politics was short-lived. The Thai right wing, both inside and outside the state, grew and was made anxious by the Communist transitions in neighboring Vietnam, Laos, and Cambodia. As 1975 wore on into 1976, farmer and worker leaders were targeted for assassination, students and others were intimidated, and conservative forces became increasingly bold. The period of political change and possibility came to an abrupt end on the morning of 6 October 1976, when right-wing state and para-state actors beat, shot, and murdered student activists massed inside the gates of Thammasat University. By that evening, there were forty-six confirmed deaths, over three thousand arrests, and a new military coup group, the National Administrative Reform Council (NARC), was in power (Zimmerman 1978, 48). Two days after the coup, the NARC appointed Thanin Kraivichien, a staunchly royalist right-wing judge as prime minister. Thanin remained in office until 20 October 1977, when General Kriangsak Chomanan staged a coup against him, and Kriangsak remained in office until he retired on 3 March 1980. During both Thanin's and Kriangsak's regimes, the human rights situation was grave, with arbitrary detention, torture, and forced disappearances documented by Thai and international human rights groups.

The decline in the importance of maintenance of human rights standards for the Thai state was reflected starkly in the realm of human rights reporting and the entry submitted to the UN *Human Rights Yearbook* after 6 October 1976. The contribution to the yearbook, which had become a biannual publication, indicated a return to an even stricter form of pro-security reporting than had been seen during the Sarit years. The first paragraph of the report for 1975–1976 notes that the 1974 Constitution has been abrogated and "The new Constitution consists of only 29 sections. Its objective is to restore the democratic form of government by means of an appropriate national administrative reform which provides for gradual development" (UN 1981, 267). With respect to rights and liberties, the report notes that, "Obviously, this Constitution fails to elaborate the way in which the rights and liberties of the people are safeguarded," and further explains that rights and liberties will be preserved, "in so far as they are not contrary to or inconsistent with the provisions of the new Constitution" (UN 1981, 267). While this statement leaves the question of protections of rights open and unspecified, the objectives of the regime, and what rights they were willing to restrict, were made explicit in the discussion of newly renewed measures for arbitrary detention.

With respect to arbitrary arrest and detention, the report notes the repeal of Decrees 21 and 43 during the prior three years, and then notes that the laws passed by the prior government, which still allowed for vocational training but placed it within the usual court system rather than outside it, "were not appropriate tools for solving social problems" (UN 1981, 269). An explanation of why is not given, but in response, the NARC issued Orders 22 and 34 in October 1976, which they noted "dealt with the question [of social problems] in the same manner" as Decrees 21 and 43 issued by Sarit (UN 1981, 269). Yet, while the Sarit government confidently and unself-consciously reported the success of Decrees 21 and 43 in solving the problems caused by those deemed to be "hooligans," there were no reports submitted about the successes, or failures, of Orders 22 and 34. In fact, the report in which the measures were described was the final report that the government of Thailand submitted for inclusion in the UN *Human Rights Yearbook*. Although the *Yearbook* continued to be compiled through 1988, there were no entries for Thailand for the years 1977 to 1988. While other countries at times failed to send reports, Thailand's twelve-year absence, particularly given the regularity with which reports were sent prior to this period, is striking.

While it is impossible to definitively ascertain the reasons why the subsequent governments chose not to report on human rights conditions, and on the implementation of Orders 22 and 34, an examination of other state documents about them suggests reasons why they must be included in any serious examination of human rights after 6 October 1976. Rather than the category of "hooligan," Orders 22 and 34 permitted the detention and re-education of individuals deemed to be a "danger to society" (*phai to sangkhom*). Order 22 began with the following explanation of its *raison d'etre*:

> As it is apparent that there are kinds of individuals whose actions are a danger to society, individuals whose behavior disturbs the peace and well-being of the people, or whose actions are a threat, or cause economic or security loss for the nation, it is appropriate to proceed by bringing the individuals with these aforementioned behaviors to return to be good citizens, for the peace and well-being of the people and the progress of the homeland.[13]

Through arbitrary detention and reeducation, the wayward dissidents were promised *return*. In the preamble that I cited above, there is an allusion to the creation of an undivided nation. The first step to this undivided, progress-and-happiness-filled nation was to identify individuals already existing within it who were a (potential) *danger* to it. Then, once these "dangers to society" were reformed and returned as good citizens, happiness and progress would ensue.

Order 22 defined and categorized individuals who are a "danger to society" as those who:

(1) bully, harass, coerce, or terrorize other individuals; (2) do not have a permanent residence, are vagrant, and do not earn an honest living; (3) make a living in a way that disturbs the peace and order or the good morals of the people; (4) illegally stockpile guns, bullets, or bomb-making supplies, either for the purpose of selling or in order to commit other illegal activities; (5) incite, provoke, use, or support the people to create confusion or unrest in the homeland; (6) cause the people to respect or go along with another form of government that is not a democracy with the king as the head of state; (7) establish an illegal casino or brothel, or deal in gambling sweepstakes or illegal lottery; (8) hoard commodities in order to make a profit, or illegally raise prices; and (9) organize to strike, or illegally stop work.[14]

Like Decrees 21 and 43 under Sarit, the administration of Order 22 and Order 34 (which specified the enforcement of Order 22) was placed in the hands of the Ministry of Interior and decentralized. Roles for the Bangkok Metropolitan Police, the Department of Corrections, and provincial governors were created within the text of the order. In addition, human rights and candid reports suggest that the army and the Internal Security Operations Command (ISOC), the interagency counterinsurgency coordinating body, were also involved in detentions under Order 22. Once an individual was identified as a potential "danger to society"—by the police, ISOC, army, or civilian informer—Order 22 allowed detention for up to thirty days while an investigation into the suspected individual was ongoing. After the initial thirty days, if in the opinion of the Director of Police in Bangkok or the provincial governor outside of Bangkok the suspected individual continued to display actions or behavior that was a "danger to society," then she or he could continue to be held. The Ministry of Interior was charged with the construction of re-education centers and the establishment of review committees. These committees were to decide every sixty days if each individual should be detained further or released. No limit was specified regarding the total length of detention.[15] In other words, indefinite detention was possible.

The Ministry of Interior was also assigned the task of identifying and securing the detention centers for individuals deemed a "danger to society." Shortly after Order 22 was issued, a plan to construct five re-education centers to accommodate the mass arrests was announced. Allotted a budget of forty-five million baht for construction, the centers were to be under the administration of the Department of Corrections and were planned for Rangsit, Lampang, Ayutthaya, Nakhon Ratchasima, and Khon Kaen (*Bangkok Post*, 29 October 1976, 5). As the planned centers would not be finished until mid-to-late 1977, the Ministry of Interior designated a number of temporary reeducation centers, often within already existing prison facilities.[16] In addition, while the Ministry of the Interior gave the Department of Corrections the role of constructing and administering the five new re-education centers, provincial governors and the Director of the Metropolitan Police Bureau were able to designate police stations, police and military training areas, and other sites as temporary places of detention and re-education.

With direct reference to human rights, immediately striking is the absence of the court in this order. At no point was a court or any authority other than the director of police or provincial governor required to authorize the detention of an individual. Those deemed a "danger to society" did not have the right to a lawyer or outside review of their case. The European Coordinating Committee for Solidarity with the Thai People argued that this opened a space for additional abuses. In a 1978 report, they succinctly noted that Order 22 "permits every possible abuse, and legitimates every arbitrary act of the military, the police, and the para-military groups . . . . [It] gives local officials the power to detain 'suspects' for at least 30 days without informing the legal authorities and without advancing the slightest proof of guilt" (ECCSTP 1978, 52). Perhaps the clear possibility for abuse under the order is why the Thai government chose not to send self-congratulatory reports about the detentions for inclusion in the UN *Human Rights Yearbook*. Yet there was not only an absence of reporting at the international level; domestic record-keeping about the detentions grew sparse as well.

The most basic records about Order 22 are fraught with numerical and categorical discrepancies. The total number of individuals detained under Order 22 remains unknown. Recalling that some detainees were held by the Department of Corrections, and some were held by local police, ISOC counterinsurgency personnel, or other authorities appointed by the Director of Police in Bangkok or provincial governors, this may not be surprising. The reported number of those detained varied widely, and changed during and after the period Order 22 was in force. According to a report by the Department of Corrections (1977), 2,188 people were detained as of December 1976. As of March 1977, the Co-ordinating Group for Religion in Society (CGRS), a Thailand-based human rights group established in early 1976, reported that eight thousand people had been arrested since October 1976, and perhaps two thousand remained in detention (CGRS 1977a). By June 1977, the CGRS estimated that 1,105 "dangers to society" remained in detention, with only 20 percent of that number being political detainees (CGRS 1977b, 1–2). A late 1977 newspaper account cited a source within the ISOC claiming that arrest lists included over sixty thousand names (*Siam Rat Weekly*, 18 December 1977, 16). In a US Library of Congress country study published ten years after the nullification of Order 22, John Haseman reported that twelve thousand people were detained over the three-year period the order was in force (1989, 269). The lack of a consistent record of how many individuals in total were detained under Order 22 may be both an outcome of the decentralization of its administration, as well as one of the intentions behind it. Without knowing how many people were detained, and by whom and in what locations, it is impossible to know how much of the citizenry was imagined to be dangerous to society and how they were treated.

Even in the case of the detainees under the direct supervision of the Department of Corrections, there were notable discrepancies in record-keeping. In their 1976 annual report, the Department of Corrections noted that on 13 October 1976, they changed the category of "hooligan" (*anthaphan*) to "misconduct" (*phu fuek oprom*).[17] They claimed that 2,188 people were arrested under Order 22 as "misconducts" (Department of Corrections 1977, 75). These detentions were duly reflected in the charts and diagrams showing the proportion of each kind of prisoner represented in the total national prison population. The category "misconduct" disappeared after the 1976 report (Department of Corrections 1978, 1979, 1980). Not only did the category disappear, but the diagrams showing the proportion of each kind of prisoner disappeared as well. The category, and any possible diagrams where it might be missed, ceased to be included in the reports. As arrests and detentions continued until the nullification of the law in August 1979, this absence is jarring. Given their initial willingness to report on the detentions, what caused the Department of Corrections to cease including the existence of the detainees in their annual report? Even before one questions the various violations of the human rights of detainees which may have taken place under Order 22, an official accounting of the precise number of detainees remains impossible. Even after the nullification of Order 22 in 1979, in which, resonant with the nullification of Sarit's Decrees 21 and 43, a note appended to the law critiqued the dangers presented by the arbitrary restriction of freedom normalized by the law, precise information about how many people were detained and in what conditions did not become publicly available.[18]

What may have made reporting about Order 22 difficult, even for a regime which discounted the importance of human rights, is that its very conception of categories of citizens who were dangerous was contrary to basic human rights principles. In this sense, if a recognition of this fact was behind, or partially behind, the failure to send reports for 1977 to 1988, might the failure to send reports be understood as a sign of a growing awareness of human rights inside the government? Or was the failure to report another indication of the sheer lack of respect for human rights cultivated across years of dictatorship and reflected in the active violations of human rights of citizens? Perhaps both.

Beyond the Culture of Human Rights Reporting

The reports included in the UN *Human Rights Yearbook* offer a very specific lens through which to view the Thai state's image and self-presentation of itself vis-à-vis international human rights standards. Despite Field Marshal Sarit Thanarat's clear antagonism towards the UDHR, his government felt compelled to place itself within a global frame of human rights at a time when there were no legally binding human rights instruments. The act of reporting, like the UDHR itself, represented the difficulty and tensions of making a global, suprapolitical ideal of human rights real on the ground in nations where authoritarianism was the order of the day. The depth of the authoritarianism that constituted the Sarit regime is reflected in the unironic and self-congratulatory inclusion of the arbitrary detention of hooligans as a step forward for security—and human rights—in Thailand.

After the 6 October 1976 massacre and coup, the form of the initial engagement with human rights reporting and the justification of authoritarian measures mirrored the Sarit years. The subsequent abrupt silence, present in both the lack of reports sent for inclusion in the UN *Human Rights Yearbook* and in the domestic records, is more difficult to interpret. How this absence might be analyzed is one of the ways in which querying the culture of human rights reporting and querying the culture of human rights may overlap most explicitly. Human rights reporting is a way to track the state's actions and self-representation, and increasingly under the individual human rights treaty mechanisms and as part of the UPR process, a way to directly challenge the state to be accountable. Whether absence reflects a failure of the state to recognize human rights violations, or reflects the keen awareness of their failure to protect human rights in line with relevant human rights standards, it points precisely to the locations where activists and scholars should push further for information and accountability.

Notes

1. I am grateful to an anonymous reviewer for suggesting the phrase "shadow of absolutism." Here it refers to the lingering, ingrained structures of inequality that marked absolute monarchy and made challenging both the monarchy and other powerful structures seem impossible and even unthinkable, even after 1932.

2. There were eight member states that abstained from voting on the UDHR but did not cast a vote against it.

3. The ICCPR was adopted by the UN on 16 December 1966, and entered into force on 23 March 1976; Thailand became a state party to the ICCPR on 29 October 1996. The ICESCR was adopted by the UN on 16 December 1966, and entered into force on 3 January 1976; Thailand became a state party to the ICESCR on 5 September 1999.

4. Under the UPR, every member state of the UN reports every four years on the actions it has taken to support and consolidate human rights. Supplementing, and often challenging, these self-reporting measures, other member states and nongovernmental organizations (NGOs) with consultative status, also submit reports.

5. According to the UN Working Group on Arbitrary Detention, there is no clear definition of arbitrary detention in international law. The Working Group therefore developed the following three categories of detention that is arbitrary: (1) when there is no legal basis for the deprivation of liberty; (2) when a person is deprived of liberty guaranteed either by the UDHR or the ICCPR; and (3) when a person has

been deprived of their liberty without the benefit of a fair trial (Working Group on Arbitrary Detention, n.d.).

6. Article 17 provides very broad, very wide-ranging powers: ". . . whenever the Prime Minister deems it appropriate for the purpose of impressing or suppressing actions, whether of internal or external origin, which jeopardize the national security or the Throne or subvert or threaten law and order, the Prime Minister, by resolution of the Council of Ministers, is empowered to issue orders to take steps accordingly. Such orders or steps shall be considered legal" (cited and translated in Thak 2007, 127).

7. All translations in this chapter are my own.

8. *Ratchakitchanubeksa* (special edition), 2 November 1958, Book 75, Part 89, 1–2.

9. *Ratchakitchanubeksa* (special edition), 10 January 1959, Book 76, Part 5, 2.

10. *Ratchakitchanubeksa* (special edition), 10 January 1959, Book 76, Part 5, 3.

11. The protests in October 1973 did not materialize out of thin air. Instead, in ways permissible (or able to go undetected by the regime), progressive thinkers and people were laying the foundation for protests in the streets by discussing, writing, and publishing new, democratic ideas and dreams beginning in the late 1950s (Prajak 2005).

12. *Ratchakitchanubeksa*, 19 February 1975, Book 92, Part 41, 34.

13. *Ratchakitchanubeksa* (special edition), 13 October 1976, Book 93, Part 128, 1.

14. *Ratchakitchanubeksa* (special edition), 13 October 1976, Book 93, Part 128, 1–2.

15. *Ratchakitchanubeksa* (special edition), 13 October 1976, Book 93, Part 128, 1–5.

16. Temporary centers included: Bang Khen, Phitsanulok, Songkhla, Lad Yao, Ratchaburi, and Sethsiri (Kongsak 1977, 50–72).

17. The annual reports of the Department of Corrections are bilingual. I use both the Thai and English words used by the Department here.

18. *Ratchakitchanubeksa*, 8 August 1979, Book 96, Part 135, 1–4.

References

Charnvit Kasetsiri. 2001 [B.E. 2544]. *14 Tula* [14 October]. Bangkok: Saithan Press.

Connors, Michael K. 2011. "Ambivalent about Human Rights: Thai Democracy." In *Human Rights in Asia*, edited by Thomas W. D. Davis and Brian Galligan, 103–22. Cheltenham, UK: Edward Elgar.

CGRS [Coordinating Group for Religion in Society]. 1977a. *Human Rights in Thailand Report, April 1977*. Bangkok: CGRS.

———. 1977b. *Human Rights in Thailand May–June 1977*. Bangkok: CGRS.

ECCSTP [European Coordinating Committee for Solidarity with the Thai People]. 1978. *Political Repression in Thailand*. London: Ad Hoc Group for Democracy in Thailand.

Department of Corrections. 1977 [B.E. 2520]. *Rai-ngan pracham pi 2519* [Annual report 1976]. Bangkok: Ministry of the Interior.

———. 1978 [B.E. 2521]. *Rai-ngan pracham pi 2520* [Annual report 1977]. Bangkok: Ministry of the Interior.

Haberkorn, Tyrell. 2011. *Revolution Interrupted: Farmers, Students, Law, and Violence in Northern Thailand*. Madison: University of Wisconsin Press.

Haseman, John B. 1989. "National Security." In *Thailand: A Country Study*, edited by Barbara Leitch LePoer, 225–86. Washington, DC: Federal Research Division.

Kongsak Liewmanont, ed. 1977 [B.E. 2520]. *Ruam khamsang khong khana patirup kanpokkhrong phaendin lae rabiap khobangkhap kiaokap kanpatibat to bukkhon thi pen phai to sangkhom* [Collected orders and procedures of the National Administrative Reform Council for dealing with the dangers to society]. Bangkok: Ministry of the Interior.

Morell, David, and Chai-anan Samudavanija. 1981. *Political Conflict in Thailand: Reform, Reaction, Revolution*. Cambridge, MA: Oelgeschlager, Gunn and Hain.

Moyn, Samuel. 2010. *The Last Utopia: Human Rights in History*. Cambridge, MA: Belknap Press of Harvard University Press.

Nowak, Manfred. 2010. "Report of the Special Rapporteur on Torture and Other Cruel, Inhuman or Degrading Treatment or Punishment (Addendum): Study on the Phenomena of Torture, Cruel, Inhuman or Degrading Treatment or Punishment in the World, Including an Assessment of Conditions of Detention." UN Human Rights Council, Geneva, Thirteenth Session, Agenda Item 3. A/HRC/13/39/Add.5.

Prajak Kongkirati. 2005 [B.E. 2548]. *Lae laew khwam khlueanwai ko prakot . . . kanmueang watthanatham khong naksueksa lae panyachon kon 14 tula* [And now the movement emerges . . . Cultural politics of students and intellectuals prior to 14 October]. Bangkok: Thammasat University Press.

Sarit Thanarat. 1965 [B.E. 2508]. *Pramuan sunthoraphot khong Sarit Thanarat pho so 2505– 2506*. [Collected speeches of Field Marshal Sarit Thanarat, 2505–2506 (1962–1963)]. Bangkok: Cabinet.

Thak Chaloemtiarana. 2007. *Thailand: The Politics of Despotic Paternalism*. Chiang Mai: Silkworm Books.

UN [United Nations]. 1947. *Yearbook on Human Rights for 1946*. Lake Success, NY: United Nations.

———. 1959. "Freedom from Arbitrary Arrest, Detention, and Exile." In *Yearbook on Human Rights: First Supplementary Volume*, 220-221. Lake Success, NY: United Nations.

———. 1960. *Yearbook on Human Rights for 1958*. Lake Success, NY: United Nations.

———. 1961. *Yearbook on Human Rights for 1959*. Lake Success, NY: United Nations.

———. 1962. *Yearbook on Human Rights for 1960*. Lake Success, NY: United Nations.

———. 1964a. *Yearbook on Human Rights for 1961*. Lake Success, NY: United Nations.

————. 1964b. *Yearbook on Human Rights for 1962.* Lake Success, NY: United Nations.

————. 1965. *Yearbook on Human Rights for 1963.* Lake Success, NY: United Nations.

————. 1967. *Yearbook on Human Rights for 1964.* Lake Success, NY: United Nations.

————. 1968. *Yearbook on Human Rights for 1965.* Lake Success, NY: United Nations.

————. 1969a. *Yearbook on Human Rights for 1966.* Lake Success, NY: United Nations.

————. 1969b. *Yearbook on Human Rights for 1967.* Lake Success, NY: United Nations.

————. 1970. *Yearbook on Human Rights for 1968.* Lake Success, NY: United Nations.

————. 1971. *Yearbook on Human Rights for 1969.* Lake Success, NY: United Nations.

————. 1973. *Yearbook on Human Rights for 1970.* Lake Success, NY: United Nations.

————. 1974. *Yearbook on Human Rights for 1971.* Lake Success, NY: United Nations.

————. 1975. *Yearbook on Human Rights for 1972.* Lake Success, NY: United Nations.

————. 1977. *Yearbook on Human Rights for 1973–1974.* Lake Success, NY: United Nations.

————. 1981. *Yearbook on Human Rights for 1975–1976.* Lake Success, NY: United Nations.

Waltz, Susan. 2002. "Reclaiming and Rebuilding the History of the Universal Declaration of Human Rights." *Third World Quarterly, Journal of Emerging Areas* 23 (3): 437–48.

Working Group on Arbitrary Detention. n.d. "Fact Sheet #26 of the Office of the High Commissioner for Human Rights: The Working Group on Arbitrary Detention." Accessed at http://www.unhchr.ch/html/menu6/2/fs26.htm.

Zimmerman, Robert F. 1978. *Reflections on the Collapse of Democracy in Thailand.* Singapore: Institute of Southeast Asian Studies.

6

The Politics of Scripts:
Language Rights, Heritage, and the Choice of
Orthography for Khmer Vernaculars in Thailand

~~~

Peter Vail and Panuwat Pantakod

Northern Khmer, a language spoken by over a million people in Thailand's lower northeast, has been, for the last few generations at least, predominantly an oral language. Cultural preservationists, alarmed at the widespread shift among Northern Khmer speakers to the national language, Thai, are calling for the creation—or revival, depending on their perspective—of a writing system to stem the loss of Northern Khmer precipitated by that shift. Selecting a script for Northern Khmer has proved to be politically contentious, since different stakeholders hold starkly divergent beliefs about Khmer identity, heritage, and multicultural rights in Thailand.

Language Maintenance and Shift

Thai language in daily life—in mass media, state education, and other domains—has spread at the expense of Northern Khmer. The shift is fuelled by policies integrating people into the Thai state and a social stigmatization of Khmer identity in Thailand generally (Vail 2006). Although Smalley (1988, 405) considered this shift a trend towards increasing multilingualism that posed no danger of Khmer-language loss, Northern Khmer villagers are now beginning to realize that many in their younger generations speak Northern Khmer poorly, if they speak it at all. Thai has spread into every linguistic domain, both public and private (including the home), and modern society and the wage labor market have created new, exclusively Thai-language domains unimaginable just a few generations ago. The drastic change in children's mother tongue from Northern Khmer to Thai demonstrates that Northern Khmer has reached what Dorian (1981, 51) calls a linguistic "tip"— that point at which a presumably stable bilingualism turns into widespread language shift.

Northern Khmer literacy disappeared several generations ago, a victim of state bureaucratization and the spread of Thai print media. Whereas the use of Khmer script in northeast Thailand, or Isan, was once reportedly widespread (if limited in the domains of its use—see Paitoon 1984, Tsumura 2009, and various comments by Aymonier [1895] 2000), the Thai state over the last one hundred years has marginalized and suppressed literacy in Khmer to the extent that today it survives only residually in a handful of Buddhist temples and has no wider vernacular purposes whatsoever. So thorough has been the eradication of Khmer literacy that many Northern Khmer today believe theirs is only an oral dialect (*phasa thong thin*), which they consider inferior to a "real," authoritative language with a written form such as Thai. At the same time, political friction between Thailand and Cambodia renders any linguistic connections between Northern Khmer and Cambodian Khmer ideologically controversial and highly politicized.

As efforts to maintain and revitalize Northern Khmer language now arise, questions surrounding literacy and orthography reemerge. One of the key steps in language maintenance and revival—not just for Northern Khmer, but for endangered languages throughout the world—has been the creation and propagation of writing systems (see, for example, Grenoble and Whaley 2006, 113–18). A writing system expands the potential domains for the use of a language and provides a durable medium that allows a language to overcome spatial and temporal constraints of face-to-face interaction and thus to be transmitted in ways that an oral language cannot.[1] Writing systems have been devised for oral languages in Thailand and many other parts of mainland Southeast Asia. In some cases, native speakers themselves design scripts specifically for their own language (see, for example, the Hmong scripts discussed by Smalley and Wimuttikosol 1998, and the Jruq script discussed by Sidwell 2008). But in most cases linguists, in conjunction with native speakers, have adapted preexisting writing systems to the phonology of the target oral language—for example, Roman or Thai scripts adapted for minority languages in Thailand, or Khmer script adapted for indigenous languages in Rattanakiri and Mondulkiri, Cambodia (see, for example, Kosonen 2008; Gregerson 2009).

In the case of Northern Khmer, however, the issue becomes more complex—and highly contentious—precisely because Northern Khmer historically already had a script, one still used to write Khmer in neighboring Cambodia, and which still serves esoteric religious functions in Thailand today.[2] Given Thailand's turbulent relations with Cambodia, selecting a script to represent Northern Khmer becomes a minefield of ideological and historical disagreements. Should the use of Khmer script be revitalized and expanded for Northern Khmer? Would doing so undermine national integrity? Or, given the extent to which Northern Khmer speakers have been assimilated into Thailand, should a script based on Thai orthography be used instead? Which writing system would best serve the purposes of Northern Khmer vernacular literacy? What are those purposes? Such questions may appear simple, but the issues behind them prove vexing indeed.

Language Planning and Linguistic Ideology

Choosing a script constitutes an example of language planning (Spolsky 2004; Sebba 2007). In the past, the predominant thinking in script selection concerned phonological efficiency—how well a script linguistically represented a given language. Ideally, one character in the script would represent one phoneme (see, for example, Pike 1947; Smalley 1976, 27–28), because this was believed to make a writing system easier for users to learn. Others, especially those associated with practice theory and the "New Literacy Studies" (Scribner and Cole 1981; Street 1984; Gee 1990), challenged this received view and argued instead for a sociolinguistic approach to script choice, one that recognizes and even prioritizes social, historical, and cultural factors connected to both the language and the script (see also Unseth 2005; Sebba 2007, 13).

A sociolinguistic approach inherently involves examining different linguistic ideologies. In a seminal 1984 article about minority language policies, Richard Ruiz distinguishes three pervasive linguistic ideologies—what he calls "orientations" to minority languages—that shape policies and practices based on them. These orientations consist of minority language as a "problem," as a "right," and as a "resource." Language-as-problem here refers to the common perception of minority languages as responsible for deficiencies in student learning, as obstacles to social mobility, or as problems that must be solved (Ruiz 1984, 18–20). Such a "problem" view is especially common in the context of national development, security, and modernization, including, as we shall see, in Thailand.

Ruiz (21–24), writing of the American context, traces the perspective of language-as-right to the civil rights movement: speakers of minority languages demand linguistic rights to be able to fully participate civically—for voting, education, and other basic social needs. As citizens, minority language speakers have the right to sociopolitical inclusion; therefore they have linguistic rights that necessarily undergird those civil rights. Ricento (2005, 355) critiques this orientation by pointing out that it protects individual civil rights, but does not protect the right of speech groups "to use their languages in the public sphere indefinitely." In other words, policies based on the view of language-as-right do not protect languages or speech communities per se, only minority language speakers insofar as they are not competent—or not yet competent—in the dominant language.

By language-as-resource, Ruiz (25–28) means that languages have economic or other benefits—for example, for the nation. He cites in particular the United States' "great deficiency in language capability" (26). He discusses how linguistic resources need not only be developed, but also conserved, precisely among those people who already speak minority languages. The rise of language-as-resource as an orientation sparked a broad interest in the United States in heritage languages and their instruction. The problem with this orientation, according to Ricento (2005, 357), is that its focus on utility results in ignoring actual people and in treating language as a commodity rather than a heritage—or, as an "instrument" rather than as an "identity marker."

Still, much has been made of the language-as-resource orientation in terms of multiculturalism. Hornberger (1998), for example, discusses how this orientation now envelops language-as-right: that is, minority speakers have the right to develop their languages as cultural resources—not only for the instrumental purposes of helping the nation, but for safeguarding heritage and culture. This is different from the specifically civil rights argument that Ruiz originally advanced and reflects the trend towards multiculturalism and cultural preservation found in various culturally oriented legal instruments, like the UN Declaration of Rights of Indigenous Peoples, and the Convention for the Safeguarding of Intangible Cultural Heritage. Such an orientation also requires an ethnographic or "ideological" examination of literacy (Street 1984), since it assumes that language ideology and literacy practices differ among diverse cultural groups.

Ruiz's orientations are not mutually exclusive, and they provide a useful heuristic for thinking about the ways that various relevant social actors understand languages and orthographies, and, as we shall see, they can help explain the contentiousness of script choice for Northern Khmer.

Multiculturalism in Thai Education

Recent debate over an orthography for Northern Khmer emerges in the context of Thailand's own nascent, albeit uneven, move towards multiculturalism. Thailand's 1997 Constitution codified what was a growing reaffirmation of diverse identities in an otherwise heavily nationalistic Thailand (Jory 1999; Hong 2000). Decentralizing policies stemming from the 1997 Constitution, especially the 1999 Education Act, ostensibly give new credence to local practices and knowledge and incorporate "local wisdom" (*phum panya thong thin*) into local school curricula (Jungck and Kajornsin 2003, 41). Schools can now dedicate about 20 percent of class time to teaching "local wisdom" as a subject in school; in many areas, schools opt to teach local language as one of those weekly subjects. The amount of time allocated—about an hour per week—is probably more symbolic than pedagogically efficacious, but given the heavy-handed nationalistic policies of previous education regimes, it has an important symbolic value nonetheless. However, not everyone agrees on what multiculturalism means in practice, and some even reject the concept outright. The most polarized conflict over Northern Khmer literacy stems from the introduction of local language into the curriculum and the meanings of multiculturalism that attend it.

Disagreement over Northern Khmer orthography centers on the nature of Northern Khmer identity and on what speakers allegedly want from a written form of their language. One side, which advocates using a Thai-based script to write Northern Khmer, characterizes ethnic Khmer citizens as a Thai minority who see themselves as "Thai who speak Khmer" (Thomas 1989, 49) and who want to orient themselves exclusively towards Thai society and nationhood. According to this camp, Northern Khmer speakers have little interest in, or palpable connections to, the Khmer-speaking community in Cambodia. Conversely, proponents of using a Khmer script argue that Northern Khmer want to identify with a broader Khmer ethnic identity and still be Thai citizens at the same time. They recognize that some Northern Khmer shun their Khmer identity and want to be Thai, but see this tendency as stemming precisely from forced assimilation and historical injustices inflicted by a chauvinistic Thai state. They argue that Northern Khmer speakers in a newly emergent multicultural milieu can now reclaim their long-suppressed Khmer identity.

Writing Northern Khmer in Thai Script

Among the first proponents of Northern Khmer language maintenance was Mahidol University's Institute of Language and Culture for Rural Development (ILCRD), which runs literacy projects for many of Thailand's minority languages, including Northern Khmer. Mahidol's programmatic aims are twofold: to effectively help Khmer-speaking children make the transition to the national language, and to preserve Northern Khmer language and culture (Suwilai 1998, 21–22). The program employs a writing system based on Thai script, adapted for use with Northern Khmer phonology.

The first effort to design an orthography for Northern Khmer using Thai script began as early as 1958 with missionary linguist William Smalley, and in earnest in 1964 (Smalley 1976, 12, 45). Smalley's work is worth reviewing here, since it plays a key role in Mahidol's current orientation. His aim, besides Bible translation, was to help minority language speakers improve their Thai, in order to facilitate greater social inclusion (11–12, 14). Although not explicitly a language-as-right perspective as Ruiz describes it, Smalley's orientation was comparable. Minority language speakers did not know Thai well, or at all, and were therefore socially and politically marginalized. He strongly advocated the use of Thai scripts to write minority languages, arguing that doing so would facilitate learning Thai language later. It would have the further benefit of requiring "preliterate" and "semiliterate" minority people to learn to read only once (11–13). Turning specifically to Northern Khmer, Smalley (44) discusses how the Thai government at that time made a strong push to assimilate Northern Khmer speakers by establishing elementary schools. He further notes (45) that at the time of his research in the early 1960s, few Northern Khmer could read Khmer script, and that by his estimation, Northern Khmer and "Phnom Penh Khmer" were linguistically sharply different. Northern Khmer speakers could thus not readily understand Cambodian radio programs, evidence that they were more sociopolitically oriented towards Thailand (see also Jenner 1974).

Smalley's orientation and insights must be understood in their historical, Cold War context. Smalley himself says little about Northern Khmer history—suggesting only that the presence of Khmer speakers in Thailand "is due to a centuries-long history of shifting borders between Thailand and Cambodia" (43). He does not examine the history of using Khmer script, and, despite the speakers' presumed orientation to Thailand, he implicitly frames his discussion of minority languages in a discourse of state security, writing that "even today I think it is probably fair to say that in spite of the mushrooming government interest in the problem created by linguistic diversity as ethnic minorities threaten national unity, there is still no over-all government language planning for minority groups" (15).[3] Smalley argues that the main Khmer-speaking population in Isan did not live near the border, but closer to the railway line further north, and uses this fact to argue that Northern Khmer people had no connections to Cambodia. The subtexts of national unity and Cold War politics are evident in all his early writing on minority language. Important to note is that in Smalley's time, minority language preservation was decidedly *not* the issue at stake, although he held out the hope that the Thai government would not "stamp out" minority languages (14). Furthermore, he was adamant that, given the density and size of the Northern Khmer-speaking population, the Northern Khmer would not lose their language, but would only become more multilingual.

The Mahidol program adheres closely to Smalley's early vision of, and justification for, minority language literacy, including for Northern Khmer. In the late 1980s, linguists from the Summer Institute of Linguistics (SIL) and Mahidol University put into final form and disseminated a Thai-based script for Northern Khmer that Smalley had created, arguing, among other things, that using Thai script would help local, "semi-literate" Northern Khmer-speakers better prepare their children for a transition from their mother tongue (Northern Khmer) to the national language (Thai) in school. But, by the 1980s, Mahidol linguists also recognized the beginnings of a broader language shift from Northern Khmer to Thai, and therefore argued also that Northern Khmer should have a writing system so that villagers could participate in preserving their own culture and local wisdom (Suwilai 1998, 21–22; see also Thomas 1989; Suwilai and Sophana 1990 [2533]). Like Smalley before them, the Mahidol team understood that the Thai-centric immersion policies of the Ministry of Education forced minority children into Thai-language curricula for which they were ill prepared.[4] Unable to understand the language of instruction, it is entirely unsurprising that minority children did poorly in school (in the case of Northern Khmer, see, for example, Saengrunee 1995 [2538]). As an alternative to immersion, Mahidol advocates a linguistic bridging program for minority-language speakers intended to allow children to learn in their mother tongue when they begin school, and to transition to Thai after approximately two years. Literacy is key to the program: following Smalley, Mahidol advocates using a Thai-based script so that reading skills in the mother tongue can be readily transferred to reading Thai language.

However, deploying this bridging project for Northern Khmer speakers raises a number of ideological and practical issues. First, the Mahidol project assumes that Northern Khmer envision themselves unequivocally as Thai, and not as Khmers in any broader sense; that Northern Khmer speakers do not see rekindling literacy skills as part of their ethnic heritage, or as useful to foster or restore ties with Khmer speakers across the border in Cambodia. Yet cross-border ties do exist (and have been reinvigorated since the end of the Cold War), and the reason such relations reached something of a nadir in the Cold War period in the first place has everything to do with the heavy-handed nationalistic state assimilation policies, such as immersion education in Thai, that Mahidol is purportedly challenging. We have argued elsewhere (Vail 2007) that the Cold War provided the ideological framework to assimilate Khmer speakers in Thailand—to encourage Northern Khmer speakers not only to disavow their Khmer-ness, but also to despise Cambodia. The Mahidol program does nothing to challenge such nationalistic rhetoric, and, by positing Northern Khmer speakers as fundamentally different from, and uninterested in, Cambodian Khmer, even passively endorses it.

Furthermore, it is simply not the case today that Northern Khmer children do not speak Thai. In Smalley's time, two to three generations ago, this was the case, and it may even have been residually the case in the late 1980s when SIL's and Mahidol's work on the Thai orthography accelerated, but it is not the case now. Even local teachers participating in Mahidol's own program told us outright that bridging to Thai language is not necessary, as the children speak Thai already. The problem, they say, is that the children's Northern Khmer skills are so poor. From our observations in those classrooms where Northern Khmer was being taught, it was abundantly clear that, instead of transferring to Thai the literacy skills they learned by using Thai script to write Northern Khmer (as envisioned by Mahidol), children were using their Thai literacy skills to decipher how to write Northern Khmer using Mahidol's Thai script system.

Mahidol's case for using a Thai script, then, stems from a transitional pedagogy which treats minority language as a problem, coupled with myopic notions of heritage that derive from a national narrative in which Northern Khmer are seen as different from other Khmer and remarkably similar to Thai. Nevertheless, the bridging strategy for minority languages overall could be seen as an important salvo against the rigid immersion policies and practices that Thailand's Ministry of Education had pursued in the past, because it inspired a linguistic consciousness among some rural teachers and challenged Bangkok-centric assumptions about the purpose and scope of national education. But in the case of Northern Khmer, it nevertheless appears largely anachronistic, since it relies on assumptions about Thai-language proficiency and Northern Khmer identity dating from the Cold War period. It also enshrines a view of Khmer heritage that distinguishes Northern Khmer from a broader Khmer ethnic affiliation, meaning the multicultural diversity Mahidol champions is one that is confined strictly to regional variations on a Thai national theme.

The Case for Using Khmer Script

If proponents of a Thai-based script for Northern Khmer envision Khmerness narrowly as a subnational identity—a variant of being Thai—the chief advocates of using Khmer script cast Northern Khmer speakers as part of a much broader pan-Khmer identity. This extends spatially from southern Isan through Cambodia to the Mekong Delta in Vietnam, which is populated by Khmer Krom speakers, and temporally back to the heyday of the Khmer empire based in Angkor. Arguments for using a Khmer script derive also from the historical use of Khmer script in past generations, and from notions of heritage based on essentialized constructions of ethnic identity.

By far the most vocal and active proponent of using Khmer script is Cheymongkol Chalermsukjitsri, founder of the Khmer Language Project, and active in teaching Khmer using Khmer script since 2007. Cheymongkol is widely regarded in the Surin-Sisaket region as having made substantial sacrifices to revitalize Khmer literacy: he teaches for a pittance, or even for free; he works tirelessly to raise funds and to garner any resources that may be of use in revitalizing Northern Khmer; and he donates old computers, books, teaching materials, and copious amounts of time to anyone interested in learning to write. He homeschools his own children in both Khmer and Thai, and he maintains and makes available a sizable library about Khmer language and culture, with books in Khmer, Thai, English, and French.

Cheymongkol has taught Khmer in several districts in Surin, and he frequently visits Cambodia as a local cultural liaison and to obtain teaching materials. He is also a vociferous critic of using Thai script to write Northern Khmer, arguing that this debases Khmer identity, obscures Northern Khmer literary and cultural heritage, and simply serves as a tool to further assimilate Northern Khmer into a Thai identity. Cheymongkol frames his crusade for using Khmer script explicitly as an issue of cultural rights—not in Ruiz's sense of rights as civic inclusion and enfranchisement, but as a right, and interestingly also as a *duty* incumbent on a culture-bearer of preserving ethnic identity and heritage. He takes particular issue with others among the Northern Khmer intelligentsia who fail to transmit Northern Khmer to their children; he argues it is a linguistic and cultural obligation for them to embrace and propagate their Khmer heritage, and to serve as role models for claiming cultural rights. He often frames this in very personal terms:

for example, he argues that if Mahidol's ethnic Khmer participants and researchers cannot recognize bridging as cultural oppression and erasure, then they must implicitly despise themselves—something along the lines of false consciousness— having internalized their own cultural subordination.

Cheymongkol had arranged with the Ministry of Education to teach Khmer (using Khmer script) in at least three Surin province classrooms. He wanted (even at one point challenged) Mahidol to teach their Thai-script method in the same district, so that the two programs could be directly compared. But the Ministry reneged, which Cheymongkol conspiratorially interprets as a behind-the-scenes manipulation by Mahidol to ensure that the teaching of Khmer uses only Thai script. Because he has a signed contract that he believes was violated, Cheymongkol plans to sue the district. This demoralizing episode has also prompted him to suspend much of his language teaching, and he now focuses instead more heavily on cultural revitalization and exchange with Cambodia, such as with traditional *kantruem* musicians.

Insisting on his rights to teach using Khmer script, Cheymongkol draws heavily on his interpretation of legal instruments, including UN documents and the Thai Constitution. Unfortunately, these instruments obfuscate linguistic rights—a point to be discussed in more detail below. Nevertheless, Cheymongkol insists that these instruments affirm the right to use Khmer script when teaching Northern Khmer language, and he is dismayed—even disgusted—at the utter lack of "rights-claiming behavior" (Munger 2006/7) he witnesses among fellow Northern Khmer speakers.

In contrast to the Mahidol project, Cheymongkol cites strong connections between Northern Khmer and Cambodian Khmer speakers (and even Khmer Krom speakers in Vietnam), and aims to revitalize those historical linkages. He regards the Cold War and Thai ultra-nationalism as transient phenomena, and believes there is a more enduring ethnic commonality among Khmers that should be revived. While he does not aim to undermine or challenge the legitimacy of the Thai state (and he has never entertained ideas of Northern Khmer secessionism or ethnic rebellion), he believes one should be able to be ethnic Khmer and Thai citizen at the same time. Most important for him in this regard is the maintenance and propagation of Northern Khmer language and its intrinsic connection to a broader Khmer heritage. For this reason he is appalled at the misleading belief prevalent among many Northern Khmer speakers (one which he attributes to government- and even Mahidol-derived misinformation) that Northern Khmer never had an orthography of its own.

If Mahidol is too myopic in interpreting the scope of Northern Khmer identity and heritage, Cheymongkol's perspective may be too broad, or at least too essentializing. Cheymongkol glosses over regional differences within the Khmer-speaking world. That is, he simplifies regional and ethnic history by implicitly assuming that Khmer language evidences a common pan-Khmer identity. He does not distinguish between cultural and historical links with northwestern Cambodia (those areas geographically and dialectically contiguous to Northern Khmer-speaking regions and that have a long history of Siamese suzerainty), where residual trade and cross-border kin networks still obtain, and with central or south Cambodia, like Phnom Penh, with its more remote, and even imagined ethnic ties. In other words, he imputes an essentialized Khmer-ness to speakers of all varieties of Khmer language, and interprets historical evidence within this essentialized ethnic framework. So Cheymongkol's historical perspective is not empirically historical, but ethno-historical, assuming the vitality and meaningfulness of a unified Khmer identity based chiefly on shared language, and asserting a narrative in which all Khmer people therefore also necessarily share a common history.

Cheymongkol also takes issue with an implicit double standard in Mahidol's bridging program, one that assumes that rural Northern Khmer children are "pre-" or "semi-literate," and that they can only endure learning one script, as Smalley had long ago argued and as Mahidol maintains today. In Cheymongkol's view, this denigrates rural children, and places the blame on them as poor learners rather than on the state for offering substandard schooling. Cheymongkol questions why, when Bangkok or foreign students learn Khmer as a second language (i.e., as a resource), they learn Khmer script, while rural Northern Khmer students, when they learn to write their own heritage language, are compelled to write in a Thai script. Furthermore, other languages that Northern Khmer learn in their local schools are not taught this way—English is taught with a Roman script, Chinese with Chinese characters—so clearly there is a double standard operating when Northern Khmer is taught using a Thai script. He perceptively identifies an underlying, naturalized ideology of monolingualism as driving the marginalization of minority languages, and observes how resource languages are only those deemed to have lucrative market value.

Discussion: Rights, History, and Iconicity

Mahidol's literacy program and Cheymongkol's Khmer Language Project are not the only stakeholders in Northern Khmer literacy, but they illustrate the spectrum of contentious issues at stake—that is, heritage, identity, and the rights to social resources accessible through literacy. Both are concerned with the fading future of the Northern Khmer language as speakers shift to Thai, but they offer starkly different solutions. Other stakeholders complicate this picture, including teachers and students in various programs, education officials in Surin province, monks who still use Khmer script, and a wide array of villagers—especially older villagers—in Surin and Sisaket provinces who have knowledge and memory of Khmer literacy and its applications.

By way of preface, it should be mentioned that dispiritingly few of the people we talked to had any well-formed opinions about Khmer literacy one way or the other. Nearly everyone we interviewed was apathetic concerning the prospects for, and utility of, Northern Khmer language (see also Vail 2006), and uncritically assumed that Northern Khmer would always somehow be transmitted even as they noted its current decline (an enigma endemic to language loss worldwide). Most only articulated their views because we elicited them. Opinions were shifting, tenuous, and often self-contradictory, and we therefore hesitate to rank any one of the opinions expressed as definitively more authentic, representative, or valid than any others. Nevertheless, it is illuminating to examine the range of views that people held, as well as the orientations they used to frame their understanding of literacy, and they can serve as a useful supplement or corrective to the more polemical and intractable views offered by the Khmer Language Program and by Mahidol. Particularly instructive are the views people held on the connection between literacy, Khmer heritage, and linguistic rights. We interpret the ambiguity and ambivalence we encountered in interviews as evidence that Khmer linguistic heritage is intrinsically fluid, contextually dependent, and polysemous, and also that the linguistic ideologies and orientations have become what Scollon and Scollon (2004, 136) call "submerged discourses"; that is, they have become part of people's habitus, deeply engrained, unarticulated, and perhaps even banal (in Billig's sense [1995]).

Linguistic Rights

It was mentioned earlier that Cheymongol of the Surin Khmer Language Project is especially adamant about casting the use of Khmer script as a cultural and linguistic right. He regularly cites the 1997 [2540] and 2007 [2550] Constitutions of Thailand, the Universal Declaration of Human Rights, UN Declaration on the Rights of Indigenous Peoples (DRIP), UNESCO's Universal Declaration on Cultural Diversity, and, most of all, Thailand's National Education Act of 1999, as instruments that support the right of Northern Khmer speakers to learn, preserve, and revitalize Khmer language, and to use Khmer orthography for doing so. But linguistic rights codified in all such instruments are notoriously vague.[5] Unspecific and open to vastly different interpretations, such instruments do not lend themselves well to concretely asserting specific linguistic rights. Such indeterminacy is a problem endemic to linguistic rights not only in Thailand, but worldwide.[6]

The Thai Constitution of 2007 [2550], and the 1997 [2540] Constitution on which it is largely based, are even more vague than the various international instruments about the role and status of language. The 2007 Constitution, for example, discusses *customs* and *local knowledge* but does not specify language:

> Part 12
> Right to Assembly Section 65: Persons so assembling as to be a traditional community shall have the right to conserve or restore their customs, local knowledge, arts or good culture of their community and of the nation and participate in management, maintenance, preservation and exploitation of natural resources and environment in a balanced and sustainable manner and persistently.

Most contentious of all is no doubt Thailand's National Education Act of 1999, a product of the decentralization requirements spawned by the 1997 Constitution, and a reaction to that year's fiscal crisis, in which the Office of the National Education Commission blamed Thailand's financial decline on an overdependence on Western education at the expense of "local knowledge" (see, for example, Jungck and Kajornsin 2003, 28). The Education Act allows for 20 percent of a school's curriculum to be designed by local boards, and to thereby incorporate local traditions, practices, language, and knowledge.

However, local knowledge is here framed as part of a broader, and somewhat nebulous "*Thai* wisdom," meaning that, whatever local knowledge gets incorporated into a school's curriculum as a result, educational rights are intended to be—or imagined to be—an instantiation of Thai wisdom, and not an alternative to it or, worse, a subversion of it.

The 1999 Education Act, then, is at once the education rights instrument that makes the teaching of Khmer language in Isan classrooms possible, but that at the same time ideologically subsumes it as part of an exclusively "Thai" national culture. Pan-Khmer identity as envisioned by Cheymongkol, and implicitly the medium of Khmer orthography, poses a critical challenge to that Thai-centric assumption, because it potentially connects Northern Khmer to a radically different national tradition in Cambodia—a heritage that contradicts the Thai national myth, and a history often at outright odds with Thailand's own. On the other hand, Mahidol's program, because it frames Northern Khmer literacy in a Thai script, readily subsumes Northern Khmer as part of "Thai wisdom."

Educational and linguistic rights, both those derived from international legal instruments and those stemming from Thailand's decentralization are, in short, vague on the role of language, silent on the status of orthography, and, in the case of the Thai laws, deeply intertwined with a Thai national identity that is not easy to reconcile with a Khmer identity that may challenge it. Indeed, Khmer language and literacy have been clearly regarded by state authorities, both in the past and at present, as an obstacle to national integration, a subversive identity—a view which sadly persists despite the lip service paid to nascent multiculturalism.

Such lingering suspicions over potentially perfidious Khmer identity surfaced frequently over the course of our research. For example, a teacher from Phum Pon village in Surin province, who participates in both Mahidol's Thai-based literacy project and offers after-school lessons to students using Khmer script, told us of a Mahidol project meeting she attended in which she questioned the utility of teaching Khmer using Thai script. The principal from another school in the project, at Ban Pho Thong, jingoistically denounced the idea of using a Khmer script, accusing the teacher of being "in collusion with Hun Sen." I encountered precisely the same attitude in a discussion with Burin Thongmaen, educational supervisor for Surin's District 1 (and himself an ethnic Kui). He, too, disparagingly suggested that proponents of Khmer script held secret allegiance to Hun Sen, and that they were implicitly a threat and not to be trusted.[7] The headman in one of the villages where Cheymongkol teaches actively discouraged the students from attending the class, saying that learning Khmer script was tantamount to collaboration with Hun Sen. More insidiously, Cheymongkol recently discovered that he has been placed on an Internal Security Office watch list for "causing an ethnic division"—ironic, of course, since his goal is so clearly multicultural. Such official distrust stems in part from Cheymongkol's having been adopted as something of a local hero among Cambodian nationalists for reviving Northern Khmer—numerous articles about him appear in nationalistic blogs like KI-Media, Khmerization, and newspapers like *Koh Santepheap*. This puts Cheymongkol in a difficult position. On the one hand, he actively fosters such publicity because of his pan-Khmer perspective and because he derives financial support and teaching materials from Cambodia and other overseas Khmer. On the other hand, the same Cambodian nationalists who praise Cheymongkol also virulently deride Thailand as imperial invaders, inflaming the already tense international disputes between the two countries, and making Cheymongkol a target of Thai nationalists.

Official hostile attitudes towards pan-Khmer language and identity are lingering prejudices born of Cold War tensions, exacerbated by current political disputes with Cambodia, in which Northern Khmer people were and are seen as potentially subversive to the state because of a secret allegiance to Cambodia (Vail 2010, 130). Only a Khmer identity utterly disassociated from Cambodia, one subsumed as a regional variety of Thai-ness, with no cross-border interests or historical connections to a broader Khmer-ness, is tolerated. The result is that the state sees Khmer when learned by central Thais as a resource, but sees Khmer when learned by heritage language learners as a threat.

Furthermore, the view that linguistic rights were simply those granted by policies of the Ministry of Education was surprisingly pervasive. A teacher in Ban Phran, Sisaket province, for example, explained how teaching local language had never even crossed their minds. The received view—that schools were for teaching Thai language, and that only Thai was a "real" language—was so thoroughly entrenched that it was beyond question or examination, a discourse entirely submerged in social practice and banal in its obviousness. But neither is this simply a case of false consciousness. Historically, state schools were used to spread Thai language and literacy; moreover, the relative poverty of rural areas compared to urban ones implicitly constructs Thai language as the crucial avenue of social mobility. Even today, rural schools are still fighting for good education in, and sufficient funding for, Thai, so teaching Khmer appears to many to be counterintuitive. Having lived through the erasure of Khmer literacy, and having been inculcated with the ideological denigration of Khmer language, many are deeply ambivalent about Thailand's nascent multicultural language instruction in schools (cf., Dauenhauer and Dauenhauer 1998). So deeply is this linguistic ideology entrenched, that many regard teaching Khmer as anathema to the whole purpose of school to begin with. The resultant lack of linguistic rights-claiming behavior, the implicit dependence on Thai state education policy, and the adherence to a Thai historical narrative about the limited scope of Khmer identity, as alluded to earlier, are precisely what Cheymongkol finds so distressing.

Khmer Script as Heritage/Resource in the Temple

Khmer literacy persists in a handful of the region's temples, where monks still use palm leaf manuscripts written in sacred Khmer *mul* script for sermons, protective tattoos, and to dispense astrological advice. Several of these monks also teach reading or writing, but even in the domain of Buddhism, where we might expect a more uniform religious explanation for the importance of Khmer writing (Tsumura 2009), we find instead entirely disparate ideological orientations. For example, in Thatum district, Surin province, the abbot at Wat Thungsawang requires his monks and novices to learn Khmer script so they can read palm leaf manuscripts. The abbot does so, he says, out of the belief that it represents village culture and tradition; he does not frame his Khmer-ness as connected to Cambodia at all. He teaches only reading, not writing, and uses as texts only genuine palm leaf manuscripts—written in the arcane language and difficult *mul* script that the novices find daunting.

In contrast, the abbot at Ban Phran temple in Sisaket province requires that his novices learn to read and write modern Khmer using *crieng* script, arguing that novices need diverse skills; once they leave the monkhood they could potentially use Khmer literacy to do business in Cambodia. Although he regards Khmer language as part of local religious heritage, he insists he teaches Khmer only to equip his monks with lucrative skills. His orientation is clearly language-as-resource, Khmer literacy as a potential tool for economic mobility.

The Iconicity of Khmer Scripts

The contrasting views of these monks, and indeed of all stakeholders in Khmer literacy, illustrate what Sebba (2007), drawing on work by Judith Irvine and Susan Gal (2000), calls the *iconicity* of orthography. He writes that iconicity

> involves a transformation of the sign relationship between linguistic features (or varieties) and the social images with which they are linked. Linguistic features that index social groups or activities appear to be iconic representations of them, as if a linguistic feature somehow depicted or displayed a social group's inherent nature or essence. (Sebba 2007, 82–83)

Though the linkage may be "only historical, contingent or conventional," it has, to those who have this interpretation, the appearance of being inherent.

Iconicity can involve the meta-meaning expressed by an entire language (as in code switching), or it can hinge on linguistic minutiae—a slight difference in the sound of a vowel, or spelling variations of a single letter. The choice of Thai or Khmer script clearly indexes the imagined extents of Khmer ethnicity, but surprisingly so too does the *style* of writing Khmer. *Mul* and *crieng* script styles are functionally identical, in that they represent the phonology of Khmer in the same way (Huffman 1970). But in terms of iconicity, they evoke starkly disparate histories, nationalisms, literacies, and identities.

Monks, villagers, and teachers we interviewed affirm that *mul* script used in the domain of religion constitutes part of their Northern Khmer religious heritage, but the same informants believe that *crieng* script belongs exclusively to Cambodians. Proponents of a pan-Khmer identity, such as Cheymongkol, reject that distinction, and say that all styles of writing constitute (Northern) Khmer heritage, for the simple reason that they are Khmer—a clear example of how Cheymongkol glosses over historical nuances in favor of an essentialized Khmer identity.

In Cambodia, the two script styles are found everywhere: in general, *mul* is used for ornamentation and *crieng* for common print. Often they appear in the same documents, as headline and text (comparable, for instance, to the ornate font of the *New York Times'* logo versus the font of its text). But historically, the only script widely used among Northern Khmer was *mul*, not *crieng*. The disparity has to do with the rise of print culture, mass literacy campaigns, and nationalism in both Cambodia and Thailand. Paitoon (1988) discusses how Khmer literacy was supplanted by Thai beginning about 100 years ago. Khmer *mul* was regarded by Northern Khmer as a sacred script, and used for religious tracts, magical tattoos, and other purposes closely tied to religion (Tsumura 2009).[8] Paitoon (1988, 95) cites a government report from 1900 that states that, even as Siamese language was being introduced, the predominant scripts in circulation were still Lao and Khmer *mul*. Following the religious reforms of 1902, Thai writing began to be taught in Surin area temple schools; secular schools also expanded rapidly in the beginning of the century, with the goal of providing universal literacy in Thai. Thai gradually displaced Khmer in temples, too, and there was a virulent expunging of Khmer literacy after the International Court of Justice awarded the ownership of Preah Vihear temple to Cambodia in 1962. Bangkok-based sangha officials ordered temples in Sisaket and Surin to burn their Khmer-language palm leaf manuscripts, but this was widely resisted.[9] The Cold War and subsequent Cambodian civil war further alienated the two countries, and Khmer literacy dropped to a low ebb, with just a few temples still clinging to its use. So, between the beginning of the twentieth century until 1960, Thai script supplanted Khmer in temples. But it never supplanted Khmer script in state education or mass media because those linguistic domains only arose in conjunction with the proliferation of Thai literacy.

Parallel processes were occurring in Cambodia. Edwards (2007) describes the rise of Khmer print literacy associated with the creation of Khmer nationalism in the colonial period. *Mul* script, as in Northern Khmer speaking regions, was regarded as magical and sacred (2007, 105). More mundane *crieng* script was designed to propagate Khmer print literacy, itself intimately bound up with the creation of Cambodian national identity and constructed in large part as a reaction against Siam and its literate practices.[10]

This explains why Northern Khmer speakers now maintain an iconic distinction between *mul* and *crieng*. Northern Khmer did have a literate form before it was eradicated by the Thai state, but, written in *mul* style, the domain of its use was (and still is) restricted almost entirely to religious functions. *Crieng*, on the other hand, was a print style disseminated in Cambodia to construct a specifically national language, and as such it has no historical connections to Northern Khmer literacy. The push for a national language in Cambodia was spurred in part as a reaction against Thai literary influence before the retrocession of Battambang and Siem Reap, at approximately the same time that Thai was being introduced and expanded in Surin and Sisaket. In short, *crieng* script in Cambodia served the same literacy functions for nation-building that Thai language and literacy served in Surin and Sisaket.

The implications here for iconicity are complex. For example, Cambodians and Northern Khmer share a vast body of traditional Khmer stories and legends. Such stories constitute, to a Northern Khmer speaker, part of their cultural heritage. But the medium in which those stories are now transmitted in Cambodia—in books printed in *crieng* script—does not. The dissonance becomes most clear-cut when Khmer literacy is being taught: there is a strong sense among the learners we interviewed that when learning *crieng* script, as Cheymongkol teaches it, they are learning it as a resource, to gain an additional skill, or simply out of interest, not as part of their own heritage. But when they then deploy that script to read traditional Khmer tales and other cultural materials, that same *crieng* text gives them access to what they consider their own heritage. Teaching Khmer literacy using Thai orthography, however, obscures the connection to a broader Khmer heritage entirely, effectively localizing Khmer identity to southern Isan, and ignoring the broader oral and literate traditions also found in Cambodia.

Summary

Observers of northeastern Thailand may find it curious that Northern Khmer speakers are so passive about linguistic rights and apathetic about their ethnic identity and heritage, given how highly politicized, and even radicalized, southern Isan has so often proved to be in other respects. Indeed, Isan is typically at the forefront of rights-claiming behavior when it comes to political enfranchisement, resource management, and even the validation of "local wisdom"—witness the assorted *"thai baan"* participatory research projects combining all three of these politicized demands (Living River Siam n.d.). But when it comes to identity politics, Northern Khmer face a tension between being proud of their ethnic Khmer heritage, on the one hand, and being "loyal" Thai citizens, on the other. The resultant apathy towards linguistic rights in general and orthographic choices in particular, we argue, stems from a combination of two key ingredients: competing orientations to language and heritage, on the one hand, and naturalized state discourses endorsing monolingualism in Thai, on the other.

Unquestionably, government-led inculcation of Thai nationalism plays a critical role here. State-driven linguistic ideologies have become hegemonic because they have become so deeply submerged into everyday practice. This is especially true in the case of education, a domain where Thai language has become so entirely naturalized as part of schooling that few think to question it, let alone contest it. Indeed, most people in rural areas still struggle to get an adequate, quality education, so linguistic rights are still largely seen as the right to Thai-language education and the social mobility it promises, not the right to instruction in or preservation of the heritage language. The largely symbolic, and ultimately anemic, state endorsement of "local wisdom" and local language preservation is ultimately bypassed by the ideological juggernaut that is education in Thai. Even the nod to nascent multiculturalism is regularly undermined by apathetic or hostile officials who either disregard it or, in the case of using a Khmer script, even characterize it as being un-Thai and subversive. Such naturalizing of Thai language education is coupled with an official denigration of Cambodian Khmer culture (Vail 2007), and a simultaneous appropriation of ancient Khmer culture into Thailand's "imperial imaginary" (Denes 2006), both of which stymie the revitalization (or construction) of an ethnic consciousness extending beyond national borders.

There is an inherent conundrum in the fact that literacy for Northern Khmer is being posited as a means to recover and revitalize a largely pre-literate past. Moreover, the potential orthographies for Northern Khmer each index different orientations to language and heritage, and force the question of whether being Northern Khmer entails being a subset of Thai, or whether being Northern Khmer can transcend national boundaries and connect to a pan-Khmer identity beyond Thailand. These orientations, in turn, connect to an array of rights-claiming behavior (or their absence). Whereas Mahidol's vision for Khmer literacy arises mainly from the perceived need for, and right to, civic inclusion among non-Thai-speaking minorities, Cheymongkol at the Khmer Language Project frames the issue of orthography as one of cultural rights and heritage. Others we encountered make no mention of rights at all—except, perhaps, for their right to a Thai-language education and as yet unrealized equity in the quality of their schools. This is not to say such people are necessarily uninterested or uninvested in their Khmer heritage; rather, by and large they do not regard ethnolinguistic heritage as an issue of rights, and they are only beginning to sense the impending loss of Northern Khmer language.

Notes

1. Some linguists, like Peter Mühlhäusler (1990, 205), dispute the necessity (and benefits) of literacy, and suggest that introducing scripts to oral languages may undermine oral traditions and thus do more harm than good.

2. The script, called *mul*, is an ornate style, and commonly distinguished from *crieng* script, which is more of a modern print style. The sociolinguistic difference between these script styles will be elaborated.

3. Note Smalley's overall orientation of "language-as-problem"—not only do minority languages potentially impede learning the national language, but language diversity inherently subverts the state.

4. For a scathing critique and summary of the Thai state's monolingual policies, see Esman 1990.

5. For example, of all these instruments, only Article 13 of the UN Declaration on the Rights of Indigenous Peoples (2007) explicitly mentions orthography. UN DRIP, however, is non-binding in international law, and even when Thailand signed it, the Thai delegate did so with the caveat that the Declaration did not create any new rights and that any benefits that flowed from the Declaration would be based on the laws and Constitution of Thailand. [See United Nations General Assembly 2007]. Thailand has not ratified other UN instruments that encourage the preservation of language diversity, such as the UNESCO Convention for the Safeguarding of the Intangible Cultural Heritage (2003) or the UNESCO Convention on the Protection and Promotion of the Diversity of Cultural Expressions (2005).

6. Skutnabb-Kangas (e.g. 1998, 2000) shows how wording concerning language rights in UN and UNESCO documents is so watered down that applying it in domains like education becomes futile. She tracks how the discussion of language changes over the course of an instrument from a clear affirmation in descriptive sections to qualified

and contingent versions in the more practical and applicable sections. For example, a descriptive section may declare that "states *shall* protect . . . linguistic identity," but the practical sections then dilute this to "states *should* take *appropriate* measures . . . *wherever possible*" (1998:6-7; italics in original).

7. Burin, despite being the officer in charge of multiculturalism for the district's classrooms, breezily opined that local languages would not die out and that it did not much matter if they did—the students all spoke Thai already. Furthermore, in Burin's view, people had the right to learn their local languages because the Ministry of Education decreed it, not because of any inherent linguistic right that people enjoyed; even then he could not see the point in teaching them. Burin was utterly apathetic, even hostile, to the idea of local languages gaining any sort of legitimacy through state education.

8. Various passages in Aymonier's Isan travel accounts (2000 [1895]) suggest that court officials could read Khmer, since Aymonier's travel letters and documents were at least partly in Khmer. Aymonier does not specify whether the letters were in *mul* or *crieng* style.

9. A common story concerning this resistance relates how the one monk who complied purportedly went blind as a result.

10. As Heder (2007, 294) summarizes it, "French administrators in dialogue with Francophone Khmer . . . saw the vernacularization of Khmer as part of this nation-saving and nation-building project, and this was intended to give Cambodia's nationalism what they called a 'national language' and thus a linguistic dimension cordoning it off from Laos, Thailand, and Vietnam. . . ."

References

Aymonier, Étienne. 2000 [1895]. *Isan Travels: Northeast Thailand's Economy in 1883–1884*. Translated by Walter E. J. Tips. Bangkok: White Lotus Press.

Billig, Michael. 1995. *Banal Nationalism*. London: Sage.

Dauenhauer, Nora Marks, and Richard Dauenhauer. 1998. "Technical, Emotional and Ideological Issues in Reversing Language Shift: Examples from Southeast Alaska." In *Endangered Languages: Current Issues and Future Prospects*, edited by Lenore A. Grenoble and Lindsey J. Whaley, 57–98. Cambridge: Cambridge University Press.

Denes, Alexandra. 2006. "Recovering Khmer Ethnic Identity from the Thai National Past: An Ethnography of the Localism Movement in Surin Province." PhD diss., Cornell University.

Dorian, Nancy. 1981. *Language Death: The Life Cycle of a Scottish Gaelic Dialect*. Philadelphia: University of Pennsylvania Press.

Edwards, Penny. 2007. *Cambodge: The Cultivation of a Nation, 1860–1945*. Honolulu: University of Hawaii Press.

Esman, Milton J. 1990. "Language Policy and Political Community in Southeast Asia." In *Language Policy and Political Development*, edited by Brian Weinstein, 185–201. Norwood, NJ: Ablex.

Gee, James Paul. 1990. *Social Linguistics and Literacies: Ideology in Discourses*. London: The Falmer Press.

Gregerson, Marilyn J. 2009. "Learning to Read in Ratanakiri: A Case Study from Northeastern Cambodia." *International Journal of Bilingual Education and Bilingualism* 12 (4): 429–47.

Grenoble, Lenore A., and Lindsay J. Whaley. 2006. *Saving Languages: An Introduction to Language Revitalization*. Cambridge: Cambridge University Press.

Heder, Steve. "Cambodia." 2007. In *Language and National Identity in Asia*, edited by Andrew Simpson, 288–311. Oxford: Oxford University Press.

Hornberger, Nancy H. 1998. "Language Policy, Language Education, Language Rights: Indigenous, Immigrant, and International Perspectives." *Language in Society* 27 (4): 439–58.

Huffman, Franklin E. 1970. *Cambodian System of Writing and Beginning Reader*. New Haven, CT: Yale University Press.

Irvine, Judith, and Susan Gal. 2000. "Language Ideology and Linguistic Differentiation" In *Regimes of Language: Ideologies, Polities and Identities*, edited by Paul V. Kroskrity, 35–83. Oxford: James Curry.

Jenner, Philip N. 1974. "Observation on the Surin Dialect of Khmer." In *South-East Asian Linguistic Studies*, edited by Nguyen Dang Liem, 61–73. Canberra: Department of Linguistics, Research School of Pacific Studies, Australian National University.

Jory, Patrick. 1999. "Political Decentralisation and the Resurgence of Regional Identities in Thailand." *Australian Journal of Social Issues* 34 (4): 337–52.

Jungck, S., and Kajornsin Boonreang. 2003. "'Thai Wisdom' and GloCalization: Negotiating the Global and the Local in Thailand's National Education Reform." In *Local Meanings, Global Schooling: Anthropology and World Culture Theory*, edited by K. Anderson-Levitt, 27–49. New York: Palgrave Macmillan.

Kosonen, Kimmo. 2008. "Literacy in Local Languages in Thailand: Language Maintenance in a Globalised World." *International Journal of Bilingual Education and Bilingualism* 11 (2): 170–88.

Living River Siam. n.d. *Thai Baan Research*. Accessed at: http://www.livingriversiam. org/work/tb_research_en.htm.

Hong, Lysa. 2000. "Twenty Years of *Sinlapa Watthanatham*: Cultural Politics in Thailand in the 1980s and 1990s." *Journal of Southeast Asian Studies* 31 (1): 26–47.

McDaniel, Justin. 2008. *Gathering Leaves and Lifting Words: Histories of Buddhist Monastic Education in Laos and Thailand*. Seattle: University of Washington Press.

Mühlhäusler, Peter. 1990. "'Reducing' Pacific Languages to Writings." In *Ideologies of Language*, edited by John Earl Joseph and Talbot J. Taylor, 189–205. London: Routledge.

Munger, Frank. 2006. "Culture, Power and Law: Thinking About the Anthropology of Rights in Thailand in an Era of Globalization." *New York Law School Law Review* 51: 817–38.

Paitoon Mikusol. 1988. "Education and Socio-Cultural Assimilation in Northeastern Thailand." *Asian Review* 2: 87–110.

Pike, Kenneth L. 1947. *Phonemics: A Technique for Reducing Languages to Writing*. Ann Arbor: University of Michigan Press.

Ricento, Thomas. 2005. "Problems with the 'Language-as-Resource' Discourse in the Promotion of Heritage Languages in the U.S.A." *Journal of Sociolinguistics* 9 (3): 348–68.

Ruiz, Richard. 1984. "Orientations in Language Planning." *Journal of the National Association for Bilingual Education* 8 (2): 15–34.

Sangrunee Meeporn. 1995 [2538]. "The Abilities in Reading Thai of Matayomsuksa I Students Using Different Dialects in the Expanding Basic Education Project under the Office of Surin Provincial Primary Education." Master's thesis, Sukhothai Thammathirat University.

Scollon, Ron, and Suzanne Scollon. 2004. *Nexus Analysis: Discourse and the Emerging Internet*. London: Routledge.

Scribner, Sylvia, and Michael Cole. 1981. *The Psychology of Literacy*. Cambridge, MA: Harvard University Press.

Sebba, Mark. 2007. *Spelling and Society: The Culture and Politics of Orthography Around the World*. Cambridge: Cambridge University Press.

Sidwell, Paul. 2008. "The Khom Script of the Kommodam Rebellion." *International Journal of the Sociology of Language* 192: 15–25.

Skutnabb-Kangas, Tove. 1998. "Language Rights and Human Wrongs: A Future for Diversity?" *Language Sciences* 20 (1): 5–27.

———. 2000. *Linguistic Genocide in Education, or Worldwide Diversity and Human Rights?* Mahwah, NJ: Lawrence Erlbaum Associates.

Smalley, William A. 1976. "Writing Systems in Thailand's Marginal Languages: History and Policy." In *Phonemes and Orthography: Language Planning in Ten Minority Languages of Thailand*, edited by William A. Smalley, 1–24. Canberra: Department of Linguistics, Research School of Pacific Studies, Australian National University.

———. 1988. "Multilingualism in the Northern Khmer Population of Thailand." *Language Sciences* 10 (2): 395–408.

———. 1994. *Linguistic Diversity and National Unity: Language Ecology in Thailand.* Chicago: University of Chicago Press.

Smalley, William A., and Nina Wimuttikosol. 1998. "Another Hmong Messianic Script and Its Texts." *Written Language and Literacy* 1: 103–28.

Spolsky, Bernard. 2004. *Language Policy.* Cambridge: Cambridge University Press.

Street, Brian V. 1984. *Literacy in Theory and Practice.* Cambridge: Cambridge University Press.

———. 1995. *Social Literacies: Critical Approaches to Literacy in Development, Ethnography, and Education.* London: Longman.

Suwilai Premsirat. 1998. *Using the Local Vernacular for Preserving Local Culture and Producing Reading Materials for Non-Thai Populations: The Northern Khmer Case Study.* Bangkok: Center for Language and Rural Development, Mahidol University.

Suwilai Premsirat and Sricampa Sophana. 1990. *Formulating a Thai-Based Northern Khmer Orthography.* Salaya, Thailand: ILCRD, Mahidol University.

Tambiah, Stanley J. 1968. "Literacy in a Buddhist Village in North-East Thailand." In *Literacy in Traditional Societies,* edited by Jack Goody, 85–131. Cambridge: Cambridge University Press.

Thomas, Dorothy. 1989. "Changing the Northern Khmer Orthography." *Notes on Literacy (SIL)* 57: 47–59.

Thomas, David. 1990 (B.E. 2533). "On the 'Language' Status of Northern Khmer." *Journal of Language and Culture (Phasa lae watthanatham)* 9 (1): 98–106.

Tsumura, Fumihiko. 2009. "Magical Use of Traditional Scripts in Northeastern Thai Villages." In *Written Cultures in Mainland Southeast Asia,* edited by Masao Kashinaga, 63–77. Osaka: National Museum of Ethnology.

UNESCO Convention for the Safeguarding of the Intangible Cultural Heritage. 2003. Paris: UNESCO. MISC/2003/CLT/CH/14. Accessed at: http://unesdoc.unesco.org/images/0013/001325/132540e.pdf.

UNESCO Convention on the Protection and Promotion of the Diversity of Cultural Expressions. 2005. CLT-2005/CONVENTION DIVERSITE-CULT REV.2 Paris: UNESCO. Accessed at: http://unesdoc.unesco.org/images/0014/001429/142919e.pdf.

United Nations Declaration on the Rights of Indigenous Peoples. 2007. NY: UN. G.A. Res. 61/295, Annex, U.N. Doc. A/RES/61/295 (13 September). Accessed at http://www.un.org/esa/socdev/unpfii/en/drip.html.

United Nations General Assembly. 2007. *General Assembly Adopts Declaration on Rights of Indigenous Peoples, 13 September 2007.* GA/10612. Sixty-first General Assembly Plenary 107th & 108th Meetings (AM & PM). New York: UN, Department of Public Information, News and Media Division. Accessed at: http://www.un.org/News/Press/docs/2007/ga10612.doc.htm.

Unseth, Peter. 2005. "Sociolinguistic Parallels between Choosing Scripts and Languages." *Written Language and Literacy* 8 (1): 19–42.

———. 2008. "The Sociolinguistics of Script Choice: An Introduction." *International Journal of the Sociology of Language* 192: 1–4.

Vail, Peter. 2006. "Can a Language of a Million Speakers Be Endangered?: Language Shift and Apathy among Northern Khmer Speakers in Thailand." *International Journal of the Sociology of Language* 178 (1): 135–47.

———. 2007. "Thailand's Khmer as 'Invisible Minority': Language, Ethnicity and Cultural Politics in North-Eastern Thailand." *Asian Ethnicity* 8 (2): 111–30.

———. 2010. "Cambodian Views of Thailand: Identifying Discourse and Ideology in Social and Linguistic Practice." Bangkok: Thai Research Fund.

7

Negotiating with the Center: Diversity and Local Cultures in Thailand

———∞∞∞———

Sirijit Sunanta

Introduction

In the past two decades, there has been a shift towards a more inclusive notion of Thai national identity and a new emphasis on pluralized and localized "Thai-ness." Ethnic and cultural diversity have become important subjects in Thai academic and popular discourses. Thai state agencies, following international organizations and nongovernmental organizations, have started to make use of the vocabulary of cultural diversity, local wisdom, and community-based development (Connors 2005a). The 2007 Thai Constitution protects community rights to local culture and resource management. The state allocates significant resources for revitalizing local and ethnic cultures, supporting local livelihoods, and regenerating local histories. This trend is both a response to an international discourse that promotes cultural rights for ethnic minorities, as well as a product of the contemporary local context—the democratization movement, the growth of civil society, and the increasing sense of national security after the Cold War.

However, when discussing diversity and local heritage in Thailand, many relevant parties, particularly state agencies, cannot abandon the dominant national discourse in which Thai-ness is rooted in Bangkok-centered narratives and institutions. In Thailand, diverse local cultures are often portrayed as the subjects of royal support and patronage; the Thai king's fatherly benevolence is seen to reach across the whole kingdom, transcending ethnic and regional lines. In May 2010, the Office of the National Culture Commission (ONCC), together with the Network of Indigenous Peoples in Thailand, combined the occasion of the UN World Day for Cultural Diversity for Dialogue and Development with the sixtieth anniversary of King Bhumibol's coronation to honor the king as the prime supporter of cultural diversity in Thailand. In Thai official cultural policies, the recognition of cultural and minority rights seems to be subsumed under the more dominant trend towards economic and developmental localism, which has a tendency to perpetuate state-centric nationalism (Connors 2005a, 2005b). State promotion of local cultures in Thailand uses, at least in part, a rural development paradigm rooted in the Thai and US governments' anti-Communist campaigns of the 1950s–1970s.[1] As will be illustrated in this chapter, the preservation and revitalization of local cultures often have developmental ends—tourism, self-sufficiency economy, local industry, and business—that do not directly promote consciousness of cultural rights or egalitarian relationships among ethnic groups and between ethnic minorities and the state.

In this chapter I will explore the interface between the international cultural rights framework and Thai understandings of ethnicity and rights through a study of a Phu Tai village in Mukdahan province in Thailand's northeast region. The Phu Tai, who speak a Tai language that differs from the Thai-Lao language spoken by the majority of the population in the northeast and from central Thai, the national language of Thailand, are recognized as a *klum chatiphan*, or ethnic group, in Thailand.[2] My study examines the ways in which a growing trend towards economic and developmental localism challenges or reifies center-periphery relations in Thailand and how that affects the ways and domains in which rights are articulated. Drawing on ethnographic data from the village, the study takes into account villagers' agency in the context of Thailand's development anxiety and the domination of the official nationalist discourse. I will show that Phu Tai villagers have maneuvered and benefited from the state-centric development discourse and from Thailand's pervasive hierarchical social structure.

The concept of ethnic relations is highly context-specific, and to begin to understand the politics of diversity in Thailand, local conceptions of race, ethnicity, majority, minority, self/other, and citizenship will need to be explored.

Race, Ethnicity, and the Politics of Diversity in Thailand

Literature on ethnicity in Thailand and Southeast Asia indicates that "race" and "ethnicity" in a scientific, biological sense were not prominent social categories before the beginning of the modern nation-state in the nineteenth and twentieth centuries. It was the term "civilization" that marked the differentiations between the social positions of different groups. Cultural differences in the Siamese empire, as in other parts of the premodern world, were understood in terms of locality, kinship, and relationship to a "civilization" transmitted primarily through authoritative textual traditions (Keyes 2008). Indic influences, particularly the adherence to Theravada Buddhism and the possession of one of several Tai scripts, constituted "civilization" in the premodern Siamese empire (Turton 2000). Pointing out incongruent understandings of "race" in the perception of Western colonizers and local peoples in Southeast Asia in the early twentieth century, Anthony Reid (2010, 32–34) described census-taking in colonial Malaya as the British imposing the "scientific" category of race on a population who were unaware of it, thus causing frustration and confusion for both census-takers and local peoples. Scholars of Southeast Asia have noted that ethnic categories were unstable and non-biological. The term *Tai* could be associated with both ethnic and social status (Turton 2000a, 13, quoting Jit Phumisak) in relation to the term *kha,* which referred to uncivilized peoples who lived in the peripheries of Tai states. Ethnographic studies in the region have shown that peoples could and did shift their "ethnic" identities as they relocated and switched farming methods (Leach 1970; Evans 2000).

The system that operated in the Siamese empire of marking social identities by a group's relationship to "civilization" was inherently hierarchical. The ruling group constituted the "civilized" people who lived in the *mueang* (town, city) or the center of civilization, while peasants lived in the *ban* (roughly translated as village, or group of households), which was considered a constituency of the *mueang.* The wild, uncivilized folk were those who lived in the forest, often in the highland frontiers where state power was weak. Thongchai Winichakul (2000) convincingly argues that because of their geographical and cultural distance from the civilized center, the *khon bannok* (rural peasants) and the *khon pa* (wild people) constituted the Other for the Siamese ruling elite.

The premodern Siamese empire was both hierarchical and heterogeneous. Its subjects included natives, migrants, and war captives who inherited diverse cultural heritages. Under a tributary system where weaker states submitted tribute as a symbol of subordination to stronger states, Siamese kings once considered themselves kings of the Lao, Mon, Khmer, and to some extent, the Malay (Keyes 2008). Subordination in the tributary system was more symbolic and ritualistic than actual: in most cases, states maintained relative autonomy under the rule of local lords.

Key changes took place when a new concept of state was imposed through Western influence during the peak of French and British colonization in Southeast Asia in the nineteenth century and at the end of Western colonization in this region after World War II. In the Western concept, the modern nation-state requires sovereignty over a fixed boundary and, ideally, a homogenous population. In order to escape colonization, King Chulalongkorn of Siam decided to play by the rules of the day and started a reform that converted the Siamese empire into a modern nation-state. In an attempt to prevent the loss of territory to Western colonizing nations, Bangkok centralized power and integrated its former tributary states into the modern Siamese state in a manner that Loos (2006, 2010) calls "competing colonization." The "multiethnic" subjects of the empire were thus converted into citizens of the new nation-state in which their different cultural heritages did not bar them from being part of the Siamese (later Thai) citizenry (Streckfuss 1993). Under Bangkok-centric nationalism and pro-integration policies, their differences were to be viewed as "ethnoregional"—variants of the common national heritage (Keyes, 1967, 2008).

Like the definition of Siamese subject-hood in the past, Thai-ness is cultural rather than biological. From the early days of Thai nationalism, King Vajiravudh posited that what the Thai people shared as a national heritage was a common language (Thai), a common religion (Buddhism), and a shared subservience to the Bangkok (Chakri) monarchy. Any person could "become Thai" no matter what their background, as long as they spoke Thai (even if they also spoke other languages), adhered to Buddhism (no matter which other particular religious customs they might also observe), and were subjects of the king as manifest in their citizenship (Keyes 2008, 22, 24). The rather homogeneous character of the Thai citizenry today is the result of national compulsory education, language policies, the construction of national historical narratives, the establishment of national and religious (Buddhist) holidays, and the media. Although the Thai state has adopted a largely inclusive and integrative approach to diversity, there are groups who have fallen out of the national imaginary of Thailand as the land of various strands of Tai or Thai peoples, namely the Malay Muslims in the south and the non-Tai-speaking hill populations. While people from the provinces consider themselves Thai, they are conscious of their marginal place in the dominant national narratives that place Bangkok at the top of the cultural hierarchy and as the norm from which regional variants differ.[3] Historically, the inclusive approach that Bangkok rulers have adopted was not an act of mere benevolence or openness, but a strategy by the Bangkok elites to ward off external threats and retain their power.

Introducing Ban Phu and the Phu Tai

My research was focused in Ban Phu village, Nong Sung district, Mukdahan province. Consisting of 250 households, the villagers of Ban Phu are mostly related to each other and are of the Phu Tai ethnic group, one of the major ethnic groups in northeast Thailand. Ban Phu is known as an outstanding model for community development projects and has won a number of titles in this regard. More recently, the village has also been chosen as a site for community culture projects. In 1998, Ban Phu was selected as Mukdahan's "Best Cultural Village." In 2007, it was chosen as a pilot village for the Office of the National Culture Commission's Local Historians Training Project. Ban Phu won the Best Community Industry Award in 2008 for its outstanding community tourism business. In 2009, the Bank for Agriculture and Agricultural Cooperatives nominated Ban Phu as a Model Sufficiency Economy Village Level 3; the village received a cash award from Mukdahan's *Wattanatham Thai Sai Yai Chumchon* Project the same year.

Entitled to full Thai citizenship rights, the Phu Tai in northeast Thailand today are descendants of Phu Tai migrants forced to move from the west side of the Mekong River during the war between Siam and King Anu of Vientiane in the first half of the nineteenth century. They were among tens of thousands of Lao, Phuan, Saek, Kaloeng, and So group members relocated in Siam's attempt to empty towns and cities on the western side of the Mekong to permanently destroy the Lao kingdom and cut off supply lines to Vietnam, Siam's main competitor at the time. Groups of Phu Tai were settled in what are today Mukdahan, Nakhon Phanom, Sakon Nakhon, Kalasin, and Udon Thani provinces. Speaking a language in the Tai-language family, they constitute a minority group among the dominantly Thai-Lao speaking population of the northeast. Despite their active political role in the Free Thai Movement and the Communist Party of Thailand (CPT) during and after World War II (Piyamas 2002), the Phu Tai were generally perceived as a "good" and non-threatening ethnic group in post-Cold War Thailand. They have become known in the wider Thai society as the *Wiang Ping*[4] of the Isan region for their exotic culture and beautiful women. Phu Tai silk textiles, *pha prae wa* (brocaded silk scarves), produced under Queen Sirikit's Arts and Crafts Project, are known as "the queen of silk textiles" and have become a highly prized commodity.

In rural areas of the multiethnic province of Mukdahan, the Phu Tai seem to fare better than other ethnic groups in terms of their educational attainment and overall economic status. Ban Phu is a case in point. Although agriculture remains the main livelihood, almost every household has a child who has obtained higher education and is employed in a government office. This trend is not new. Writing in the 1960s about Ban Nong Sung, a Phu Tai village six kilometers from Ban Phu, Kirsch (1967) noted that the villagers were eager to assimilate into the Thai nation and to participate in social and geographical mobility particularly through secular education and employment in government offices.

Under Thailand's administrative centralization, government officials are considered *chao nai*, or the ruling class. The term *chao nai* has an ethnic connotation since the majority of state officials have been sent from Bangkok to rule the provinces, and the ruling class uses central Thai language and etiquette to deal with official matters (Diller 1991). Thai class structure has been transformed over decades of economic development and democratization, but this notion of ethnicized class differentiation prevails. Ban Phu villagers, the key informants for this study, work hard to give their children education so that the younger generation can become *chao nai*: as the local saying goes, "send them off to school so they can become bosses" (*song pai rian nangsue hai pen chao pen nai*). A senior member of Ban Phu mentioned that some Phu Tai government employees in the village, particularly teachers, use central Thai when talking to their children because these parents want to raise their children as *chao nai*, or educated urban people.[5] Although entitled to legal citizenship, the Phu Tai feel that they inhabit a marginalized position in Thai class, ethnic, and spatial hierarchies compared to the *chao nai* from Bangkok, who are entitled to full Thai cultural citizenship and enjoy greater access to cultural resources and national belonging.[6]

Building Ties with Officials and Higher Institutions

The location of Ban Phu in the CPT's area of influence during the Cold War put the villagers in constant contact with military personnel who, according to the villagers, frequently visited Ban Phu partly because of the reputation of the beauty of Ban Phu girls. Since the 1960s, Ban Phu villagers have built connections with high-ranking military officers, provincial government officials, and wealthy merchants from Mukdahan town by inviting them to join *kathin* and *pha pa* Buddhist fundraising events at the village. These public events were organized by the Khiri Nakhon Youth Group, a group led by young schoolteachers who were among Ban Phu's first generation to obtain higher education. Formed in 1968, the group's main goal was to mobilize community development. The funds raised in the *kathin* and *pha pa* events went to support the village temple and other public facilities.[7]

I was told by villagers in their sixties on more than one occasion that General Saiyud Kerdphol, chair of the Thai-American Friendship Foundation and former director of the Communist Suppression Operations Command, became acquainted with Ban Phu during the 1960s through Sing Pothisai, a Phu Tai schoolteacher from a nearby village who was arrested and sent to Bangkok for alleged involvement in Communist activities. According to the villagers, Uncle Sing, as he was called, proved that he was not a Communist, and the military asked him to work with the Communist Suppression Operations Command at their Suan Ruenrudi office.[8] Uncle Sing brought General Saiyud Kerdphol into close contact with Ban Phu, an association that Ban Phu villagers highly welcomed. Association with high-ranking government and military officials was very beneficial for Ban Phu's development.

Since the 1960s, Ban Phu villagers have aligned themselves with Thai institutions of power; becoming *chao nai* or forging alliances with them is a source of pride.[9] Achan Sawat (pseudonym), an informal leader of Ban Phu, proudly noted that Ban Phu has had the privilege of receiving *chao nai* and building connections with them:

> From 1965 on, Ban Phu received *pha pa* groups. There were important people who came in and built relationships with Ban Phu people. They helped out with many things. For example, in 1965 soldiers came in and helped build the roof for our school. Ban Phu has had the opportunity to welcome important people, even General Saiyud Kerdphol and high-ranking soldiers such as Wing Commander Prakob Pakaranang ,who frequently visited Ban Phu and almost became one with the Ban Phu people (laugh). If Ban Phu needed anything, he would quickly respond.[10]

An audience Ban Phu villagers had with the king and queen in 1974 is the story most often recited to Ban Phu's visitors. According to Ban Phu villagers' accounts, it was their initiative to travel to Bangkok and seek an audience with the king and queen. The story began in 1973 when the king and queen paid a royal visit to an area near Ban Phu and "Grandma" Suthin from Ban Phu, then thirty years old, was in the crowd wearing handwoven silk. Queen Sirikit came to her and commented approvingly on "Grandma" Suthin's silk *pha sin* (women's wraparound skirt). The Queen asked Grandma Suthin to weave a piece of beautiful silk and send it to the palace, which she agreed to do. When Ban Phu villagers heard the story, the village headman along with other villagers saw this as an opportunity. They decided that Ban Phu villagers would present their silks to their majesties in person instead of sending them. The villagers then asked General Saiyud Kerdphol to help them to seek an audience. Taking this event as an example, Achan Sawat commented that Ban Phu villagers have been progressive thinkers compared to people from other villages:

> There were people from different villages in the crowd when the king and queen visited. The queen was interested in silks from Ban Phu and elsewhere. But Ban Phu villagers thought outside the box. Once we knew that the queen had asked Mrs. Suthin to weave the silk, the village headman thought about seeking a royal audience.

During the audience with the monarch, when asked if they needed anything, Ban Phu villagers told their majesties that they wished to have a high school near their village so that going to school would be easier for Ban Phu children. The Ban Phu villagers' wish was realized. The construction of the high school was completed in 1975, and the military performed a parachute show to celebrate the opening of the school.

Figure 7.1. A large vinyl poster at Ban Phu Community Learning Center shows Ban Phu villagers' audience with the king and queen of Thailand at Chitralada Palace in 1974. Photo by Sirijit Sunanta, 26 May 2011.

Considering Cold War politics surrounding Ban Phu's relations with the military and the palace during the 1960s and 1970s, the generosity and attention that Ban Phu received was part of the military's strategy to control the influence of Communism in the area by trying to win the hearts of rural people and keeping close contact with them. Craig Reynolds suggests that the Community Development Department, opened in the 1960s, was a mechanism through which the Cold War Thai state tightened its control over rural communities as well as aiding in monitoring them (Reynolds 2003).

Whether Ban Phu villagers were aware of the military's agenda was not clear, but the villagers certainly took advantage of the situation.

Eager for Development

Ban Phu villagers have been preoccupied with development since the 1960s. The Cold War period is not a very distant past for Ban Phu villagers in their 50s and 60s, former members of Khirinakhon Youth Groups, who are still active as leaders in the community in 2011. Four decades ago, Ban Phu's Khirinakhon Youth Group and its sister group, Thai Phithak Thin, set out to bring development to the village. Ban Phu's members considered their village a united and progressive community. Led by the Khirinakhon Youth Group and the Thai Phithak Thin Group, the villagers developed participatory mechanisms, such as holding meetings to reach collective decisions about village activities. A senior villager recalled that, "We had a meeting every Friday to discuss the village's business." Ban Phu's collective strength and democratic community mechanisms were devoted to community economic development. Connections with the military and the palace were also exploited towards this end. The story villagers in their 50s and 60s often proudly recall is of the villagers' assertive demand for and timely acquisition of electricity, schools, and paved roads—key development infrastructure in the 1960s and 70s.

"Aunt" Wassana, sixty years old, previously a member of the Khirinakhon Youth Group and now the head of Ban Phu's cotton weaving group, shared her opinions about her village in the 1960s and 1970s, as well as Khirinakhon Youth Group's role in village development:

> We Ban Phu villagers are serious people. If we want something we have to get it. We wanted a school and we got one. Some [provincial] officers said that we were just a small village of rural people; we would never get our own school. They said the government would give a school to Ban Nong Sung [where Nong Sung's District Office is located], but we thought if Ban Nong Sung got a school we had to get one too. And we did get a school, thanks to the Khirinakhon Youth Group. We were highly motivated people (*fai raeng*). We also fought to get a road. We asked for explosives to blow

up a huge boulder so we could use it to build a road. We went to Bangkok
to ask for explosives. After we got explosives, we brought in a truck to build
the road with those rocks.

Aunt Wassana talked about her own contribution in the building of the
road:

> I went to Bangkok to see the doctor. I stopped by to see Uncle Sing. I was
> a radical after all when it came to helping the villagers. I discussed with
> Uncle Sing and novice Sinthu about what we could do with that boulder if
> we wanted to use it to build a road. Uncle Sing took me to Suan Ruenrudi.
> We already had some friends there. When we got to the gate, we gave the
> guard our name card, and [General Saiyud's] aide came to get us, joking
> that we were Communists coming from Khamchaii district.

Ban Phu villagers actively joined government-initiated development
projects that focused on rural development. They worked closely with the
Community Development Office in forming occupational groups such as
weaving groups. Since the 1970s, Ban Phu has been one of the villages under
the Voluntary Development and Self Defense Village Program, a government-
funded program that closely links development and security concerns. On
the assumption that economic development is the solution to the nation's
security problems, this program targets mostly rural villages in sensitive areas;
in the 1970s, this included many villages in the northeast. Apart from forming
a set of special village committees, villages under the Voluntary Development
and Self Defense Village Program received paramilitary training. Apparently
Ban Phu did well under this program: in 1988 it was recognized as the best
Voluntary Development and Self Defense Village in the northeast region.

The villagers have adopted a series of developmental initiatives and
techniques from outside, mostly those introduced by the Community
Development Office, which they combine with their own ideas and
innovations. A village cooperative, weaving groups, and handicraft-making
groups have been set up. When the idea of the "Sufficiency Economy"
emerged as the dominant official discourse, Ban Phu was selected by the
Community Development Office as a site for the "Model Village in Sufficiency
Economy Program" in 2006. And as local culture gains momentum in Thai

state policies, the villagers are mobilizing this trend to their advantage, most visibly in new tourism and homestay projects.

Culture for Economic Development: Ban Phu Homestay Project

The Ban Phu Homestay Project exemplifies the way in which culture and development have been interwoven in Thailand's rural policies. The Nong Sung district Community Development Office introduced the homestay project to Ban Phu in 2007. The first guests Ban Phu received were a group of 168 Community Development Office staff members from seven northeastern provinces, who visited Ban Phu on an official trip to learn about its community development and Sufficiency Economy projects. After the inaugural visit, Ban Phu continues to provide a site for official and educational tourism, receiving guests who visit in groups mostly from local and provincial administrative organizations, schools, and other government offices.

Once the visitors get off their bus at Ban Phu, they are greeted and handed fresh flower garlands by villagers dressed in Phu Tai costumes. A drum dance parade leads the visitors to the Community Learning Center, located within the village temple. Here, an informal Ban Phu leader introduces the village to the visitors, giving a brief history of the village and describing the villagers' activities and development projects. The visitors then tour the village to view Ban Phu's Sufficiency Economy activities. The highlight of the visit is a Phu Tai reception dinner accompanied by music and performances. Villagers welcome the guests with the Phu Tai blessing ceremony. Most available village members participate in these guest-welcoming activities, especially the elderly, women, and children, for which they receive payment in return. The compensation ranges from twenty to over one hundred baht, depending on the number of visitors in each group. The village's products—hand-sewn Phu Tai-style shirts, sarongs, *sin*, handwoven cotton shoulder cloths, and other handicrafts—are displayed for sale during the guest visits. The Ban Phu Homestay Project has proven profitable; in 2007, Ban Phu's total homestay income was 1,856,660 baht.

Some aspects of Phu Tai culture—music, dances, and dress—have been revived for tourism purposes. The villagers put together their memories, inventions, and imaginations when they designed the Phu Tai "uniforms" that they wear when receiving guests. They decided that a woman would wear a blue or black Phu Tai-style top and a particular woven pattern of cotton *sin* when receiving visitors. In the past, Ban Phu's women's *sin* came in different woven patterns; the particular one they have chosen to use for guest receptions was formerly worn only by older women. The male guest-welcoming outfit is a Phu Tai-style shirt and a cotton sarong. In the past Ban Phu men often wore indigo-dyed cotton pants. But since indigo-dyed cotton shirts and pants (*mohom*) are already well known as local cultural products from Phrae province (in northern Thailand), Ban Phu villagers sought to construct their own trademark costume.

Ban Phu's tourism is special in that the village offers official and educational tourism experiences mostly for groups of government employees. Approximately half of the visiting groups are brought to the village through the Community Development Office. Ban Phu tries to reach out beyond the

Figure 7.2 Ban Phu villagers in Phu Tai traditional clothes greet their homestay visitors. Photo by Sirijit Sunanta, 14 October, 2010.

existing target group, but faces significant limitations. Having become geared toward community development, Ban Phu has not positioned itself well for commercial tourism. Development activities and Sufficiency Economy projects do not attract individual urban visitors, who seek more exciting and exotic escapes. Compared to hill populations in the north, the Phu Tai are too developed and domesticated for ethnic tourism.

As a result of the Community Development Office's continuous campaigns, villages and communities across Thailand have produced local products often with no clear marketing guidelines. A member of a weaving group in Ban Phu commented that the Community Development Office actively promotes the production of local goods but does not pay enough attention to design and marketing. More often than not, the consumers of local products are local and provincial government officials. The Ban Phu silk-weaving group supplies their invented *lai kaeo mukda* silk, a symbol of Mukdahan province, to provincial government officials of various ranks who are bound by provincial government policies to wear *lai kaeo mukda* silk on Thursdays. In neighboring Kalasin province, government officials are required to put on *pha phrae wa* silk, Kalasin's provincial product, on Fridays. From production to consumption, the local culture industries are closely linked with the government sector.

The promotion of the local culture industry, including tourism, contributes to the revival of Phu Tai weaving, dress, and performances, but not to all aspects of the Phu Tai heritage. Villagers noted that the Phu Tai language is still spoken in the family and community, but is changing rapidly as younger Phu Tai speakers use more central Thai terms in their speech. Some young children do not speak Phu Tai at home. Ban Phu villagers have almost completely lost their ability to read the ancient Lao Buddhist palm leaf manuscripts that the previous generations left them. Traditional *yao* healing practices have already disappeared from Ban Phu. The younger generations are reluctant to continue the practices of *yao* healing and traditional medicine because of the strict adherence to bodily regulations and rules it requires for persons dealing with the spirit world.[11]

Demanding Recognition?

Having benefited from development projects and connections with state and military institutions, most Ban Phu villagers do not feel that the state discriminates against them or their culture. Asked if she feels state policies marginalize the Phu Tai, Pi Cho, a district cultural officer who is herself a Phu Tai, immediately replies, "No, I have never felt that way. We are proud to be Thai. We are not *chon klum noi* [ethnic minority]." The term *chon klum noi* seems to be reserved for those who cannot fully assimilate into the national imaginary of Thai citizens, such as the non-Tai-speaking highland ethnic groups (*chao khao*). The Phu Tai feel that they are not the most marginalized group in Thailand's ethnic and cultural hierarchy. In the multiethnic northeast region, the Phu Tai view themselves as more civilized or developed than the Bru and So people whose languages are not in the Tai language family. Portraying the Phu Tai as needing minority rights, the Phu Tai feel, is akin to grouping them with the *chao khao*. They reject this as a grave misunderstanding of the Phu Tai perspective. A Ban Phu member tried to correct me when I brought up the issue of ethnic relations and cultural rights: "We are the Phu Tai ethnic group, we are not *chao khao*!" Even among the Phu Tai, Ban Phu villagers seem to differentiate themselves from Phu Tai in other villages on the basis of class and their relative degree of progress. The view of an informal leader of Ban Phu toward his own village is that, "[Among the Phu Tai from the west side of the Mekong], we are the descendants of the ruling class. We value education and we have progressive ideas. We are different from Phu Tai from the periphery [of the Phu Tai civilization's center]." Ban Phu villagers are willing to assimilate into the Thai nation in order to seek advancement within the national system. Kirsch (1967, 57) noted this trend in Ban Nong Sung back in the 1960s:

> The Phu Thai of today do not look back to their past as a "golden age" of Phu Thai separateness. If anything, there is a degree of self-satisfaction as they see themselves and their children becoming "more civilized"—which is interpreted as becoming more "Thai-ized." This is not to say that they have repudiated their Phu Thai-ness, or that they see no incompatibility with being both simultaneously. Being a Phu Thai is merely being a special kind of a Thai.

While Ban Phu villagers have explicitly demanded rights to education and development, locating cultural rights is more complicated. The Ban Phu high school teaches a local curriculum in accordance with the Ministry of Education's guidelines, but the school chooses not to teach Phu Tai language. Courses with local cultural content in the curriculum are devoted to cultural performances and cooking, useful skills for Ban Phu's tourism projects. A deputy headman and father said he considers enhancing children's English language skills more important than including the Phu Tai language in the school curriculum. Generally, villagers do not express anxiety over the loss of their Phu Tai identity. Many say the Phu Tai language will not disappear, as it is still spoken in every household in the village, although the vocabulary has changed over time. At the conclusion of the ONCC's project on Local Historians Training, villagers' interest in compiling local history subsided.

The Phu Tai's relationship with the Thai state today is still framed by the legacy of premodern hierarchical relations among groups and between citizens and the state. In premodern Southeast Asian inter-state relations, submission of weaker states to stronger powers and multiple allegiances were not uncommon; in fact they were important survival strategies for weaker states. According to Kirsch, the narrative of the Phu Tai migration legend illustrates the normalization of flexible allegiances that explains the ease with which the Phu Tai on the east bank of the Mekong shifted their allegiance from Chao Anu of Vientiane to the king of Siam in the nineteenth century. Ban Phu's locally constructed village history recognizes that the ancestors of Ban Phu villagers came from the west bank of the Mekong River, which is today the Lao People's Democratic Republic, but the political background of the relocation and any intimation that force was involved are not acknowledged. Today, Ban Phu villagers explicitly display their allegiance to the Thai nation and their submission to the Thai king, most visibly through the decoration of Ban Phu's Community Learning Center, where the Thai flag, a Buddha image, portraits of the king and queen, portraits of General Saiyud Kerdphol and Uncle Sing Pothisai, as well as the image of Thao Suranari's monument,[12] are prominently exhibited.

Memories of oppressive relations between villagers and the state, or state officials, are not completely absent. On rare occasions, the story about the forced relocation from the west bank of the Mekong comes up. During a quiet conversation, Achan Sawat revealed to me his empathy towards nearby

CPT villages during the peak of the Cold War, acknowledging that those villagers were heavily oppressed by state officials in ways similar to the Thai government's handling of the conflicts in southern Thailand today. He also relayed his memory from the 1970s when police and forestry officers hunted down villagers who cut down trees to build houses, but secretly cooperated with investors to cut down trees on a massive scale for their own enrichment. Aunt Wassana briefly mentioned the death of a Ban Phu villager who was shot dead in his own house by a mysterious gunman one night during the peak of the Cold War. The man had been sick and bound to his bed, and the villagers believed that he was killed by the authorities, who mistook him for another man in a neighboring village with the same name. The execution of those suspected of involvement in Communist and anti-government activities was not uncommon. These resentments have not developed into collective actions against injustice and state control, however. Unlike the celebratory stories about Ban Phu villagers' audience with the king and queen in 1974 and the connections with high-ranking military and administrative officials, these negative memories of the state and state officials are hardly ever recounted publicly.

While Ban Phu villagers are not overly concerned about their cultural rights, they firmly guard their rights to political participation. The villagers actively participate in local and national politics and closely follow national political news in the media. During Thailand's post-2005 political conflicts, Ban Phu villagers actively voiced their political opinions among families and neighbors, recognizing that national politics greatly affects their lives in the village. Ban Phu's voter turnout for the national general election in 2007 was as high as 78 percent, and some villagers strongly expressed their resentment of the 2006 military coup that overthrew the elected government. About ten men from the village joined the Red Shirt protests in Bangkok in 2010. Ban Phu members and other northeastern villagers' strong support for participatory democracy reveals the conflicting and competing discourses about the Thai social order and national imaginary, as well as the divergent meanings of citizenship. The contestation over the kind of citizenship Ban Phu villagers should aspire to is manifested in the village head's and informal leaders' ambivalence about Ban Phu members' participation in the Red Shirt movement. The village head asked his villagers not to join the Red Shirt protest in Bangkok telling them that it would cause troubles for people in

Bangkok including many of their own relatives who now work in the capital city. Village leaders have been aware of the representation of the Red Shirts as rural trouble makers who defy established order from the center and feared that the village's involvement with the Red Shirt movement might tarnish Ban Phu's reputation as a model (and compliant) rural village.

Because Ban Phu villagers are invested in political participation at both local and national levels, differing political opinions and support for different candidates have been an important cause of divisions among people in the community. The last village head election in 2009 was a close competition between a new candidate and the former village head. The election of the new candidate left supporters of the former village head disappointed and posed a challenge for the new village head in gaining popular acceptance and cooperation. In the course of Thailand's ongoing political crisis, the majority of the population in the northeast, including Ban Phu villagers, have overwhelmingly supported the Pheu Thai Party associated with former Prime Minister Thaksin Shinawatra. The 2011 national election, in which over 90 percent of Ban Phu votes went to the Pheu Thai Party, testifies to the local support for the Pheu Thai. Achan Sawat, Ban Phu's informal leader, was not successful in his election bid for the position of Ban Pao municipality's mayor in 2009 partly because of his known support for the Democrat Party.

Government Localism Projects and Cultural Rights

The localism discourse in Thailand today, particularly in state development and cultural policies, is partly responsible for the underdevelopment of concepts of cultural rights among groups such as the Phu Tai. The localism discourse portrays Phu Tai culture as a rural or agrarian way of life from the past that is under threat because of the penetration of modernity and capitalist relations. This outlook frames the report of the ONCC's Local Historians Training Project conducted in Ban Phu (Kiriboon and Mareaam 2005). The report describes Phu Thai heritage as encroached upon and threatened by time and modernity rather than by Thai national policies and cultural assimilation. The report suggests that the younger generation is ignorant about Phu Tai culture because they are becoming modern (*khon than samai*), not because they have become absorbed into the dominant culture.

Launched in 2004 by the ONCC, the *Wattanatham Thai Sai Yai Chumchon* projects aim to promote the transmission of local knowledge, mobilize local cultures, and strengthen Thai communities by making use of existing social capital. The project's official rationale stresses the importance of community participation and collaboration between governmental and nongovernmental parties. With its emphasis on local cultures and community participation, this project seems to be compatible with cultural rights for ethnic minorities.

A close analysis of the project and its implementation, however, reveals that *Wattanatham Thai Sai Yai Chumchon* is another form of the "culture-for-development" agenda long promoted by the Community Development Department. The six components of *Wattanatham Thai Sai Yai Chumchon* are: (1) local wisdom, (2) local art and culture industry, (3) morality and ethics, (4) cultural activities, (5) local museums, and (6) information and public libraries. To participate in the project, a village or community has to organize these six activities designated by the ONCC in Bangkok. None of the six components directly encourages the formation of an awareness of cultural rights. Rather, the project aims to coach rural people to be good Thai citizens who follow state guidance. The national template of activities to be carried out under the project promotes uniformity rather than diversity among villages and communities across Thailand.

Government projects and funding delivered through bureaucratic structures do not facilitate an open space for people to think and act outside the framework of the traditional hierarchical administrative structure of village (*muban*), subdistrict (*tambon*), district (*amphoe*), and province (*changwat*). Collectivity is thus formed around these formal administrative units rather than transcending them. Government projects encourage Ban Phu villagers to imagine themselves as part of Nong Sung subdistrict and Mukdahan province rather than as a part of the Phu Tai ethnic group in Thailand. The benefits that Ban Phu has received from government projects prevent the villagers from aligning with other Phu Tai villages or other ethnic minority groups. Villages compete with each other for resources and recognition from national and provincial officials. When the head of Ban Phu's silk-weaving group invented a weaving pattern that won the provincial competition and was selected as a symbol of Mukdahan, the villagers took pride in their accomplishment. They are proud to be part of Mukdahan province, which is in turn part of the Thai nation. The province does not specifically recognize that the pattern was invented by Phu Tai weavers, and the villagers do not take issue with this. When Kalasin province organized the first International Phu Tai Day on 9–11 March 2012, a grand event that was presided over by Prime Minister Yingluck Shinawatra, most Ban Phu villagers chose not to take part. Unlike Mukdahan provincial activities, Ban Phu villagers did not feel they had a place in the International Phu Tai Day organized by Kalasin province.

Over the long history of Thailand's centralization of state power, national policies have deeply influenced the lives of all Thai people. State-led development constitutes an overarching frame within which rural citizens have to learn to maneuver in order to succeed, as one of Ban Phu's deputy headmen remarked:

> We need to adjust to the government's policies. If we don't, we won't get anything. In this system dominated by officials, we have to go along with the situation. For example, after the next election if Abhisit's time is over, we have to see what the next government will pay attention to. If Thaksin is back, he will bring back OTOP[13] and we will go back to OTOP, too. It is like a circle. But if Abhisit is back, he will promote the Sufficiency Economy. Thaksin promoted OTOP and OTOP is related to the Sufficiency Economy. But Abhisit will only support the Sufficiency Economy because it's the king's project. He doesn't care about OTOP. Our village will have to take the government's policies as our guideline. If we do not adjust (to government policies), our village won't be successful.

It is important to note that Ban Phu's success does not derive from the villagers' self-sufficiency and simple agrarian life, as preached by supporters of the localism agenda. On the contrary, the Ban Phu people have arrived in their current position because of their ambition, their determination to build connections with powerful actors and institutions, and their outward-looking disposition. Ban Phu's strong economy has been a result of over three decades of livelihoods diversification and the high percentage of village members in government employment. Almost all households receive financial support from family members who work as government employees or as migrant wage-earners in cities. This support enables the Ban Phu villagers who stay to continue working in the village and carry out community development activities. In terms of the Thai ethnic and cultural hierarchy, the Phu Tai people of Ban Phu have fought to improve their position by moving closer to "modernity and civilization" rather than challenging the existing hierarchy itself. Although administrative decentralization has been on the official agenda in Thailand for years and culminated in the 1997 "People's Constitution," practices on the ground and public attitudes are slow to change.[14] The Ministry of Interior's old style of governing, in which the central government transmits administrative power down along its hierarchical structure—from province to district to subdistrict to village—continues to dominate the Thai political and social landscape.

Conclusion

In this chapter I have examined the ways in which the dominant trend towards economic and developmental localism challenges or reifies center-periphery relations in Thailand and how this affects the articulation of rights. In the context of Thailand's state centralization and hierarchical relations, Ban Phu villagers present themselves as good, rural Thai citizens who are development-oriented and loyal to the monarchy. They recognize the roles of key institutions—the military, government officials, and the monarchy—and strategize to forge hierarchical alliances with them. Ban Phu villagers have demanded rights to development, particularly to education, which they embrace as their main route to social mobility. Under the guidance of government officials, the villagers deploy their Phu Tai-ness towards economic development particularly through tourism and the local culture industry. Having identified with the Thai state, Ban Phu villagers have little interest in forming intra- or inter-ethnic allegiances or demanding rights to preserve their ethnic identities; they choose to strategically display their difference in a state-endorsed and non-threatening manner. Phu Tai cultural identities are mobilized in the service of Thai hegemony, particularly that of the national-security and developmental state. As for the Thai state, the support that Ban Phu has received illustrates that the recognition of ethnic difference and minority groups is limited to ethnic representations and displays that do not challenge the cultural and political hegemony of Bangkok. Cultural rights in Thailand are substantially defined by and oriented towards compliance with state authority and the dominant values of Thai-ness.

Symbolic gestures of openness to difference divert attention away from more pressing demands—for example, for land rights or citizenship—from groups that are less fortunate than the Phu Tai in Ban Phu.[15] While granting cultural rights to more domesticated Tai-speaking ethnic/cultural groups, the state eschews the demands of Malay Muslims in the south for cultural authority and rightful representation in the overwhelmingly Buddhist state. Apparently ingrained in policies and everyday social interactions, Thai state hegemony has continually been challenged, however. The presence of local Red Shirt activities in Ban Phu disrupts the apparent cultural consensus and obedience to the bureaucratic state. Both challenges to Thai state hegemony and reactionary efforts to maintain the status quo have been ever more vehement in Thailand's current polarized political landscape and will likely only intensify the contestation over the meanings of citizenship and rights.

Notes

1. Craig J. Reynolds (2009) traces the use of the term *chumchon* (community) in Thailand to anti-Communist rural development and the government's goal to restructure the village.

2. Thai-Lao identity, however, is commonly understood as "ethnoregional," a regional variant of Thai national identity. See Keyes 1967, 2008.

3. See, for example, Diller's account (1991) of the establishing of central Thai as the national language.

4. *Wiang Phing* refers to the old kingdom of Lanna in the north of Thailand. In the dominant imaginary of central Thais, Lanna represents the mystical and desirable Other.

5. One such parent I talked to said he was proud of being a Phu Tai. Yet, self-declared pride does not necessarily lead to the revitalization of minority languages. No interviewees stated that they were ashamed of their Phu Tai ethnic identity, but inner feelings toward one's minority identity are at times too personal for informants to discuss openly with outsiders.

6. See Mills 2012 on the distinction between legal and cultural citizenship in Thailand and the unequal entitlement to Thai cultural citizenship between urban and rural subjects.

7. During the *kathin* and *pha pa* events, the guests were warmly welcomed at a dinner reception accompanied by dance and music performances. The guests could also join in the *ramwong kan kuson* (charity dance), during which the guests made

donations in order to dance with Ban Phu women. These *kathin* and *pha pa* receptions in the 1960s were the model after which the current Ban Phu homestay reception has been modeled.

8. The villagers' accounts of their Cold War experience belie the highly repressive history of Thai politics in which dissidents were harshly suppressed by the Thai military government. Accused of Communist involvement, dissidents were arrested, kidnapped, and executed both secretly and in public. See, for example, Thak 2007 and Somsak 1993.

9. From my personal observation of the Tai Song Dam ethnic group in Thailand's central provinces, this trend is not unique to the Phu Tai in Ban Phu. Forced to migrate from the west bank of the Mekong as were the Phu Tai, the Tai Song Dam today play up their relations and loyalty to the monarchy, stressing their forebears' close service to the Siamese court. The books *Khun nang song* (Song Nobles) and *Chao chom song* (Song Consorts) are often displayed in Tai Song Dam cultural gatherings.

10. Interview with Achan Sawat, July 2010.

11. Thirty to forty years ago, there were about thirty *mo yao* (traditional healers) in Ban Phu. The number gradually decreased, and they totally disappeared twenty years ago. Old *mo yao* passed away without replacements. Many *mo yao* decided to undergo a ritual at the Buddhist temple to break their connections with the spirits and stopped practicing. The abandonment of *yao* healing in Ban Phu coincided with the villagers' access to modern medical treatments through roads and district health stations.

12. Thao Suranari is a Thai heroine who helped the Siamese army defeat Chao Anu in Khorat during the war between Chao Anu and Siam in 1826.

13. One Tambon, One Product (OTOP) is a Thai government program initiated under former Prime Minister Thaksin Shinawatra from 2001–2006 to support the locally made and marketed products of each Thai subdistrict (*tambon*).

14. See Nidhi 2003 and Reynolds 2003 for discussions of the unwritten or "cultural" constitution—the way power is actually exercised in Thailand, as opposed to what is written down as the nation's formal legal frame.

15. Hayami 2006 offers a critique of the multicultural gestures of the Thai state.

References

Castellino, Joshua, and Elvira Dominguez Redondo. 2006. *Minority Rights in Asia: A Comparative Legal Analysis*. Oxford: Oxford University Press.

Connors, Michael Kelly. 2005a. "Democracy and the Mainstreaming of Localism in Thailand." In *Southeast Asian Responses to Globalization: Restructuring Governance and Deepening Democracy*, edited by Francis Loh Kok Wah and Joakim Öjendal, 259–86. Singapore: NIAS Press.

————. 2005b. "Ministering Culture: Hegemony and the Politics of Culture and Identity in Thailand." *Critical Asian Studies* 37 (4): 523–51.

Diller, Anthony. 1991. "What Makes Central Thai a National Language?" In *National Identity and Its Defenders: Thailand 1938–1989*, edited by Craig J. Reynolds, 87–132. Chiang Mai: Silkworm Books.

Evans, Grant. 2000. "Tai-Ization: Ethnic Change in Northern Indo-China." In Turton 2000, 263–89.

Hayami, Yoko. 2006. "Redefining 'Otherness' from Northern Thailand: Notes Towards Debating Multiculturalism in Thailand and Beyond." *Southeast Asian Studies* 44 (3): 283–94.

Keyes, Charles. 1967. *Isan: Regionalism in Northeastern Thailand.* Data Paper 65. Ithaca, NY: Cornell University Southeast Asia Program.

————. 2008. "Ethnicity and the Nation-States of Thailand and Vietnam." In *Challenging the Limits: Indigenous Peoples of the Mekong Region*, edited by Prasit Leepreecha, Don McCaskill, and Kwanchewan Buadaeng, 13–53. Chiang Mai: Mekong Press.

Khomun khrong kan wattanatham thai sai yai chumchon [Project information: Community culture connection project]. N.d. Accessed at http://saiyai.culture.go.th/index.php?option=com_content&view=section&layout=blog&id=7&Itemid=28.

Kiriboon Jongwutiwes and Maream Nillapan. 2005. *Khrongkan suepkhon prawattisat watthanatham thongthin kan rianru krabuankan soem sakkayaphap kan wichai chumchon nai phuenthi amphoe wanyai lae amphoe nongsung changwat mukdahan* [Local history and culture: Community research development in Wan Yai and Nong Sung districts, Mukdahan province]. Nakhon Pathom: Silpakorn University, Education Department.

Kirsch, A. Thomas. 1967. "Phu Thai Religious Syncretism: A Case Study of Thai Religion and Society." PhD diss., Harvard University.

Leach, Edmund R. 1970. *Political Systems of Highland Burma: A Study of Kachin Social Structure.* London: Athlone Press.

Loos, Tamara. 2006. *Subject Siam: Family, Law, and Colonial Modernity in Thailand.* Ithaca, NY: Cornell University Press.

————. 2010. "Competitive Colonialisms: Siam and the Malay Muslim South." In *The Ambiguous Allure of the West: Traces of the Colonial in Thailand*, edited by Rachel V. Harrison and Peter A. Jackson, 75–91. Hong Kong: Hong Kong University Press.

Mills, Mary Beth. 2012. "Thai Mobilities and Cultural Citizenship." *Critical Asian Studies* 44 (1): 85–112.

Narong Ardsmiti, Theeraphong Bunrugsa, and Wassana Suaykred. 2009. *Kan tittam lae pramoenphon khrongkan oprom choeng patibatkan nakwatthanatham chumchon nai kan sang khrueakhai watthanatham* [Follow-up and evaluation of the workshop on cultural network building for local cultural officers]. Nakhon Pathom: Research Institute for Languages and Cultures of Asia, Mahidol University.

Nidhi Eoseewong. 2003. "The Thai Cultural Constitution." *Kyoto Review of Southeast Asia* 3. Accessed at http://kyotoreview.cseas.kyoto-u.ac.jp/issue/issue2/index.html.

Phillips, Anne. 2007. *Multiculturalism without Culture.* Princeton, NJ: Princeton University Press.

Piyamas Akka-amnuay. 2002. "The Phuthai People and Their Political Roles on the Phu Phan Ranges During 1945–1980." Master's thesis, Mahasarakham University.

Reid, Anthony. 2010. *Imperial Alchemy: Nationalism and Political Identity in Southeast Asia.* Cambridge: Cambridge University Press.

Reynolds, Craig J. 2003. "Thailand's Democratic Traditions." In *The Development of Thai Democracy: Proceedings of the Thai Update 2003,* 25–42. Canberra: National Thai Studies Centre, Australian National University, 29–30 April.

———. 2009. "*Chumchon*/Community in Thailand." In *Words in Motion,* edited by Carol Gluck and Anna Lowenhaupt Tsing, 286–305. Durham, NC: Duke University Press.

Somsak Jeamteerasakul. 1993. "The Communist Movement in Thailand." PhD diss., Monash University.

Streckfuss, David. 1993. "The Mixed Colonial Legacy in Siam: Origins of Thai Racialist Thought, 1890–1910." In *Autonomous Histories, Particular Truths: Essays in Honor of John R. W. Smail,* edited by Laurie J. Sears, 123–53. Madison: University of Wisconsin, Center for Southeast Asian Studies.

Taylor, Charles. 1994. *Multiculturalism.* Princeton, NJ: Princeton University Press.

Thak Chaloemtirana. 2007. *Thailand: The Politics of Despotic Paternalism.* Chiang Mai: Silkworm.

Thongchai Winichakul. 2000. "The Other Within: Travel and Ethno-Spatial Differentiation of Siamese Subjects, 1885–1910." In Turton 2000, 38–62.

Turton, Andrew, ed. 2000. *Civility and Savagery: Social Identity in Tai States.* Richmond, UK: Curzon Press.

———. 2000a. "Introduction to *Civility and Savagery.*" In Turton 2000, 3–31.

8

Culture and Rights for Urban Minorities in Bangkok

──◦◦◦──

Matthew Mullen and Mike Hayes

Introduction

The human right to culture—and other human rights related to culture—
remain dynamic and contested issues. At a definitional level, we need to
distinguish these two types of rights. The *human right to culture* is a specific
right that is detailed in the Universal Declaration of Human Rights and then
given a legally binding definition in Article 27 of the International Covenant
on Civil and Political Rights (ICCPR). *Human rights related to culture* are the
rights people need to be able to practice their culture (for instance, freedom
of movement to get to a cultural site, or the right to health care in order to be
well enough to practice one's culture). This chapter, in examining the human
right to culture in urban minorities, explores the first category of cultural
rights, that is the specific right of an individual to participate in culture. Article
27 of the ICCPR gives this as:

> In those States in which ethnic, religious or linguistic minorities exist,
> persons belonging to such minorities shall not be denied the right, in
> community with the other members of their group, to enjoy their own
> culture, to profess and practise their own religion, or to use their own
> language.[1]

An obvious shortcoming of this definition of the human right to culture is that it sees culture as a set of practices and activities and not as a negotiated and fluid identity: culture is a thing to be done, and not a dynamic identity. However, since we wish here to compare the status of rights across different minority groups in an effort to understand why some cultural rights are protected and others are not, we use this more essentialized standard as a heuristic tool.

In vibrant and rapidly transforming cities such as Bangkok, there is debate about how and under what circumstances urban minorities[2] can practice their culture. Urban minorities practice their culture within the context of a larger struggle between contemporary trends that promote multiculturalism, transnationalism, and the protection of distinct identities, on the one hand, and forces that threaten the identity of minorities, such as assimilationist or discriminatory policies, on the other. There is little research on the particularities of realizing the human right to culture in urban settings, especially on how culture, identity, and rights of minority communities are practiced, promoted, and protected. We do not yet fully understand why certain groups can practice their culture within a city without discrimination, while other groups cannot; why do some groups live in relative harmony in a city, while others face discrimination and exclusion? For example, there are few cases of city dwellers protesting against a "Chinatown" in their midst, yet many examples of protests against the presence of mosques. The ability of a minority to live harmoniously in a city is, at one level, an issue of human rights—the rights to speak one's language, to practice one's religion, and to share one's culture with family and community. Yet the achievement of these rights is patchy at best. Acceptance may be based on a minority community's long and stable history, its willingness to adapt, or the majority community's tolerance of its religion. The rejection of a minority community could be due to racial stereotyping, the undocumented or illegal status of its members, or a perception that the community has a negative impact on the economy. Most likely it is a combination of these factors within the unique context of the urban environment. This study looks at the potential factors affecting urban minorities and their right to culture.

Urban minorities' ability to pursue their right to culture is made problematic because, unlike indigenous groups, they may have neither land nor history to ground their cultural claim. For example, Thailand's hill tribes have a connection to the land or to a "pre-nation-state" history to anchor their cultural acceptance, but urban minorities must somehow *earn* this status as their communities establish themselves. As our research posits, the process by which urban minorities earn acceptance of their right to culture could be described as a continuous negotiation between the urban minority community and various entities within the broader urban majority, whether this be state authorities, members of the majority culture, or the media, among others.

This research explores the process of negotiation by examining three urban minority groups in Bangkok that vary in terms of history, size, socioeconomic status, and cultural practices. The groups were selected for their variety: first, the Sikh community, which is a well-established group whose culture is respected by the majority Thai culture; second, the migrant Burmese Mon community,[3] which has long historical connections to Thailand, but still faces some discrimination due to its members' status as predominantly migrant workers; and, third, the West African community, a group that has only emerged in the last decade, faces significant discrimination, and has limited opportunity to practice its culture.

Research in Thailand on the cultural rights of minority groups has mainly focused on citizenship and related issues for the hill tribes located in the north of the country, and on the Muslim minority in the south.[4] The study of urban groups has for the most part remained limited to the domain of geographers and population scientists concerned with demographics and sector-specific issues such as public health, traffic, and zoning.[5] There is little, if any, literature on the three groups of this study.[6] The original assumption in this research was that by selecting three groups quite distinct in the level of their cultural acceptance (from the near complete acceptance of the Sikhs to the near complete rejection of the West Africans), the process of acceptance could be delineated to explain why and how cultural rights are attained or denied.

The study found that there is no single dimension or simple causal relationship that can explain the attainment of the right to culture. Though the process of acceptance is dynamic and unique, there are some important factors in this process: Historical links and legal status contribute greatly to the ability of the minority culture to claim acceptance. Longevity of residence in a city strengthens claims to allow the continuance of cultural practices such as religious worship, language use, and cultural performances. Secondly, the group's self-identification is crucial in its acceptance, for some groups choose to live apart from the majority society. Finally, economic independence is valued as contributing to, rather than taking from, the Thai state, in the sense of taking jobs, money, or opportunities away from the Thai people. Cultural identity for minorities is not the product of a single party (either what the majority *allows* or what the minority *practices*), but rather an in-between result that depends on the context of the city, the standards of rights, and other factors. The main conclusion we can infer from the research was that cultural acceptance was not an accumulation of achievements or a gradual realization of rights, but rather that each of these communities was engaged in a multifaceted negotiation around cultural practices and identity in relation to their position in Bangkok society, and it was within this negotiation that rights' claiming is made.[7] By considering culture as negotiated, though, we are not arguing that good negotiating tactics result in a strong culture, or that cultures can be understood by a variety of negotiation skills and theory. Rather, viewing rights claims to culture as a negotiated position recognizes the importance of context and the fluidity of culture. Minority and majority cultures engage in a rights-claiming process in which a cultural identity is being constantly produced. The claims may be aggressive (in criticizing discrimination, for instance), or passive (adopting clothes or hairstyles of the majority population).

Bangkok is exemplary of a contemporary "global city."[8] The rapidly growing economy, the mix of nationalities, and the relative openness are underscored by a competition for services and opportunities between capital and labor, citizens and non-citizens, and young and old generations. In what Greenstein et al. (2000) have called the "systemically uneven space," urban minorities must consider integrating to gain their security, both culturally and economically, by adjusting behavior and redefining interactions. This has been considered a test of social resilience—particular groups' "ability to cope with and adapt to environmental and social change" (Adger et al. 2002, 358). But does resilience mean giving up on cultural rights? The process of urban minorities' forming a community and maintaining their community identity is mutually dependent on the human rights framework. To be functioning members of the city the people living there need to have the freedoms recognized as human rights, such as the freedom to participate culturally in public space, to have access to urban services, and to be considered a member of the city itself. Indeed, human rights takes on greater importance for these groups who may not get the protection afforded by the national laws and government officials because they are deemed non-citizens or ineligible for such protection. Thus, it is useful to address the right to culture, albeit using the essentialized and limited view of culture-as-practice as set out in the ICCPR.[9]

Our research was undertaken by three small groups of researchers who interviewed community leaders and members about their culture and rights. Each group asked community members a similar set of questions about their cultural values and practices and their freedom to engage in cultural practices. Community leaders (for the Sikh and Mon groups) were asked more detailed questions about the community's history and culture and how the community practices its culture. The researchers made site visits to the communities, where they made field observations and conducted interviews from December 2010 to February 2011. The data collection tools were expert interviews of community leaders, oral history interviews of two to three community members to elicit life stories, and respondent interviews with about twenty members per group to gain a broader understanding of any social discrimination the communities had experienced. The analysis of the expert interviews, the interviews of community members, and the individual life stories led to an understanding of how integral cultural rights are to the fundamental rights of people and to the secure enjoyment of culture by minority communities in Bangkok.

Interview questions for the groups centered on how groups felt they fitted into the urban culture and how they constructed and participated in cultural spaces. There were five clusters of issues covered: First, the importance of the history of the group, assuming long-established groups have more legitimacy. Second, there were questions about the similarities of the cultures of minority and majority groups. Though cultural proximity may be a problematic concept, we wanted to test the idea that cultural practices similar to Thai culture could be claimed more easily. A third category was the contribution to the broader society, on the assumption that communities providing a service would find it easier to claim a cultural right. Fourth, we asked community members about their willingness to integrate, compromise, or adapt their cultural values to achieve acceptance. Finally, we asked questions about relations with local authorities (such as the police, the municipal government, or the local community), and about experiences of discrimination or rights violations. Embedded within our analysis of the research results for each of the three communities is a brief life story to highlight parallels between individual experiences and community practices. The life stories are intended to show how people uniquely deal with their rights to cultural practice. To conclude the chapter, we briefly discuss some of the human rights ramifications of the findings for urban minority studies.

The Bangkok Sikh Community

Sikhs consider themselves to be highly integrated into the Thai community. According to the Sikh community, Sikh families started to settle in Thailand in the 1870s, and Bangkok quickly became the center for settlement. Early migration was oriented towards economic opportunity, but in 1947, after the partition of India, Sikhs began to receive Thai citizenship, marking a shift to more permanent settlement. Currently there are approximately fifty to sixty thousand ethnic Sikh-Thai citizens. The population is scattered across Thailand, but the vast majority reside in Bangkok, where they tend to be involved in the textile, real estate, or hotel businesses.

Community member interviewees referred to the open values of Sikhism, such as universal equality and the positioning of all religions and people as equal in the eyes of God, when trying to explain why the Sikh community is treated so "favorably." Indeed, they saw the values within the community as strong assets in the establishment of the Sikh community in Bangkok. The strength of this historical narrative to the Sikh community is clearly important, since most Sikhs know and recount this history. The historical narrative itself is reified to exemplify the harmony between Thais and Sikhs, given that there are few alternative historical narratives to challenge it.[10] Interviewees noted that there was an adjustment period for Sikhs in Thailand, but no one gave any historical accounts of serious discrimination against Sikhs in Thailand, and their reflections on the settlement process in Thailand were overwhelmingly positive. At most, some Sikhs mentioned "some minor gaps, [but] not that much as compared to other migrant communities." This view was consistent across the community, from the leaders to younger Sikhs. In terms of self-identification, this was exemplified by one interviewee who identifies himself as having equal parts "Thai-ness" and "Sikh-ness." The ability to maintain a cultural minority identity while simultaneously feeling a part of the larger Bangkok community shows that Sikhs' cultural rights have been respected by the Bangkok community, and currently there are few rights-claiming activities. It should be noted that some respondents said that Sikhs feel more discriminated against in India than in Thailand. Not only does this underline that discrimination can be relative, but it also shows that, for some, discrimination is judged contextually. Furthermore, that no respondents gave examples of discrimination does not mean it does not exist, but it is not talked about.

The fact that the Sikhs have attained recognition of their human right to culture can be attributed not directly to human rights advocacy, but rather to a sense of mutual understanding and mutual benefit instead of competition. Interviewees noted that the lack of historical conflict between the Sikhs and Thais is because of similarities in cultural practices. Informants described the Sikh and Thai identities as "one and the same." The exact proximity of the cultures is clearly debatable, but the point here is that the Sikhs represent themselves as culturally similar when negotiating their cultural space. The narrative of their transition—from migrants, to residents, to Sikh-Thai citizens—forms a reified history of cultural acceptance. It is worth noting that Sikhs do possess advantages in their negotiation. They have forged what they described as a mutually beneficial relationship with Thais over the past 150 years. Given the long presence of Sikh culture over several generations, there is obviously a certain legitimacy their legal residence in Thailand has conferred. Further, interviewees noted that economically the Sikhs have made a positive contribution to the Thai economy. They pointed out that Sikhs did not rely on government services; the community actively donates funds to the Thai state for relief efforts; they work in their own businesses; and they often pay for their own education and health. The idea that Sikhs are "good contributors" is a belief that contributes to a respect for the community's culture and rights. That the Sikhs have viewed the state positively also bolsters the perception of them as "contributors." According to the president of the *gurdwara* (Sikh temple), the Thai government and the Sikh community have been mutually supportive. Doubtless this plays a role in continuing negotiations of cultural identity and rights and gives the Sikhs leverage when claiming their cultural rights.

Life Narrative of Singh[11]

Singh's grandfather migrated to Thailand in 1904 from Punjab, in what is now Pakistan, to improve his livelihood. The grandfather was first approached to go to Brazil for agricultural work, but his friends told him that Thailand was a better option as it is geographically closer to Punjab, and many Sikhs had already settled there. Even during his grandfather's time, Singh said, Sikhs rarely faced discrimination. In his opinion, this was because they did not participate in politics or seek government jobs. In addition, he said that the influence of the British in Thailand meant the Sikhs had a level of recognition through the expatriate community, which may have assisted in reducing their discrimination. Since he was born in Thailand in the late 1950s, he said, the most discrimination he had faced was teasing at school, but never anything more persistent or negative. Singh went back to Punjab to attend primary school because the family wanted him to maintain his links to their homeland. Singh is now in his fifties and is heavily involved in various community organizations. As a reasonably successful businessman running his own company for the past thirty-eight years, he has put his children through the Thai Sikh International School, and they are now studying at university.

Singh says he is proud that cultural practices remain a centerpiece of Sikh life in Bangkok. He noted that Sikh commitment to tradition persists to the point that marriages and the child-naming ceremony must take place within the Sikh temple if they are to be registered. Such cultural practices, and many others, have never been challenged.

He considers that both Thais and Sikhs have made mutual accommodations, such as male Sikhs working in the private sector who had to cut their hair to fit in to the Thai workplace. Sikhs do face discrimination, for example because of their turbans: one of Mr. Singh's relatives claimed he was rejected in the interview round for a government job after passing the exam because he wore a turban. In the end, the relative gave up and cut his hair in order to find a job.

As the above narrative shows, the Sikh community is underpinned by a set of priorities related to their religion and the maintenance of a distinct cultural identity. The community members place central importance on the *gurdwara*, which forms a critical part of the Sikhs' history. Asvin Singh Sachthep, a member of the committee of Sri Gurusingh Sabha (the central organization for Sikhs living in Thailand), stated in an interview that for a large part of the Sikhs' history in Thailand there were no *gurdwara* in Thailand. One temple was built in Pahurat, which acts as the main temple for the Thai-Sikh population.[12] That temple continues to serve as a social center where Sikhs gather, pray, and teach the next generation about Sikh history and culture. Non-Sikh Thais attend the temple on occasion, showing the local acceptance that exists between the Sikhs and the broader Thai society in Bangkok. The Sikh temple organization also encourages and promotes Punjabi language, though language teaching is now more formalized in the Thai Sikh International School, which is integrated into the Thai education system and has around 1,200 students. The impression is that Thai Sikhs have essentially integrated themselves into the mainstream of Thai society, even though they study at their own schools, pray at their own temples, and work in their own businesses.

Although the Sikh community may have compromised in terms of cultural identity or rights in the process of assimilation, it appeared that such compromises were mainly voluntary and symbolic. Informants said that many males in the community who work in the white-collar sector had to cut their hair to integrate into the Bangkok business society. The wearing of the turban among young Sikhs, though still widespread, is optional. Not many younger Sikhs speak Punjabi; they mostly speak Thai and English, and there are some Hindi speakers.

However, some social changes show areas of concern to the community. Elderly people in the community expressed a concern with intermarriages. Though most Sikhs would prefer marriages within the community, marriages between Sikh men and Thai women are increasing. The concern about intermarriage relates to what informants perceived as the integrity of the Sikh community. In order to maintain their position as a deeply integrated and accepted community, intermarriage must be allowed. Yet marrying out of the community can be seen as a threat to the community if Sikh traditions are not passed on to future generations. The pattern of Sikh men marrying Thai women, rather than Sikh women marrying Thai men, which is very rare, supports this view: Sikh women marrying outside could result in women leaving the community. A Thai woman marrying a Sikh, on the other hand, would be expected to be become a part of the Sikh community. In a sense, when the Sikh community seeks greater tolerance with the Thai community, the price for them is to allow intermarriage. While clearly many elders in the community do not support intermarriage, it is a concession they need to reluctantly make.

Mon Migrant Worker Community in Bangkok

Over the last two centuries, the Mon went from being one of the more dominant cultural presences in mainland Southeast Asia to a group marginalized by colonialism and nationalistic sentiments in Burma and Thailand. Mon migration to Thailand dates back to the late Ayutthaya period, and also to communities in Phra Pradaeng to the south of Bangkok (where the Mon new year's festival is still celebrated a week after the Thai festival of Songkran) and in Pak Kret to the north of Bangkok.[13] However, a significant addition to the community identity occurred with the more recent arrival of Mon migrants in Thailand, most of whom came largely for economic reasons during Bangkok's rapid economic expansion in the 1980s and 1990s. Some Mon settlements are over a hundred years old, and Mon cultural and national activities have often been celebrated in them, but there is little connection between the situation of those who arrived after 1990 and the earlier group of settlers. Indeed, these two periods of migration (before and after the 1990s) essentially describe two separate Mon groups within Thailand, and it is the second, more recent, group that is the focus of this study. While there has been research on migrant workers in Bangkok, some of which addresses the concerns and challenges faced by the Mons, research has not explicitly investigated the human rights to culture of Mon migrant workers.[14]

The Mon interviewees felt that they had been able to secure a cultural identity within Samut Sakhon, but they still faced constraints. The insecure and complex legal context for migrant workers leaves them open to abuse and mistreatment by police, government officials, and business operators. The protection of the right to culture is partial at best. Cultural practices often require approval from local authorities. For instance, leaders of the Mon community had to gain permission from Thai officials to build each of the two Mon temples in the community, and Mon National Day is typically the only celebration in which the authorities allow large numbers of Mons to gather and celebrate. The festivities have taken place for sixty-four years, though there are no records documenting how long this celebration has taken place in Samut Sakhon.[15] The policing of cultural practices is explicit in the community. For instance, at the Mon National Day celebration on 18 February 2011, there was a high level of security at the entrance to the outdoor concert.[16] At most Thai concerts, attendees would be minimally and automatically scanned when they walked through an entranceway. At this concert, however, policemen were conducting full body searches of all attendees. Some concert attendees explained that this was voluntarily agreed to by the organizers to prevent Thai authorities from claiming bogus security issues caused by the festival. The Mons must thus accept stricter security procedures in order to protect the right of the Mon community to hold large festivals in the future. The discrimination the Mon face is not limited to discrimination from authorities. Informants noted several disturbing accounts of local youths beating and robbing Mon men, accounts of murdered Mon workers, and many accounts of the rape of Mon women by Thai locals. The brutality these accounts describe suggests the risks the Mon take when living in Thailand. The scene of heightened security at the concert reflected some tense imbalances in how rights are protected: while the local authorities may see the Mon as a threat, they are more commonly the victims of poor security.

Another area of concern is with symbols that reflect Mon nationalistic sentiment: on Mon National Day no Mon flags may be displayed. Even though the Mons are close in cultural terms to the Thais—sharing the same religion (Theravada Buddhism), and similar cultural practices, such as the Songkran water festival at new year in the Buddhist calendar (April), and ceremonies for a baby's first haircut—Thai authorities show little sympathy for Mon cultural identity. While the authorities' explicit reason may be to avoid being seen as supporting secessionist movements in a neighboring country, this may be an example of reified histories in competition. Some respondents hinted that the shared history of juxtaposed kingdoms has had a negative impact on their cultural rights, since in a sense they are competing for ownership over the same cultural practices as found in Thailand (in other words, it could appear that Thai culture is a descendant of an older Mon culture, as some claim). There is always a complex interaction between nationalism and cultural identity. For the Mons, cultural pride and religion are priorities.

However, what complicates their negotiations with the Thais is the Thai state's desire to control non-Thai nationalist sentiments within Thailand, either for security reasons, or, in this case, to appease neighboring Burma and avoid accusations of harboring secessionists. For many Mons, expressing cultural pride and national pride are integrated, especially in a symbolic sense. But they are forced to bargain away some of their nationalistic identity in order to minimize tensions and secure other priorities.

Life Narrative of Samon[17]

Samon was a pro-democracy activist during the August 1988 ("8/8/88") student protests in Burma. He joined thousands of political refugees fleeing from Burma after 1988 and began his work in human rights along the southern Thai-Burmese border by monitoring the flood of thousands of Mon internally displaced people (IDPs), refugees, and migrant workers caused by the ongoing conflict and human rights abuses in Burma. He moved to Samut Sakhon in the 1990s for work. After 2000, the poor living conditions of many Mons in Burma pushed them to improve their economic conditions by moving to Thailand. The influx gradually changed from people fleeing conflict to people seeking economic security. Since that time, Samon explained, while abuses faced by Mon migrant workers due to law enforcement problems, corruption, and lack of labor protection are still prevalent, the situation has improved greatly. The difficulties Samon faced are common to Mon migrant workers: he has no national identity card, which means he cannot move outside the district, cannot own land, cannot apply for jobs, and is much more vulnerable to arrest. If he returns to Burma, he may be suspected of having connections to armed groups and may face persecution, yet his application for a Thai work visa requires proof of Burmese citizenship, which for Samon was difficult to obtain.

Samon maintained that the Mon people are able to keep a very strong group cultural identity, stronger than in Burma where cultural freedom is very limited. He felt that overall the situation for migrant workers is improving, and that the Thai government may officially recognize Mon and other migrant workers. He noted that young Mons born in Thailand can sometimes obtain Thai citizenship. Samon now has an identification card, which increases his mobility.

The Mon migrant workers' rights to participate in and practice cultural activities must often be subordinated to the more practical concerns of legal status and economic survival. However, there are aspects of cultural identity that the Mon interviewed considered as non-negotiable, such as religious practices and weddings, although they are willing to make some compromises in order to undertake these practices, such as holding weddings in private rooms. Another example relates to the wearing of the *longyi*, the Burmese traditional male wrap-around cloth. In 2008, the Samut Sakhon authorities tried to ban anyone in the province from wearing a *longyi*. This ban had no basis in law, as the authorities only have the right to control public decency but not the right to control what people wear.[18] An interviewee, Hong, went to the local government office with his Mon friends to challenge this ruling while wearing their *longyi*. Security guards stopped them, but the group was eventually let through to make their case. The ban on *longyi* was rescinded.

A definitive characteristic of rights-claiming among the Mons and Thais is the former's lack of power. The Mons' socioeconomic contribution to Thailand is mostly ignored, as the labor the Mon and other Burmese minority groups provide is interpreted as taking jobs away from local Thais. From the Thai majority community's perspective, the relationship with the Mons— poor, vulnerable migrants—is not seen as one of mutual benefit, and the Mons are forced to negotiate from a weaker position. Claiming the right to culture is weakened because the Mon migrant workers are seen as essentially economic migrants with no cultural or historical legitimacy to claim rights. The two incidents mentioned above—seeking permission for the building of two Mon temples, and tight security at the annual Mon festival—show that cultural claims require compromise. The balancing act of promoting Mon identity without promoting Mon nationalism can be seen on the front pillars of one of the two Mon temples. On one pillar is a traditional Thai mythological bird (*krut*, or *garuda*) and on the other pillar is depicted a Mon mythological swan (*hintha*), presumably symbolizing the Mon presence in the Thai nation-state. Similar to the other groups in this study, the Mons consider such concessions to be necessary in order to practice their culture.

Like other groups, the Mon migrant workers find living in Thailand comparatively better than in their home country for security, safety, or economic reasons. It is understandable, then, that some of the Mon informants provided somewhat contradictory responses when questioned about discrimination: for instance, a reference to discrimination might be quickly followed by examples of acceptance. In particular, young interviewees were positive about Thailand and praised the availability of reliable electricity and of work opportunities. They were content to be married in their small, one-room apartments or willing to miss festivals if they could not get the time off work. To cope with discrimination and threats to their security, the Mon have, to a certain extent, isolated themselves from the larger community, living together in particular neighborhoods and shopping at the same markets. Despite overcrowding, many respondents seemed uninterested in moving out to live among the broader Thai society, as the confines of the community provided a sense of security, and it was within this reduced space that they could practice their culture.

West Africans

There are a number of African communities in Bangkok, mostly forming loose, relatively heterogeneous identities, for example, as Muslims, or as West Africans. Our research focused specifically on the West Africans who inhabit an area around Sukhumvit Soi 3, the so-called "West African *soi*." This group has gained attention for being suspected as criminals involved in drug dealing and other crimes. The group was chosen because it inhabits a specific space and identity in the city. While not as culturally homogenous as the Sikhs or Mons, the West Africans of Soi 3 do share values, a living space, and an identity. Although this may stretch the definition of "community," it is a necessary concession as we wanted to include a nascent minority culture, which in this case only manifests a limited sense of community. The West African group itself can be divided into two large sub-groups. First, there is the Muslim West African group. These individuals tend to identify themselves first as Muslim, and second as African. They are integrated into the larger Middle Eastern community around Soi 3/1 and are culturally defined by their business, prayer, dress, recreation, and food. The Muslim group's access to resources and services differs from the other West Africans, as they are able to make use of networks available to the larger Arab and Muslim community. In the West African community we studied, many members identify themselves with a more criminal façade, and tend to associate themselves more with

American gangster dress, music, speech, and ideas.[19] These individuals have been spatially segregated, as most of their activity is hidden down a sub-*soi* of Soi 3. The relationship between these two divided communities is tense and divisive, as Muslim respondents emphasized how the West Africans are different. One West African interviewed for the project stated, "We don't hate each other, we just don't interact." The West African *soi* probably started as an offshoot of the more established "Arab" or "Middle Eastern" *soi* (Soi 3/1), which has a number of Middle Eastern restaurants, travel agencies, and import-export businesses. Around 2011, after some complaints about illegal activities resulted in high-profile raids, the police forced the people living on the African *soi* to move to a sub-*soi* that is hidden from view, off the main street.

Historical information on the group at Soi 3 is elusive and ambiguous, largely because the community is transient—most individuals contacted during this research had no intention of starting a family, or staying long-term in Thailand, and knew little of those who had arrived before them. Further, many individuals knew nothing about Thailand prior to coming. The number of women and children from West Africa appears to be very small, and interviewees explained that men with a wife and children had been advised to migrate without their families. There are a small number of women who work in commercial sex work, but they were not involved in our interviews. The lack of history is a challenge for the group to establish cultural practices. The West Africans at Soi 3 exemplify a group that has been both spatially and socially excluded from the surrounding Thai urban society. Interviewees suggest that the exclusion is generated by both external forces and by the internal wishes of the group, in order to differentiate themselves from their surroundings. Members of this West African community assert their identity by emphasizing "otherness." This otherness is not based on an African identity, but a criminal one: as one interviewee states, "Why would I eat African food or dress African? Everybody is already scared of me. I can't change their minds, so I fit where I fit. I listen to 50 Cent and Lil Wayne, and I work for the American dream; what do I have to lose?" Surrounded by the Nana entertainment district and near to the Grace Hotel—both venues with a reputation for illegal activities—West African interviewees admitted that they had gained a reputation for engaging in underground economies such as drug dealing, smuggling, and prostitution, and we were repeatedly reminded of the scope and pervasiveness of the sex and drug trade in and around their community. While the number of West Africans involved in clandestine activities is unknown, all the informants felt that they were being associated with these activities by default. However, interviewees were also quick to admit that the criminal image ascribed to them was in part legitimate, since there were few other options for group members to earn money, and because any positive contributions the community had made were never acknowledged. While some interviewees embraced their "otherness" as West Africans, others despised it, and wanted to forge a positive image of the community. The criminal image of their community has ramifications for other West African communities in Bangkok. In selected interviews with West Africans not associated with the Soi 3 group, there was open criticism of the activities on Soi 3 and concern for the image of West Africans in general because of the potential to generalize and stereotype all West Africans as criminals.

Life Narrative of B[20]

B is a twenty-six-year-old man who came to Thailand from Liberia just over a year and a half ago. Though for B life in Thailand is not great, he admits that it is better than in Liberia. While in Thailand B engages in a mixture of legal business, such as exporting goods (mainly cheap clothes), and illegal activities, such as selling drugs. He will be in Thailand for the duration of his visa, and longer if he can extend it. B didn't see any point in asserting his culture or identity, as he didn't feel he had a place in Thai society. The extent of his desire to contribute to and integrate with Thais was limited to paying for documents and visa stamps. Yet he did consider that he felt a strong sense of brotherhood with his West African friends and emphasized loyalty and dedication to them. What held him and his friends together was a common commitment to defying the system and society. B considers that he will always be discriminated against in Thai society because his skin color marks him clearly as different and because Thais have fixed perceptions about his place of origin as a site of violence and chaos.

West Africans and Thais are complicit in maintaining sharp divisions that paradoxically have elements of both hostility and cooperation. The hostility is largely a product of racial discrimination, stereotypes, and an unwillingness to forge any better understanding. Most West Africans are transient, only stay for two or three years, and have no connection to the Thai community; there is little incentive to relate. Much of the discrimination described by the informants was racially based. One interviewee said, "They can see we're different [by skin color] from the other side of the road, and they already 'know' what we're about." Yet, this identity of "otherness" is something the Soi 3 West Africans seem to utilize to their benefit. Beneath the outward tension is a clandestine cooperation in which many of the Soi 3 informants described friendly business relationships with local authorities who collude in and get benefits from underground operations. What emerges is a twofold relationship with the authorities, who must appear to be policing the behavior of this community (in the form of sporadic raids) while simultaneously conniving at and benefiting from their activities. In such an environment, inclusion and acceptance are unlikely, but the minority group maintains enough power to secure a space for their culture and identity

One might assume that a community that is stereotyped so negatively would be powerless to claim any rights, let alone cultural rights, but the Soi 3 West Africans posited a different view. The reality is that they are a ghettoized group who have an imposing presence. Many interviewees explained that they were treated as outsiders with nothing to lose, and they were willing to assert their identity this way. Informants explained their intimidating power as a "force that you can't just play around with." The community members seem to share a similar worldview—in terms of backgrounds and interests— resulting in high levels of camaraderie and solidarity. When asked about "unacceptable treatment," one informant replied that the West Africans in Soi 3 only "put their foot down when the police come around to arrest people and tell people what they can and can't do." Therefore, they were careful about maintaining up-to-date visa documentation, since they recognized that migrants' legal status was an area in which the authorities would not compromise.

It was unclear whether the Soi 3 West Africans were satisfied with their circumstances or not. Many informants suggested that they were quite willing to make any compromises necessary to ensure that their businesses ran smoothly. Rather than attempting to determine which cultural rights could be claimed, the more appropriate question may be why this community is willing to embrace such an excluded existence. The West Africans of Soi 3 do not pursue traditional cultural rights in the sense of practicing a culture from their home. Rather, cultural rights were subordinated to the desire for autonomy and space, and economic freedom—the capacity to make money. In order to make money, the interviewees explained, they needed space. Similar to the Mon migrant workers, the West Africans felt a level of safety in their own space. One interviewee noted, "When you've seen what I've seen, you're happy to have a safe place to sleep, and you're not so worried about being treated with a lot of respect." Like other groups in this study, the comparative safety of Bangkok is a valid reason to limit their rights claims to only those that are most essential: privacy, economic activities, and security.

Conclusion: Human Rights in a Negotiated Space

From the description given of the three groups a number of themes emerge. First, history plays an important role in the identity of the community. As previously noted, a reified history can be used by communities as a form of legitimacy, as in the case of the Sikhs' well-defined history of compatibility and compliance with the larger Thai society. But history can also create challenges, as in the Mon migrant workers' case, in which their historical aspirations for nationhood conflict with a reified Thai historical narrative. Communities without history, such as the West Africans in Bangkok, face much greater challenges to gain acceptance.

From the communities, we learned that a claim for cultural rights is a strategic choice. The community may feel they do not have the power to assert the right to culture because of their precarious legal status, as with the Mon migrant worker community. On the other hand, urban minorities sometimes choose not to pursue their cultural practices: the West Africans identified themselves not with an indigenous African culture, but with an urban gang culture. The groups have a variety of responses to alienation: they can further separate themselves from the population; they can assimilate into the majority culture; or, by engaging in rights claims, they can assert their cultural practices. There are elements of each of these responses across the three groups studied. The Sikh groups often border on assimilation, and their members identify themselves as Thai and prioritize Thai cultural practices. At the other extreme, the African groups often deliberately separate themselves spatially and culturally from Bangkok society with little intervention.

The lack of acceptance of the minority community may push them into unprotected environments such as informal economies, insecure tenure, areas with no police protection, or unregulated social services. This is true for the Mon migrant worker groups who face vulnerability to exploitation because their attempts at rights-seeking have found little sympathy with the broader Bangkok society. Communities escaping conflict and poverty, such as the Mons and West Africans, may be willing to forfeit a great deal for space and opportunity. It appears that in these unprotected environments, claiming cultural rights is hardly a priority, as the desire for economic security, privacy, and personal safely take precedence. However, for some communities this is a risk worth taking; all three communities tended to compare their current circumstances in Bangkok to the circumstances in the countries they had migrated from—a sort of "better-than-home" comparison of rights. Some interviewees were willing to tolerate violations of their human rights to culture, and of other, broader human rights, because when compared to war and poverty, these seemed to be relatively minor concerns.

Across the three groups discussed in this chapter, there are clues to how cultural acceptance is gained. It seems that it may not be necessary for a cultural practice to be deliberately articulated as a claim; many cultural practices are not defended, or groups may voluntarily forgo them in order to focus on other rights. Rights claims emerge only when the majority society resists what is seen as a necessary right to culture. It should be added, though, that by assuming that cultural rights are claim-dependent does not exonerate a city or state from addressing human rights issues, or from their duty to provide basic protections or opportunities.

Assumptions that cultural proximity or a minority culture's contribution to society could enable more cultural rights were often inconclusive, and it appeared that these assumptions were interpreted to fit the existing values: Sikh economic contribution was praised, while Mon migrant worker contributions were condemned. It appears that the strongest basis for these values was the sense of legitimacy the majority culture assigned to the minority culture; this can be a legitimate history, legitimate legal status, or legitimate work. Yet, much like social contributions, even legitimacy is a status that can be arbitrarily awarded or withdrawn, such as for the West Africans, whose existence depends on their visa status. Without a strongly grounded standard of cultural rights, it is easy for the minority culture to face discrimination and harassment. Such a situation represents a loss for both majority and minority groups. A respected urban minority is a safe and productive one. Once respect is withdrawn, and the ability for a minority to develop its own cultural systems is constrained, then fear, suspicion, and vulnerability are what define its status.

Notes

Field research was conducted by teams of graduate students from the Institute for Human Rights and Peace Studies, Mahidol University, including Abhay Luthra, Salem Bidyalaxmi, Emma Vick, Vivienne Daeppe, Ussarin Kaewpradap, Brooke Mullen, Mahbubul Haque, Saleh Mohammed Samit, Phyu Myat Thwe, Hlaing Yu Aung , Thuytien Vinh Truong, and Sasiprapa Jampian.

1. This paper uses the ICCPR definition because the treaty has been ratified and is thus legally binding in Thailand.

2. We choose to use the term "minority" in this chapter because it is used in the major human rights literature, and because it signifies that the groups have a minority status with respect to the majority culture. This is not to suggest that the majority or minority communities are homogeneous groups, for clearly there is no single "majority" Thai or Bangkok culture. Rather, the use of majority and minority in this research denotes the relative disparity of power that the groups possess in the Bangkok context.

3. The Mon community selected was actually based in Samut Sakhon, which is technically outside Bangkok—it is a satellite city approximately fifty kilometers from the city center. We chose this site because of the high number of Mon and Burmese workers there, and the existence of their communities. Most Mon or Burmese workers within Bangkok are dispersed at their places of work (whether in houses where they are domestic workers, or at building sites where they frequently live while working).

4. For a general overview of studies on minorities in Thailand, see Toyota 2005, Magallanes and Hollick (1998), and Neef (2005).

5. Notable exceptions include Marc Askew's *Bangkok* (2002), which traces the lives of specific inhabitants (such as middle-class residents of a *mu ban*, an inner city slum, and sex workers) and the body of research on the well-established Chinese minority. For examples of the latter, see Balbo (2005); Murakami et al. (2005); Bishop et al. (2000); Fraser (2002); Setchell (1995); Lee (1998); Vanlandingham and Hirschman (2001); Tong and Chan (2001); and Juree (1979).

6. On the Sikhs, one of the only studies is Manjit Sidhu's *Sikhs in Thailand* (1993). Most, if not all, studies on the Burmese in Thailand focus on the concerns of refugees and forced migration, or the protection of Burmese migrant laborers, while the large body of work on the Mon is almost exclusively on the established community and not the recent Mon migrant workers. Aside from recent media reports, there has been no focused study on the West Africans in Bangkok. A recent example of press coverage is the *Bangkok Post*'s report on drug dealing in the "African *soi*" (Wechsler 2011).

7. It is important to note that our research does not claim to present a two-sided analysis of the negotiations. It is interested exclusively in the negotiation process as seen through the eyes of the minority community. Understanding the negotiation process from the point of the majority group (state and civil) would provide a different analysis of the relations between the two groups, but this is beyond the scope of the research.

8. Saskia Sassen (2001, 2005) argues that global cities have become the main producer of capital, technology, and innovations, and are not products of the national economy or nation-state. What is of interest for Sassen is how cities operate together, almost to the neglect of the state system of which they are a part. Two issues from Sassen's work are of relevance here: that the culture of a city is already highly globalized and hence should be more conducive to acceptance of minority cultures, and that identity at the city level is distinct from the national level, and cultural tensions should be sought not between a national culture and a minority (which most human rights standards posit), but rather between the values of a city and that of the minority community.

9. The ideas here are based on the concept of "rights to the city" that has been used in UNESCO-based research. See especially Kristiansen and Brown (2009). In their UNESCO report, the authors are more directly interested in the status of "urban citizenship," which adds value to human rights by increasing participation at the urban level, and thus gives a greater franchise to communities (as opposed to nations), and further addresses politics at the urban, rather than the national, level.

10. There are few counterexamples to the story of Sikh integration into Thai society. In the *Thailand: Country Survey Series 1957* produced by Yale University's Human Relations Area Files, Indian groups are "considered a transient group, not likely to be assimilated. . . .[Their] economic competition is resented" (HRAF 1957, 70). Further, it states that "Sikhs are traditionally night watchmen for business or private premises" (69). Other reports from this time, for example the *Thailand Official Yearbook 1964*, only state that the Sikhs number approximately ten thousand and have two associations: one hospital, and one school.

11. The name Singh is a pseudonym to conceal the identity of the interviewee. For the Sikh community, nineteen respondent interviews were conducted with community members around the Paruhat temple in January 2011. It should also be noted that each life story—Sikh, Mon, and West African—was collected by different

groups of researchers working under different conditions; hence the three narratives are not always comparable.

12. The original wooden temple was built around 1911, and the current *gurdwara* at Pahurat was completed in 1980. There are now seventeen *gurdwara* in Thailand.

13. The Phra Pradaeng and Pak Kret communities have largely assimilated into the Thai majority over the past century and so were not selected as communities to study for this research.

14. One of the few works on Mon history is South (2003). See also Bauer (1990). These studies do not, however, look at Mon communities in Bangkok.

15. For more details, see Mon Unity League (2008), which states, "The Mon National Day commemorates the inception of the Mon Nation, the founding in 825 AD of the Hongsawatoi Kingdom by two brothers, Sammala and Vimala, in what is now Pegu in Lower Burma. . . ."

16. The research team observed the Mon National Day celebration.

17. Samon requested that the research team use his real name in the study. For the Mon community nine respondent interviews were conducted during two site visits in February 2011.

18. This was part of a larger process called the "Provincial Decrees" that attempted to limit Burmese migrants' rights in response to public outcries over the number of migrant workers. The decrees included a ban on owning mobile phones and motorcycles, and restrictions on migrants' movements. These decrees were eventually overturned after numerous protests, including by the National Human Rights Commission of Thailand. See Human Rights Watch (2010).

19. It should also be noted that there is a third category of West Africans: those who are neither Muslim nor live near Soi 3; these include the many teachers, staff of embassies, athletes, and students who also live in Bangkok.

20. "B" is a pseudonym. We conducted thirteen respondent interviews among the West African community around Sukhumvit Soi 3 during January and February 2011.

References

Adger, W. Neil, P. Mick Kelly, Alexandra Winkels, Luong Quang Huy, and Catherine Locke. 2002. "Migration, Remittances, Livelihood Trajectories, and Social Resilience." *Ambio* 31 (4): 358–65.

Askew, Marc. 2002. *Bangkok: Place, Practice and Representation*. London: Routledge.

Balbo, Marcello, ed. 2005. *International Migrants and the City*. Nairobi: UN-HABITAT and Venice: Universita Iuav di Venezia.

Bauer, Christian. 1990. "Language and Ethnicity: The Mon in Thailand and Burma." In *Ethnic Groups across National Boundaries in Mainland Southeast Asia*, edited by Gehan Wijeyewardene, 14–47. Singapore: ISEAS.

Bishop, Ian, Francisco Escobar, Sadasivam Karuppannan, Kasemsan Suwannarat, Ian Williamson, and Paul Yates. 2000. "Spatial Data Infrastructures for Cities in Developing Countries: Lessons from the Bangkok Experience." *Cities* 17 (2): 85–96.

Fraser, Evan. 2002. "Urban Ecology in Bangkok, Thailand: Community Participation, Urban Agriculture and Forestry." *Environments* 30 (1): 37–50.

Goodman, Alan. 1971. "The Political Implications of Urban Development in Southeast Asia: The 'Fragment' Hypothesis." *Economic Development and Cultural Change* 20 (1): 117–30.

Greenstein, Rosalind, Francisco Sabatini, and Martim Smolka. 2000. "Urban Spatial Segregation: Forces, Consequences, and Policy Responses." *Land Lines* 12 (6). Accessed at: http://www.lincolninst.edu/pubs/276_Urban-Spatial-Segregation--Forces--Consequences--and-Policy-Responses.

HRAF [Human Relations Area Files]. 1957. *Thailand: Country Survey Series 1957*. New Haven, CT: Yale University, HRAF.

Human Rights Watch. 2010. *From the Tiger to the Crocodile: Abuse of Migrant Workers in Thailand*. New York: Human Rights Watch.

Juree Namsirichai Vichit-Vadakan. 1979. "Not Too High and Not Too Low: A Comparative Study of Thai and Chinese Middle Class Life in Bangkok." PhD diss., University of California, Berkeley.

Kristiansen, Annali, and Alison Brown. 2009. "Urban Policies and the Right to the City: Rights, Responsibilities and Citizenship." MOST-2 Policy Paper. Paris: UNESCO.

Kymlicka, Will. 1995. *Multicultural Citizenship: A Liberal Theory of Minority Rights*. Oxford: Oxford University Press.

———. 2005. "Multiculturalism: Western Models, Global Trends, and Asian Debates." In *Multiculturalism in Asia*, edited by Will Kymlicka and Baogang He, 22–55. Oxford: Oxford University Press.

———. 2007. *Multicultural Odysseys: Navigating the New International Politics of Diversity*. Oxford: Oxford University Press.

Lee, Yok-Shiu. 1998. "Intermediary Institutions, Community Organizations, and Urban Environmental Management: The Case of Three Bangkok Slums." *World Development* 26 (6): 993–1011.

Magallanes, Catherine J. Iorns, and Malcolm Hollick. 1998. *Land Conflicts in Southeast Asia: Indigenous Peoples, Environment and International Law*. Bangkok: White Lotus Press.

Marston, Wilfred, and Thomas Van Valey. 1979. "The Role of Residential Segregation in the Assimilation Process." *Annals of the American Academy of Political and Social Science* 441 (1): 13–25.

Mon Unity League. 2008. *Discovery of Rehmonnya*. Bangkok: Tech Promotion & Advertising.

Murakami, Akinobu, Alinda Medrial Zain, Kazuhiko Takeuchi, Atsushi Tsunekawa, and Shigehiro Yokota. 2005. "Trends in Urbanization Patterns of Land Use in the Asian Mega Cities Jakarta, Bangkok and Metro Manila." *Landscape and Urban Planning* 70 (3–4): 251–59.

Neef, Andreas, ed. 2005. *Participatory Approaches for Sustainable Land Use in Southeast Asia*. Bangkok: White Lotus Press.

Riger, Stephanie, and Paul Lavrakas 1981. "Community Ties, Patterns of Attachment and Social Interaction in Urban Neighborhoods." *American Journal of Community Psychology* 9 (1): 55–56.

Sassen, Saskia. 2001. *The Global City: New York, London, Tokyo*. Princeton, NJ: Princeton University Press.

———. 2005. "The Repositioning of Citizenship and Alienage: Emergent Subjects and Spaces for Politics." *Globalizations* 2 (1): 79–94.

Setchell, Charles. 1995. "The Growing Environmental Crisis in the World's Mega Cities: The Case of Bangkok." *Third World Planning Review* 17 (1): 1–18.

Sidhu, Manjit. 1993. *Sikhs in Thailand*. Bangkok: Institute of Asian Studies, Chulalongkorn University.

South, Ashley. 2003. *Mon Nationalism and Civil War in Burma: The Golden Sheldrake*. New York: RoutledgeCurzon.

Thailand Official Yearbook 1964. 1964. Bangkok: Royal Thai Government.

Tong, Chee Kiong, and Kwok B. Chan, eds. 2001. *Alternate Identities: The Chinese of Contemporary Thailand*. Singapore: Times Academic Press.

Toyota, Mika. 2005. "Subjects of the Nation Without Citizenship: The Case of 'Hill Tribes' in Thailand." In *Multiculturalism in Asia*, edited by Will Kymlicka and Baogang He, 110–35. Oxford: Oxford University Press.

Vanlandingham, Mark, and Charles Hirschman. 2001. "Population Pressure and Fertility in Pre-Transition Thailand." *Population Studies* 55: 233–48.

Watts, Ann, and Thomas Watts. 1981. "Minorities and Urban Crime: Are They the Cause or the Victims?" *Urban Affairs Review* 16 (4): 423–36.

Wechsler, Maxmilian. 2001. "Busted or Bullied?" *Bangkok Post, Spectrum* (9 January), 8–10.

Wilson, Richard A., and Jon P. Mitchell, eds. 2003. *Human Rights in Global Perspectives: Anthropological Studies of Rights, Claims and Entitlements*. London: Pluto Press.

9

Controlling Bad Drugs, Creating Good Citizens: Citizenship and Social Immobility for Thailand's Highland Ethnic Minorities

Mukdawan Sakboon

Introduction

Members of upland ethnic minority groups in northern Thailand are still excluded, both de jure and de facto, from full membership in the Thai state, despite their efforts and the state's to solve the problem. There *are* government policies intended to include members of the highland minorities in a homogenous Thai polity. But the complexity of the policies, the inconsistent manner in which they have been implemented, and long-standing stereotypical assumptions about "hill tribe" people contribute to this ongoing exclusion.

This chapter argues that the national project of integration of the highland ethnic minorities in Thailand is contradictory. Due to the interweaving of the idea of "ideal citizens" and the politics of difference, the state policy to integrate ethnic minorities into a homogenous identity is enacted through a strategy of separation. These exclusionary practices are intensified in particular locales such as the highland borderlands in the northern region, where declining forestlands, mobility of people, and the presence of drugs are collectively seen as a threat to the integrity of the nation-state. These "problems" form the basis upon which administrative policies are made and national identity redefined to exclude those perceived as the source of those problems.

The chapter begins with a historical summary of the Thai government's policy on hill tribes, tracing its roots in a national integration project up through current fears of illicit drug activity and illegal migration. The next section details the implementation of the policy pertaining to citizenship requirements for the highland people in the borderlands in northern Thailand. I then discuss the difficulties in obtaining citizenship before addressing the ways in which exclusionary citizenship policies and practices restrict mobility and impose other forms of discrimination and marginalization on the highland peoples. After discussing the role of local politics and corrupt practices in regards to citizenship-seeking processes, the chapter concludes with a brief look at the responses of the highland peoples to the state's methods of exclusion and the ongoing challenges facing them.

Hill Tribes, Highlands, and the Thai State Development Policy

"Hill tribe" (*chao khao*)[1] people are officially defined as "original ethnic groups with unique culture, traditions, belief systems, language and livelihoods who live and work in, or whose ancestors settled in, the kingdom's highlands" (Department of Provincial Administration 2000, 2). Ten major ethnic groups are collectively called "hill tribes": the Karen, Hmong, Mien, Akha, Lahu, Lisu, Lua, Khamu, H'tin and Mlabri (ibid). The Thai state assigns the hill tribes minority status based on their numbers in comparison to the ethnic Thai majority. Official data as of 2003 put the number of "hill tribe" people at 922,957 (about 1.46 percent of the country's sixty-three-million population). Officially, there are different ethnic minority categories of which the hill tribes constitute one (Department of Provincial Administration 2002). In general use by most government officials, the term *chao khao* is understood to mean ethnic minority groups who have migrated into Thailand over the past thirty to fifty years. But using the term *chao khao* in this sense distorts the fact that some of the highland ethnic minority people, like the Lua (or Lawa or Lawoe), the Karen, the Khamu, and the Lahu, have long been settled in the highlands in northern Thailand.

Like the highlands in many countries,[2] the elevated slopes of northern Thailand have become problematic areas due to their having become a space of intervention (McKinnon 2004) in which a large number of development projects have been carried out (Van der Meer 1981; Tapp 1989; Kammerer 1989; McCaskill and Kampe 1997). The fact that the highland areas in Thailand are also borderland areas further complicates the issue. Borders, as Sturgeon (2005, 4) explains, can be understood as "the margin or edge of a nation-state, or a dividing line that links as well as separates people in two nation-states, including the social relationships surrounding that line." Borders are markers of statehood (Horstmann 2002); they play a special role in the origin and development of the state precisely because of their geographical location as border zones. The nature of the borderlands—where the sovereignty of the state is marginal or even abandoned (Horstmann 2002, 8)— has led the state to distrust ethnic minorities living within this "lawless" zone. Due to their "plastic" nature, the borderlands have assumed prominent roles in the geographies of citizenship (Sturgeon 2005) which impair state regulatory capacity, challenge the sanctity of territorial sovereignty, and blur the populations' sense of belonging. Consequently, in its national integration policy the Thai state has set as its key objective the creation of a sense of loyalty among the people who reside in the borderlands through the key programs of citizenship registration and highland education.

Amidst the fear of Communism in the Southeast Asian region from the 1950s to the 1980s, and the pressure applied by the United States and international organizations such as the United Nations on countries in this region to eradicate opium cultivation, the highland ethnic minorities have been presented as "troublemakers" who pose a grave threat to "national security" in the eyes of authorities (Tapp 1989; Pinkaew 1998). The state penalized the hill villagers for growing opium, practicing swidden cultivation, and being perceived as Communist sympathizers. Their impermanent settlements were translated by the state as implying a lack of national loyalty. Accordingly, since the 1950s, the highland ethnic minorities have been the focus of state policies and programs that aim to secure borders and put an end to opium cultivation. In frontier areas such as the hills of northern Thailand, where state sovereignty is blurred and border crossings are difficult to regulate, new types of border control have been employed that shift the focus onto the people through the use of identification cards. In this way, border demarcations are redrawn and inscribed on the bodies of the moving subjects as a means of achieving surveillance and control of the highland ethnic minorities.

The "hill tribe discourse" (Pinkaew 1998), which has classified the mobility of people and goods as "illicit," has led to the increasing vulnerability of marginal ethnic minorities in the border areas and to manipulation and exploitation by centrist administrations (Tapp 1989). In the national project to integrate the rural highland people, terms such as "highlanders" and "hill tribes" were applied to create distinctions and divisions that allowed for better surveillance, discipline, and control by the state, similar to what Foucault has termed "governmentality." Therefore, the highlands in northern Thailand, as a geographical location at the periphery, were given distinctive *identity* as a development-deficit space in need of intervention (development and control). In other words, the interweaving of the politics of space, identity, and allegiance has rendered the highlands a specific category of space manageable by state administration and control. Likewise, the highland residents—the ethnic minorities there—have also been presented as people in need of "development" in all aspects. State intervention in the name of development and social welfare for the highland people has as its major objectives: (1) the securing of borders; (2) ending opium cultivation; and (3) improving the living conditions of the highland ethnic minority people (Wanat 1989). Activities include agricultural extension programs, crop replacement, improvement of health care and education services, and the resettlement of the highland communities in the forms of *nikhom* (self-help resettlement areas). However, guided by concerns about national security rather than reflecting the express needs of the affected people, government resettlement programs proved a monumental failure. They failed to deliver the desired reforms (Chupinit 1988; Kammerer 1989; Tapp 1989; McCaskill and Kampe 1997).

Before the change of the state policy in the 1950s, central administrators in Bangkok paid little attention to the villagers who reside in the country's highland areas in the northern and western region. For example, the first national census also excluded the highland ethnic minorities (Somchai and Nattamon 2002). Unlike their counterparts in the neighboring countries of Indochina, Burma, and India, the highland people in Thailand were never included in any census reports or district gazetteers compiled by the government (Manndorff 1965). However, this changed after authorities considered the villagers' residency in the highland and their shifting cultivation and opium growing as threats to "national security" in the Cold War era, when Thailand was pressured to eradicate opium and its neighboring countries were rife with ideological warfare of which Thailand was believed to be the next to be affected.

Driven by security concerns, the Thai state initiated "development programs" mostly funded by foreign donors as well as international and local nongovernmental organizations. Apart from the state-led programs, several so-called Royal Projects and the Royal Initiated Projects were also set up by their majesties King Bhumibol and Queen Sirikit. Though these projects have been established in the highlands and lowlands, most of the Royal Project sites are in upland areas. Importantly, the Thai government's concern over Communism, which stemmed from conflicts in neighboring countries, won great support from the United States, which assisted the country in combating political threats and in building the infrastructure deemed necessary for development (Darling 1960, 1962; Nairn 1966; Thak 1974). Key community development programs, known as the Mobile Development Units, and the Accelerated Rural Development Programs were partly funded by the United States government (Thak 1974; Nairn 1966). The American war in Vietnam and Laos further led the community development programs in Thailand along the lines of security and military considerations (Thak 1974, 335), aiming to win the hearts of rural villagers thought to be vulnerable to insurgent sentiments. The aim was to woo them away from the insurgents by integrating them into the national state.

Demarcating Boundaries and Creating Citizens

In an attempt to control borders and citizens, the Cabinet in 1976 resolved to implement national integration policies and programs to instill national loyalty among the highland people and turn them into "able, self-reliant" Thai citizens. The Thai state's integration policies and ethnic minority programs sought homogenization through the two-pronged process of citizenship and education. Several state surveys had been conducted from the 1960s to 1980s in which officials registered highland residents with the intention of keeping records before the commencement of official citizenship registration. As one Akha villager in Phuhai (pseudonym) village, Mae Fa Luang district, Chiang Rai province, where I conducted my fieldwork, recalled of one such survey that took place in the 1980s,

Many women were so afraid of being photographed that they hid away from the officials who were told these women had gone to collect vegetables. Everyone else was photographed, and family records were kept. We were told we would become Thai citizens. (Interview, 12 October 2005).

Some Akha women from this village also went to the nearby Hin Taek village (renamed Thoet Thai after Thai soldiers forced the drug lord Khun Sa and his army out of the area) to receive hill tribe "memento coins" that were inscribed with a picture of King Bhumibol on the front and a map of Thailand on the back. Villagers said that they had no idea who the man was or what the map meant. "The officials said that without the coin, we wouldn't be allowed to live in this country," said an Akha woman (interview, 20 October 2005).

Despite the state national integration policy, of which citizenship recognition is one of the key focuses, Thailand's policy towards citizenship for the highland ethnic minorities has always been subject to changes depending on the socioeconomic and political contexts. In the 1950s and 1960s, when the government's concern about Communism and border security was the basis on which the national integration policy was formed, the status of the highland villagers as citizens was recognized, though not legally. The Thai authorities' acknowledgment of the de facto citizenship of the ethnic highland people is evident in the proposal of the Hill Tribe Committee's subcommittee on administration and registration, recorded at a meeting on 8 May 1973:

Most highland people have long been settled in Thailand's territory. Legally they are citizens whose citizenship has yet to be registered in the household document. This is not their fault, however. It is just because state authorities had failed to reach them at their locations. Thus, it is not appropriate to "give" citizenship to highland people who are already Thai citizens. A better resolution would be official registration of their citizenship in the household document.

However, this tacit understanding changed when the 1970s military-led government adopted stricter measures against members of ethnic minorities who they feared were Communist sympathizers or instigators. Citizenship status could no longer be obtained automatically by virtue of land tenure, but had to be verified through blood links with national citizens. Consequently, there were changes in related laws and policies that revoked citizenship already obtained and denied citizenship to those born in Thailand whose parents' legal status as citizens was still unverified. The effects of these changes are still being felt.

Currently, the highland ethnic minority peoples are separated into three categories with regard to their personal status. The state authorities created this classification system based on different Cabinet resolutions and laws passed at different periods. The divisions also reflect the level of the state's acceptance of the citizenship status of the highland ethnic minority people during different social and political contexts. The three categories of the highland ethnic minorities are:

Original highland people: Persons born in Thailand between 10 April 1913 and 13 December 1972. They are entitled to Thai citizenship as are their children.

Legal immigrants: Highland people who entered the kingdom either before or on 3 October 1985 can apply for citizenship through naturalization after living in the country for five consecutive years. Their children, if born in Thailand, can apply for Thai citizenship to the Interior Ministry.

Illegal immigrants: Highland people who entered the country after 3 October 1985 cannot apply for any legal status and must be repatriated, as must their children (including those born in Thailand).

The classification and criteria reflect the connections between place, existing laws and policies, the idea of citizenship, and mobility. Apparently, state officials have based their national citizenship criteria on people's connection with place, conferring birthright citizenship to those who can prove themselves to be original or "native hill tribes" (in Thai, *chao khao tit phaendin*—literally, "hill tribes tied to the land"). "Native hill tribes" are defined as those who can prove that they were born in the kingdom during the period 10 April 1913 to 13 December 1972, dating from when the first Nationality Act of 1913 was promulgated. This birthright criteria is based on the principle of *jus soli*, that is, citizenship determined by the place where one was born.

Denied, Delayed, and Restricted Citizenship

In Thailand, the ethnic "Thai" people whose parents have Thai citizenship are legally eligible for Thai citizenship. This takes the form of a Thai identification card and the registration of the card holder in the household registration document. The identification card is a must for all legal matters and all contact with authorities regarding all aspects of one's life—work, study, travel, marriage. Unlike the ethnic "Thai," members of the highland ethnic minorities must provide evidence to local officials that they are entitled to citizenship rights. They must lodge applications with authorized officials with various required documents, including certification of their parents' status, proof of residency, and witnesses' statements.

Related laws and regulations stipulate that only "original" highland people may apply to their respective district chiefs for registration of their citizenship in the household document. The district chiefs are authorized to grant application approval. If approved, their Thai citizenship is considered "birthright" citizenship and cannot be revoked. To be considered as "original" people, applicants must have been born in Thailand during the period 10 April 1913 to 13 December 1972.

Thailand-born highland ethnic minority children whose parents are considered to be "legal immigrants" by State authorities can apply to the Interior Ministry for Thai citizenship provided they submit all required documents including a birth certificate. However, this type of Thai citizenship is not considered a "birthright," and is subject to revocation in cases of convicted crimes, either drug-related or other crimes considered a threat to "national security" according to the 1965 Nationality Act (most recently amended in 2008).

There has been great confusion among government officials attempting to implement these laws and regulations, and, as a result, many mistakes have been made. Many "original" highland people who rightly claim birthright citizenship have instead been considered legal immigrants—or even illegal immigrants. Contributing to this confusion is the implementation of Revolutionary Decree No. 337 (in force from 14 December 1972 to 25 February 1992). Implemented during the height of the state's paranoia over domestic and regional Communist insurgencies, the decree aimed to reject individuals who were accused of being Communist sympathizers. The decree specifically targeted ethnic Vietnamese immigrants and their children, since the state closely associated them with the Communist insurgency (Thongchai 1994, 6). This controversial decree revoked the birthright citizenship of people born in Thailand of alien parents who had been allowed to temporarily reside in the kingdom or who had entered illegally. People whose birthright citizenship rights were revoked then became illegal immigrants.

Even though Revolutionary Decree No. 337 was ostensibly aimed at specific groups, all categories of ethnic minority people, including the highland people, suffered. State distrust of ethnic minorities and the state's "punishment" (through the denial or revocation of citizenship) for their perceived lack of loyalty has persisted through the current law on nationality. Despite the abrogation of the decree via amendment of the 1966 Nationality Act, its problematic content remains intact in law and continues to be enforced.

Article 7 of the 1966 Nationality Act states that Thailand-born children are not entitled to birthright citizenship if their parents are illegal immigrants. These children have thus become legally defined as "immigrants who entered the kingdom illegally and must be deported." Since many highland people are misidentified as illegal immigrants (due to the authorities' tardiness in approving citizenship applications), this particular article of the nationality law has negatively affected their children. These children's futures remain uncertain, and their lives are fraught with difficulty.

In addition, regulations required that applicants for Thai citizenship produce state-certified documents as evidence of their eligibility for legal status. Authorities ignored the fact that state surveys in the past—indeed even those surveys most recently undertaken—did not reach many highland villagers in their remote villages. Additionally, many mistakes were made during the process of registering the personal details of each highland villager: date of birth, place of birth, date of entry into the kingdom, and the birthplace of their parents, for example. Enforcing the policy without addressing these realities, as has been the case in many districts (Chutima 2007), has resulted in misinterpretation, bitterness, complaints, and petitions. Many original highland people who for one reason or another were not surveyed have become illegal immigrants according to the law. In several cases, the children of some families have become Thai while others remain legally defined as illegal immigrants (due to different laws and regulations related to citizenship that were in force at the time of their birth), irrespective of the fact that they were born in Thailand.

A study of the lack of citizenship among the highland villagers carried out by the Bangkok Office of the United Nations Educational, Scientific and Cultural Organization (UNESCO) found that in many districts in the northern provinces, ethnic highland peoples' applications for citizenship had been left unaddressed for many years. When villagers visit the district offices to check on the progress of their applications, they are told by district officials to "wait until [they are] informed of the result of the consideration by authorized officials." The major reason provided by many district officials to UNESCO researchers for the delay in considering the applications was shortage of personnel to handle a large volume of applications (Chutima 2007). Furthermore, lack of reliable records and required documents has contributed to many people being left with no legal status. Another UNESCO-funded research project conducted in October 2009 in a village in Mae Fa Luang district found that villagers had been waiting on average ten years for their application to be considered. According to villagers, the waiting time varied from one month to fifteen years. As a result of these long delays, a large number of highland ethnic minority people in Thailand are left without any legal status, despite the fact that they were born in the country or have been settled in the kingdom for over ten years.

Perhaps unsurprisingly, after over three decades of state national integration policies aimed at enabling the highland ethnic minorities to become Thai citizens, approximately 377,677 highland people are still without Thai citizenship according to a 2005 report issued by the National Security Council (NSC) and the Department of Provincial Administration. In Chiang Rai's Mae Fa Luang district alone, 43,000 people are without Thai citizenship compared to 34,000 people who have citizenship, according to a senior district official's report to the meeting of the National Economic and Social Development Council, held in Chiang Mai on 1–2 August 2006.

The employment of various classification categories provides authorities with convenient bases for implementing different policies depending on changing social and political environments. However, the categories are not based on real situations, but have resulted from frequently revived concerns about drug abuse, threats to national security, and environmental problems— all issues that have long been associated with highland ethnic minority identity. State authorities have continually deployed classifications of the highland ethnic minorities as effective tools in the administrative control of these people, invariably to the latter's disadvantage.

Moreover, the Thai state has also employed a color-card system to control and regulate members of ethnic minorities without Thai citizenship.[3] For example, previously highland ethnic minority people whose legal status was yet to be determined by the authorities were required to hold either a blue card (*bat si fa*) or a green card with a red border (*bat khiao khop daeng*), depending on the period when they were surveyed and registered. According to related laws, these cards could be used as documents to substantiate highland villagers' citizenship applications. A policy change a few years ago scrapped these hill tribe cards. Currently authorities issue pink, non-Thai-citizen cards to all categories of ethnic minorities who reside in Thailand without Thai citizenship.

Many former holders of the hill tribe cards commonly complained that the cards issued to them were worth less than alien migrant laborers' cards. The restrictions imposed by the "non-Thai" card resulted in many highland ethnic villagers' opting to register as alien migrant laborers so that they could travel to work for a longer period, either within their district or beyond, without having to return to their district periodically to renew their permission to travel. Holders of blue hill tribe cards employed outside of their registered district had to return to renew their permission to travel every month. Sa, an Akha villager from Chiang Rai's Mae Fa Luang district, provided the following example: "I used to have a blue card. When I came to work in Chiang Mai, I had to register as an alien migrant worker so that I could stay and work for three or six months" (interview, 10 October 2005).

Restricted Mobility and Other Forms of Discrimination and Marginalization

My sixteen-year-old student was born in Thoet Thai subdistrict, Mae Fa Luang district, Chiang Rai province. However, since he has not yet received Thai citizenship, he is considered as non-Thai and has to ask for permission whenever he needs to leave his district of residence for any purpose. He was once jailed for thirty-nine days for travelling outside his district without permission. There are many cases of students like this one whom I tried to help in their applicaitons for Thai citizenship. But I don't really have the authority to decide on this issue. (Interview with high school principal, 4 October 2005)

Beyond the intangible feelings of exclusion from the national community, lack of citizenship has very real and damaging consequences for the lives and prospects of people in the highlands. As non-citizens, their right to travel is limited by law and permissible only within their registered district. To travel beyond their own district's borders, they must first seek permission from officials to whom they must pay fees. Highland villagers without Thai nationality are not allowed to procure a driving license: thus they cannot travel freely on their own. Violators of these restrictions on mobility face fines between five hundred and two thousand baht, in line with related laws. Often, villagers are asked to pay even more. Those who cannot afford the fines are liable to a jail term of one or two days, or more.

Restricted mobility characterizes the everyday realities faced by many ethnic minority people without legal status. Members of highland ethnic minorities face stricter police screening than local *khon mueang* (northern Thai) travelers due to the prevailing pejorative stereotyping of the *chao khao* as people associated with trafficking in drugs and contributing to forest decline. The inspection of their identification cards is an example of what Bauman (1997) calls the pursuit of modern purity, which expresses itself daily in the punitive action taken against "dangerous classes." On a daily basis, the highland people risk being charged as illegal migrants when failing to produce a "hill tribe" card on demand. According to this politics of difference, or "discourse of the hill tribe," members of the highland ethnic minorities are often targeted for inspection due to local officials' attitude towards the highlanders as "different" from the local people in general. For some minority villagers, the requirement to show their "hill tribe" cards at the numerous border checkpoints exposes them to the public gaze of onlookers—further reifying their sense of otherness. An Akha man from Phuhai village in Chiang Rai's Mae Fa Luang district lamented, "I have always been an easy target. There were times when the police only asked me among many other passengers in a public bus to show my ID card. I was so ashamed" (interview, 21 August 2005).

In addition to mobility restrictions, members of the highland ethnic minorities also face other forms of discrimination and marginalization due to lack of citizenship (Chutima 2007; Wiwat 2006; Pesses 2007). Many continue to live in fear of being relocated out of areas designated as national parks, forest reserves, or wildlife conservation areas. They cannot own land or open a bank account. Job opportunities are limited, and if they are fortunate enough to find employment, they are often underpaid. Furthermore, the low-cost healthcare services (according to the thirty-baht-per-hospital-visit scheme) that they previously enjoyed were cut off when the services became nationalized and reserved only for Thai citizens (Wiwat 2006). UNESCO has identified lack of citizenship as the major risk factor for the exploitation and trafficking of highland girls and women in Thailand (Yindee 2001).

Despite a state policy stipulating that all children in the kingdom should have access to education, children whose parents are non-citizens are barred from attending school, refused opportunities for higher education, and are ineligible for any educational benefits, including state scholarships. A study by the United Nations Children Fund (UNICEF) (2000) shows that over nine hundred thousand children in Thailand do not enter school, or enter at a late age. Only 43 percent of school students complete lower or upper secondary school levels. Students without Thai nationality who want to travel outside of their place of residence must request permission from authorities each time they plan to travel. A new Education Ministry regulation approved by the Cabinet on 5 July 2005 addressed this problem by stating that students need only to request permission one time in order to leave their place of residence for as long as their studies require. In reality, however, village informants report that local district officials often ignore this new regulation.

Controlling Drugs: Redefining Citizenship at the Borderlands

The district chief arrived before noon in his four-wheel-drive truck, escorted by two armed defense volunteers and accompanied by the subdistrict headman (*kamnan*) of Mae Salong Nai subdistrict, and four other local leaders. About forty villagers gathered at the village meeting place, including seven villagers whose names had been listed for fast-track approval by the district chief. The district chief said he came to seek the consent of the village meeting before making his decision. He said more applications would be approved if villagers could show they were dedicated to controlling drugs.

> I want to approve first these seven people who have assisted the government's efforts and who have done a good deed in being our eyes and ears, so that we can live safe from drugs. These people have set an example for the rest of you. If you people are as determined as these seven fellows and cooperate with the authorities, your chance to get citizenship will be guaranteed. (Field notes, 28 August 2006)

Whereas the fear of Communism had at one time guided the Thai state's citizenship practices, today the threat of illicit drug production, trafficking, and use has gained salience in how highland people are perceived by the state. Through the imagination of a new form of national security threat engendered by the widespread presence of drugs and illegal immigrants, local officials have redefined their concepts of who has the right to belong. The state, in conjunction with local officials, has effectively used this redefinition to control and manipulate highland ethnic minorities. Villagers' eligibility for citizenship has become dependent on their level of cooperation in drug prevention and control programs. The control and creation of a new identity for the highland ethnic minorities was spurred on by the former Thaksin Shinawatra administration's harsh policy on drugs and control of people's mobility. In Mae Fa Luang district, for example, local officials were ordered to make fifty arrests per month, according to an official at the Mae Salong Nai Tambon Administrative Organization (interview, 17 September 2005).

Villagers are part of this state surveillance. Ong (1996) observes that it is not just the state that is the sole disciplinary force in the making of cultural citizens, but also civil society institutions and social groups. The Mae Fa Luang district chief set preconditions for the approval of citizenship application based on a village's ability to "wipe out" drug consumption and trafficking. This type of policy has resulted in communal pressure being forced on individual addicts or families to "kick the habit." Accompanying these measures, frequent raids are conducted in villages on the Thai-Burma border. In addition, local officials used the tool of community consensus (*prachakhom*) in which a village meeting is called and villagers either vote or are asked their opinions on important issues. In most border villages in Mae

Fa Luang and Mae Chan districts, the *prachakhom* has been widely used as a venue to verify the eligibility of villagers for citizenship approval. To obtain citizenship approval, villagers must prove to be active and contributing to communal activities, and to not be drug addicts.

As illustrated in the remark of the district chief above, the problems associated with lack of citizenship among the highland ethnic minorities living at the borderlands have resulted from (local) state officials' efforts to maintain control over the populations located along the border. These policies emerged simultaneously with the Thaksin administration's policy of a "war on drugs." Local officials at these frontier zones have resorted to using (non-Thai citizen) identification cards—as well as delaying consideration of the eligibility of citizenship applications—as effective tools of biopolitical control. This control has resulted in the production of new criteria for the inclusion of highland ethnic minorities into Thai society. In addition, it has contributed to the ongoing transformation of the subjectivity of these people, made possible by the manipulation of the pejorative stereotyping of the highland ethnic minority as "drug addicts." The ethnicizing of "addict" has thus been stressed in the official understanding of highland ethnic minorities' eligibility for citizenship.

According to Cohen and Lyttleton's study of opium detoxification in Laos (2002), the negative consequences of such programs in northwestern Laos are evident in the inculcation of an "addict identity" and in a strong sense of shame among relapsed addicts. Similarly, state agencies at the district levels in Mae Fa Luang and Mae Chan imposed this kind of "addict identity" in a discursive sense for the purpose of surveillance and control of Akha villagers. In these border villages, district officials have sought the assistance of local leaders in controlling supposed degenerate and "uncontrollable" villagers. Building upon the prevailing stereotypes of highland ethnic minorities, district officials have successfully exploited this social identity and utilized it as an instrument of control by linking an "addict identity" to the idea of a citizen.

Applying this strategy, the district chief of Mae Fa Luang boldly declared that unless villagers rid the whole area of drugs, he would not sign a single application for citizenship. As far as the officials are concerned, good citizens cannot be involved in drug consumption and trafficking. Bad citizens are inevitably engaged in such activities. The state thus sets standards of good citizenship by demonstrating what a good citizen is *not*. This understanding conveniently disregards the fact that previously the state encouraged opium growth for tax purposes, and that various forms of drug use are widespread in Thai society in general—not just among the highland people (Vichai et al. 1999; Vichai 2000).

The confluence of many factors at the borderlands—where the sovereignty of the state is blurred and national loyalty is questioned—has played an important role in the problem of lack of citizenship among villagers. How citizenship is handled in the borderland space reveals the intersection between: the politics of difference; the different conceptions of citizenship that obtain among villagers and officials; local officials' efforts to control the peoples at the border; and the abuse of power that exploits pejorative stereotyping of the hill tribes. The intersection of these factors and the use of citizenship as a tool of exclusion arouses in the minority villagers feelings of being compromised, unwanted, and excluded. Coupled with local authorities' belief that there are no more "original hill tribe" members without citizenship, this means many highland villagers have applied several times for citizenship without success (Chutima 2007; Wiwat 2006). As Aju Choemer, an Akha villager from Chiang Rai who led a villagers' protest demanding that district officials more promptly process citizenship applications, observed in a letter submitted to the Mae Fa Luang district chief, Chiang Rai, on 2 April 2008, "We have been waiting for eight to nine years, and have wasted a lot of money, but nothing happens."

Importantly, citizenship has become instrumental for the local power structure in demanding social, economic, political, and cultural cooperation from the highland ethnic minority peoples, in effect, implying to the minority villagers what they expect *good* citizens to be like. In at least one village, people have been told time and again to donate blood, to become village guards or health volunteers, and to participate in state rituals in return for special treatment of their citizenship applications. As one villager recalled,

> I remember the district chief once told our meeting of village health volunteers that he would give citizenship to all volunteers. They did not get it. Even a member of parliament from Chiang Rai pledged during the election campaign that the lack of citizenship problem must be addressed. Nothing happened. What about me? I have cooperated with them all. I am

the border defense volunteer. I donate blood whenever there is a request. The officials said whoever donates blood will get priority for citizenship consideration. (Interview, 9 November 2005)

In another case, a villager from Mae Fa Luang district in Chiang Rai told a public seminar on legal status held in Chiang Mai in June 2005 that the district chief promised to give fifty "special quotas" to villagers from his village, which won the "model village" competition for drugs prevention and control. However, when this district chief was sent to take up a position in another district, his successor ignored this promise.

Through conditioning villagers' eligibility for citizenship upon their degrees of cooperation in drug prevention and control, local officials wield their authority to consider and approve citizenship as a weapon to hold ethnic villagers hostage to national loyalty. Local authorities threaten that drug addicts' applications will not be signed by relevant parties and can thus not be validated for submission.

Or, there is the case of former Mae Fa Luang district officials who falsely promised residents of villages who were praised for their commitment to eradicating drugs that a special "citizenship" quota would be set aside for them. The district chief and his deputies in effect deployed a carrot-and-stick technique. Holding out the carrot over and over again and then withdrawing it would seem to erode the efficacy of this sort of practice. Unfulfilled promises aside, many members of the highland ethnic minorities in northern Thailand have found that there are other ways that can accelerate their citizenship registration process.

Local Politics and Corruption

If you have money, you can buy your card. My family had to pay nearly ten thousand baht to the village head before we got a Thai identification card. First we had to pay three hundred each for the application. When our applications were approved we were each asked to pay one thousand baht before getting photographed for the ID card. (Interview with an Akha woman, 16 August 2005)

In many districts in northern Thailand, local villagers have been asked by local officials to pay "fees" when applying for citizenship or any other legal status. Villagers report having to spend "lots of money" in the process, with the amount paid ranging from three hundred baht to more than twenty thousand baht (the exchange rate in 2005, when I conducted my study, was around forty-one baht per US dollar). An Akha man I interviewed on 17 August 2005 recalled, "I applied several years ago. I paid the village head five hundred baht: he told me to pay another one thousand baht if my application was approved. But nothing happened."

Some highland villagers in the village where I conducted my fieldwork in Chiang Rai, and other highland villagers in nearby villages with whom I talked, complained that the total fees paid were a large sum of money. As one hill farmer recalled, "We only earn an annual income of about twenty thousand baht to about fifty thousand baht from selling our agricultural produce (mostly maize and ginger). In some years, we earned nothing when these crops made no profit" (Interview, 21 October 2005).

District officials and village leaders play prominent roles in local politics affecting all aspects of villagers' lives. Apropos of citizenship, the powers of these officials have been further strengthened in recent years: the laws have authorized them to validate villagers' applications. In every step to apply for citizenship, applicants need the signatures of the headman and of others members of a committee authorized to validate their applications. Village informants complain that this requirement renders them easy prey to corrupt practices by local officials who extract fees in return for considering citizenship applications. Local officials have used the process of citizenship application, consideration, and approval as a means to extort money from villagers. Further exploiting the villagers' hunger for the right to belong, district officials collude with subdistrict and village heads in their attempts to extract both money and national loyalty from villagers (*Kom Chat Luek* 2005, 1).

Conclusion

Vienne (1989, 48) stated two decades ago that Thai state officials hold traditional cultures and ethnic identity accountable for security dilemmas, narcotics, and forest destruction-related problems. This holds true today in the state's current citizenship practices, which maintain that cultural differences inherent in the "nature" of the highland ethnic minorities are the source of these problems. This is evident in the citizenship conferral ritual specifically reserved for highland ethnic minorities. An extension of the disciplinary biopolitics practiced in excluding the highland people from citizenship, this ceremony, which is called *pithi prakat ton pen phonlamueang Thai* (ceremony to declare oneself a Thai citizen), is held when minorities' citizenship applications *are* approved. Participants receiving the Thai identification cards from authorities are required to make a vow in the presence of the symbols of Thai "nationhood"—portraits of King Bhumibol and Queen Sirikit, a Thai flag, and a Buddha image—that they will be "good" citizens (not involved with drugs), loyal to both nation and king. Indeed, loyalty to the Thai nation and the symbolic head of the nation has been included as preeminent among the criteria against which each Thai citizenship applicant is measured. Other qualifications require that the applicants: be law-abiding persons; show interest in using the Thai language; have good records of cooperating, assisting, or doing good service to the state and community; have a stable income and a decent occupation; are not opium growers, users, or involved in the drug trade; and are not perpetrators, promoters, or supporters of forest destruction and destruction of other natural resources (Department of Provincial Administration 2000).

As tacit recognition of their "otherness," the highland minorities are perceived to lack national consciousness and loyalty to the key institutions that most Thais hold dear. Apart from other state loyalty rituals such as "standing to pay respect to the national anthem twice a day," this ceremony at which one declares oneself to be a Thai citizen is seen as vital to the symbolic "transformation" of the highland ethnic minority bodies from which national loyalty can now be expected.

But the highland ethnic villager—like any other ethnic minority people who suffer marginalization—have also adapted, contested, and constructed their own ways of life and identity. As one means of challenging this perception and the exclusionary practices that flow from it, a coalition of people without citizenship was formed in 2007 comprised of Akha villagers and other ethnic groups in Mae Fa Luang district who have been waiting for the approval of their citizenship applications for over ten years. Through cooperation with local nongovernmental organizations, this coalition brought their cases to the attention of the parliamentary ombudsman, senators, and other local political representatives, as well as the local, national, and international media. Members of this coalition told their stories of hardship at local, regional, and international conferences, submitted a shadow report of human rights discrimination to the United Nations Commission on Human Rights, and held a series of demonstrations in front of the Chiang Rai and Chiang Mai Provincial Halls.

Another adaptive strategy that highland people have employed in their struggle to obtain citizenship rights as well as other fundamental rights is the adoption of the term "indigenous people." At a conference in Chiang Mai in September 2009, representatives of the highland ethnic minorities accepted the term "indigenous peoples" to refer to themselves. A movement, known as the "IP movement," began to take shape in 2007 when a coalition of seventeen ethnic groups formed the Network of Indigenous Peoples in Thailand and declared 9 August as Indigenous Peoples Day. With the support of other organizations that work to promote the rights of indigenous peoples and the Ministry of Social Development and Human Security's Bureau of Ethnicity Development, the Network of Indigenous Peoples in Thailand annually organize a three-day "Indigenous Peoples Festival" in Chiang Mai as a forum for indigenous peoples to express their concerns with regard to their rights and culture. Even with these adaptive strategies, the highland ethnic minorities face daunting challenges and hardships in obtaining citizenship and realizing their rights as full members of the Thai national community. This can be explained through an understanding of the nature of the relationship between the state and what are considered peripheral populations. As Mika Toyota has argued (2005, 110), the state's discourse on "hill tribe" status has nurtured the perception that ethnic Thais are the "core" of the nation-state. This perception has justified paternalism and state control of the upland people and provided grounds for discrimination against them and their denial of full Thai citizenship. Thus, adopting the discourse of "indigenous rights" is unlikely to improve this situation (ibid).

So long as the state and its local agents retain their perception of the highland peoples as "other" and inextricably link them to threats such as illicit drugs, the state's exclusionary practices will persist. Furthermore, official exclusion has also been nurtured by the explicit and implicit prejudice that still prevails among Thai people in general. Examples are abundant, as experienced and testified to by Akha villagers and other ethnic minorities in their daily lives. Even those with citizenship experience such prejudice. A 2010 study, conducted by an Akha activist hired by UNESCO to record the level of socioeconomic progress of highland villagers who have obtained Thai citizenship, found that villagers continue to face great difficulties in living their lives, when traveling, or applying for jobs or for education due to widespread prejudice. This is especially so with regard to minority group members applying for government positions: those whose citizenship rights are considered as not conferred by "birthright" have been prevented from winning positions in the police, military, or judiciary. Therefore, as Toyota (2005, 131) rightly observed, it would be naïve to suppose that granting "citizenship" status alone could solve the multiple problems currently affecting upland peoples. The crucial issue is, she argued, the recognition of equal citizenship, not the recognition of some distinctive hill tribe (or "indigenous people") status (ibid). The ongoing challenges facing the highland ethnic minorities—whether citizens or not—is thus the combination of burdensome legal procedures guided by negative attitudes and preconceptions about ethnic identity.

While on the one hand the national integration policy aimed to homogenize (boundaries and people), on the other hand it introduced conditions that would nurture difference as the means to maintain hierarchical relations of power between the ethnic majority and ethnic minority. Citizenship increasingly became an instrument of control that produced different categories of people and distinguished between citizen and non-citizen (Horstmann 2002, 21). The very same processes that were initially intended to integrate have been employed effectively as tools of exclusion and regulation. Despite the 1976 Cabinet resolution, the reality is that many highland people remain without any legal status. According to Thai law they are aliens who are temporarily allowed to stay in the kingdom pending the verification of their status.

Unlike in the past, when highland ethnic minorities might have wanted to remain outside the reach of the state to maintain their invisibility (what Scott calls lack of "legibility"), currently the ethnic minorities of northern Thailand very much want to be visible. It is important to note that the highland ethnic minorities in northern Thailand differ in significant ways from Scott's "Zomian" people who intentionally escaped state administration (2009). The development programs and the benefits citizenship rights provide led to the changes in highland ethnic minorities' aspirations for full membership in the nation-state. The ethnographic literature shows that the lack of "legibility" of ethnic groups in northern Thailand is not deliberate or the result of everyday acts of resistance on their part, either as individuals or as a group, but rather is the result of bureaucratic ineptitude or low-level state corruption. These are among the serious obstacles that must be removed before full recognition of the rights of the highland ethnic minorities—civil and political, as well as social, economic, and cultural—can be realized.

Notes

1. The British colonial practice in Burma was to call highlanders "hill tribes," and this term subsequently came into general use in Thailand and is now the standard translation (McKinnon 1989, 307). Some scholars criticize the use of the term "hill tribe" due to the evolutionist concept associated with the word "tribe." The term *chao khao* is also criticized for its pejorative connotations as a consequence of the discourse of "otherness" (Krisdawan 2000).

2. See, for example, the studies of the highlands in Indonesia by Tsing (1993) and Li (1999), and the study of highland Ecuador by Crain (1990).

3. The change in the Thai state policy in 2007 with regard to this colored-card system resulted in the issuance of one-color card (in pink) for all categories of ethnic minority in Thailand without Thai citizenship.

References

Bauman, Zygmunt. 1997. *Postmodernity and Its Discontents.* Cambridge: Polity Press.

Chupinit Kesmanee. 1988. "Hilltribe Relocation Policy in Thailand." *Cultural Survival Quarterly* 12 (4): 2–6

Chutima Morlaeku. 2007. "Report on the Lack of Citizenship among the Highland ethnic Minorities." Unpublished internal report. Bangkok: UNESCO.

Cohen, Paul, and Chris Lyttleton. 2002. "Opium-Reduction Programs: Discourse of Addiction and Gender in Northwest Laos." *Sojourn* 17 (1): 1–23.

Crain, Mary. 1990. "The Social Construction of National Identity in Highland Ecuador." *Anthropological Quarterly* 63 (1): 43–59.

Department of Provincial Administration. 2000. *Rabiap samnak thabian klang wa duai kan phitcharana long raikan sathana bukkhon nai thabian ratsadon hai kae bukkhon bon phuenthi sung pho so 2543* [The Central Registration Bureau's regulation on the registration of personal status of highland people in the household document, B.E. 2543]. Bangkok: Asa Raksa Dindaen Publishing House.

———. 2002. *Thamniap chumchon bon phuenthi sung yisip changwat nai prathet Thai pi pho so 2545* [Directory of highland communities in twenty provinces of Thailand, 2002]. Bangkok: Ministry of Social Development and Human Security.

Darling, C. Frank. 1960. "Marshal Sarit and Absolutist Rule in Thailand." *Pacific Affairs* 33 (4): 347–60.

———.1962. "Modern Politics in Thailand." *Review of Politics* 24 (2): 163–82.

Hortsmann, Alexander. 2002. "Rethinking Citizenship in Thailand: Identities at the Fringe of the Nation-state in National and Post-National Times." Unpublished paper presented at the Eighth International Conference of Thai Studies, Nakhon Phanom, Thailand, 9–12 January.

Kammerer, Cornelia Ann. 1989. "Territorial Imperatives: Akha Ethnic Identity and Thailand's National Integration." In McKinnon and Vienne 1989, 259–301.

Kom Chad Luek, 29 March 2005. Accessed at http://www.komchadluek.net/news/2005/03-29/p1-16868357.

Li, Murray T. 1999. "Compromising Power: Development, Culture, and Rule in Indonesia." *Cultural Anthropology* 14 (3): 295–322.

Manndorff, Hans. 1965. *The Hill Tribe Program of the Public Welfare Department, Ministry of Interior, Thailand: Research and Socio-economic Development.* Bangkok: Division of Hill Tribe Welfare, Bureau of Self-help Land Resettlement, Public Welfare Department.

McCaskill, Don, and Ken Kampe. 1997. *Development or Domestication: Indigenous Peoples of Southeast Asia.* Chiang Mai: Silkworm Books.

McKinnon, John, and Bernard Vienne, eds. 1989. *Hill Tribes Today: Problems in Change.* Bangkok: White Lotus.

McKinnon, Katherine. 2004. "Locating Post-Development Subjects: Discourse of Intervention and Identification in the Highlands of Northern Thailand." PhD diss., Australian National University.

Nairn, C. Ronald. 1966. *International Aid to Thailand: The New Colonialism?* New Haven, CT: Yale University Press.

Ong, Aihwa. 1996. "Cultural Citizenship as Subject-Making: Immigrants Negotiate Racial and Cultural Boundaries in the United States." *Current Anthropology* 37 (5): 737–62.

Pesses, Abigaël. 2007. "Final Report on Karen Focus Group Discussions about Birth and Citizenship Registration in Chiang Mai, within the Framework of UNESCO's 'The Highland Birth and Citizenship Registration Promotion Project: Reduction in Structural Vulnerability for Trafficking among High-Risk Populations in Thailand.'" Unpublished internal document. Bangkok: UNESCO.

Pinkaew Luangaramsri. 1998. "Wathakham wa duai chao khao" [On the discourse of "hill tribes"]. *Sangkhomsat* 11 (1): 75–87.

Scott, James C. 2009. *The Art of Not Being Governed: An Anarchist History of Upland Southeast Asia*. New Haven, CT: Yale University Press.

Somchai Preechasilpakul and Nattamon Khongcharoen. 2002. *Kan yomrap/kitkan chao khao nai krabuankan hai sanchat thai: Kan samruat kho kotmai, naeo nayobai, saphap panha* [Accommodation/exclusion of hill tribes in the process of Thai nationality conferral: An exploration of laws, policies and problems]. Chiang Mai: Faculty of Social Science, Chiang Mai University.

Sturgeon, Janet. 2005. *Border Landscapes: The Politics of Akha Land Use in China and Thailand*. Chiang Mai: Silkworm.

Tapp, Nicholas. 1989. *Sovereignty and Rebellion: The White Hmong of Northern Thailand*. Singapore: Oxford University Press.

Thak Chaloemtiarana. 1974. "The Sarit Regime, 1957–1963: The Formative Years of Modern Thai Politics." PhD diss., Cornell University.

Thongchai Winichakul. 1994. *Siam Mapped*. Chiang Mai: Silkworm Books.

Toyota, Mika. 2005. "Subjects of the Nation Without Citizenship: The Case of 'Hill Tribes' in Thailand." In *Multiculturalism in Asia*, edited by Will Kymlicka and Baogang He, 110–35. Oxford: Oxford University Press.

Tsing, Lowenhaupt A. 1993. *In the Realm of the Diamond Queen*. Princeton, NJ: Princeton University Press.

UNICEF [United Nations Children Fund]. 2000. "Kan sueksa phap ruam" [Education: Overview] Accessed at http://www.unicef.org/thailand/tha/education.html.

Van der Meer, Cornelis L. J. 1981. *Rural Development in Northern Thailand: An Interpretation and Analysis*.

Vichai Poshyachinda, Manit Srisurapanont, and Usaneya Perngparn. 1999. "The Amphetamine-Type Stimulants Epidemic in Thailand: A Country Profile." Unpublished paper prepared for WHO, Bangkok.

Vienne, Bernard. 1989. "Facing Development in the Highlands: A Challenge for Thai Society." In McKinnon and Vienne 1989, 33–60.

Wanat Bhruksasri. 1989. "Government Policy: Highland Ethnic Minorities." In McKinnon and Vienne 1989, 5–31.

Wiwat Tamee. 2006. "Rai-ngan phon kan sueksa saphap panha kan khao thueng sathana bukkhon lae sanchat thai khong chon phao lae chatiphan nai prathet thai lae kho sanoenae naeothang nai kan kaekhai panha" [A study of the problems of access to legal status and Thai citizenship of ethnic groups in Thailand and their resolution]. Unpublished paper presented at the meeting of the National Economic and Social Advisory Council, Chiang Mai Phukham Hotel, Chiang Mai, 19 August.

Yindee, Lertcharoenchok. 2001. "Searching for Identity." *Step-by-Step* 5. Accessed at http://www.un.or.th/TraffickingProject/volume5.pdf.

Contributors

COELI BARRY teaches at the Institute of Human Rights and Peace Studies, Mahidol University, and is currently writing a reference book on Cultural Rights. Her research and reading interests include literature, religion, and politics, as well as social theory.

BENCHARAT SAE CHUA is a lecturer at the Institute of Human Rights and Peace Studies, Mahidol University. Her research interests include social movements and citizenship rights.

ALEXANDRA DENES is a senior research associate at the Princess Maha Chakri Sirindhorn Anthropology Centre. An anthropologist specializing in heritage issues in Southeast Asia, her current research interests center on cultural heritage rights at the Phanom Rung Historical Park in Buriram province.

TYRELL HABERKORN is a research fellow in the Department of Political and Social Change at the Australian National University. Her book *Revolution Interrupted: Farmers, Students, Law, and Violence* was published in 2011. She is now working on a history of impunity for state violence in Thailand since 1932, as well as gender, sedition, and political prisoners in the US and in Thailand.

MIKE HAYES is a lecturer at the Institute of Human Rights and Peace Studies, Mahidol University. His current research interests include non-citizens' rights and rights-based development.

HO KONG CHONG is associate professor at the National University of Singapore, Department of Sociology. He received his PhD in sociology from the University of Chicago and currently researches globalization and inter-city competition, civic spaces and urban politics, neighborhoods and community life.

MUKDAWAN SAKBOON is a lecturer at the Department of Social Science and Development, Faculty of Social Sciences, Chiang Mai University. She received her PhD in anthropology from Macquarie University in 2010. A former journalist for *The Nation* newspaper in Bangkok for a number of years, her research interests focus on nationalism, citizenship, ethnic minority groups, human rights, and HIV/AIDS.

MATTHEW MULLEN is a PhD candidate in Human Rights and Peace Studies at Mahidol University. His research focuses on the relationship between international advocacy and diplomacy, and grassroots empowerment tactics employed by populations in the world's most oppressive states.

PANUWAT PANTAKOD is currently teaching at the Department of English for Business Communication, Sripatum University at Chonburi. He received his MA in Applied Linguistics at King Mongkut's University of Technology, Thonburi. Born and raised in a multilingual family (Thai-Lao and Khmer), his main interests have been languages and cultures of the mentioned ethnic groups.

PORNPAN CHINNAPONG is associate professor at the Faculty of Architecture, King Mongkut Institute of Technology Ladkrabang (KMITL). Ms. Chinnapong has a background in architecture and urban planning. Her areas of research include urban form, city planning, and the use of civic space in Bangkok.

SIRIJIT SUNANTA teaches in the PhD program in multicultural studies at the Research Institute for Languages and Cultures of Asia (RILCA), Mahidol University. Her current research interests include gender and globalization, Thai women and the global intimate, cultural diversity, and the multicultural debate in Thailand.

TIAMSOON SIRISRISAK teaches museum and heritage studies at RILCA at Mahidol University. His current research interests include community-based conservation of Chinatown in Bangkok and the interpretation of World War II shared heritage.

PETER VAIL is a senior lecturer in the University Scholars Program at the National University of Singapore. He received his PhD in Cultural Anthropology from Cornell University and is currently teaching on the topics of language death, culture, and the idea of the native.

Index